T0301490

China and the Multinationals

NEW HORIZONS IN INTERNATIONAL BUSINESS

Series Editor: Peter J. Buckley
Centre for International Business,
University of Leeds (CIBUL), UK

The New Horizons in International Business series has established itself as the world's leading forum for the presentation of new ideas in international business research. It offers pre-eminent contributions in the areas of multinational enterprise – including foreign direct investment, business strategy and corporate alliances, global competitive strategies, and entrepreneurship. In short, this series constitutes essential reading for academics, business strategists and policy makers alike.

Titles in the series include:

China and the Multinationals

International Business and the Entry of China into the Global Economy

Edited by

Robert Pearce

Professor of International Business Emeritus, John H. Dunning Centre for International Business and Department of Economics, University of Reading, UK

NEW HORIZONS IN INTERNATIONAL BUSINESS

Edward Elgar

Cheltenham, UK • Northampton, MA, USA

Published by
Edward Elgar Publishing Limited
The Lypiatts
15 Lansdown Road
Cheltenham
Glos GL50 2JA
UK

Edward Elgar Publishing, Inc.
William Pratt House
9 Dewey Court
Northampton
Massachusetts 01060
USA

A catalogue record for this book
is available from the British Library

Library of Congress Control Number: 2011931000

ISBN 978 1 84844 668 7

Typeset by Servis Filmsetting Ltd, Stockport, Cheshire
Printed and bound by MPG Books Group, UK

To the memory of John Dunning,
from who we all learned so much

Contents

Contributors

Peter J. Buckley – Centre for International Business, University of Leeds, Leeds, UK.

L. Jeremy Clegg – Centre for International Business, University of Leeds, Leeds, UK.

Simon Collinson – Henley Business School, University of Reading, UK.

Adam R. Cross – Centre for International Business, University of Leeds, Leeds, UK.

Bersant Hobdari – Copenhagen Business School, Copenhagen, Denmark.

Marina Papanastassiou – Copenhagen Business School, Copenhagen, Denmark.

Robert Pearce – John H. Dunning Centre for International Business, University of Reading, Reading, UK.

Evis Sinani – Copenhagen Business School, Copenhagen, Denmark.

Yanxue Sun – Nottingham University Business School, Ningbo Campus, China.

Yuxuan Tang – John H. Dunning Centre for International Business, University of Reading, Reading, UK.

Hinrich Voss – Centre for International Business, University of Leeds, Leeds, UK.

Feng Zhang – Bill Greeley School of Business, St Mary's University, San Antonio, Texas, USA.

Si Zhang – Tsinghua University, Beijing.

Acknowledgements

We dedicate this book to the memory of John Dunning. The starting point for this collection was a panel session presented at the Academy of International Business (AIB) conference in Milan in 2008. For many of us the highlight of that conference was a very appropriate and moving tribute session to John, at what, sadly, turned out to be his last major conference. Just as John's influence and guidance retains its importance in International Business generally so it pervades this collection. Most of the authors here either worked with John directly or with someone who had done so. This is reflected in the overall aims of the book and in the concerns and presentational styles of individual chapters. In a way that John would recognise and support the book has a broad theme that carries very considerable practical implications; the relation between International Business and the opening and growth of the of Chinese economy. This can then feedback interactively into techniques and methodologies that can be adapted and evolved as and when required. For us, as I think for John, good and purposeful theorising is vital, but the issues they are used to approach are paramount. One aspect of this, close to John's later interests and concerns, is the importance of institutions; how they affect MNEs *in* and *from* China, and how International Business may, indeed, affect them.

In preparing this volume I have two great debts here at Reading. Firstly, as so often, to Jill Turner who typed several chapters with her usual speed and accuracy. Secondly, to Yuxuan Tang who addressed the daunting task of converting disparate manuscripts to Elgar house style with great proficiency, initiative and patience.

Robert Pearce

1. China and the multinationals

Robert Pearce

The central theme of the chapters in this book is the understanding of multinational enterprises (MNEs) and their relationship with the economic development of China and the implications of its emergence into the global economy. That inward foreign direct investment (FDI) played, as the policy reforms after 1978 expected it to do, a major role in Chinese economic development and its repositioning in the international economy is well understood. Less systematically documented is precisely how, beyond the quantitative access to development-related resources, inward FDI supported Chinese growth and the extent to which it mediated China's entry into the global economy. A vital emphasis of one strand of the investigation here is that such important issues can be best elucidated by understanding how their operations in China fitted into the wider global strategies and competitive agendas of mature and well-established MNEs.

More recent and complementary phenomena and research agendas then concern the substantial and pervasive growth of Chinese outward FDI. Here again the main focus of the reported research is to address issues that perceive the emergence of Chinese FDI as manifest in the origins of a new breed of MNE. The ways in which such nascent Chinese MNEs resemble, or deviate from, the mature Western MNEs investing in China constitutes a topic of immense academic and practical concern. Two broad issues can underpin such investigation. Firstly, what is the purpose of FDI from China and the international expansion of Chinese enterprise? What are the aims and strategic motivations pursued through the international subsidiaries of Chinese MNEs? Secondly, what are the sources of the ability (the ownership advantages in terms of MNE theory) of Chinese firms to expand overseas and to establish operations in particular locations to pursue specific objectives? An important subtext of these two questions then derives from the extent of potential influence of the Chinese government and particular facets of its policy agenda. How much of the ability to successfully achieve specified objectives in their international operations are endowed to Chinese MNEs, through resource or policy support, by the state and government? To what extent are those objectives defined for

Chinese MNEs from contexts that reflect the wider state strategic programmes and agendas?

From this background we expect the chapters here to help elaborate
three interdependent investigative agendas. Firstly, the two contexts
analysed here, occurring simultaneously and linked around the Chinese
economy and Chinese economic interests, provide for an extended understanding of the MNE as an agent and institution. We investigate issues
that help comprehend the positioning of the MNE as integral to the ways
in which China enters the global economy. But both how Western MNEs
operate in China and the evolving nature of Chinese MNEs will challenge
and enrich our understanding of the MNEs themselves.

Secondly, and building analytically on the first set of issues, are the questions relating to how MNEs, old and new, influenced the ways in which
the opening and growth of China becomes integral within the wider global
economy. Broad perspectives on the international impact of the emergence of China have focused on its exporting performance and massive
trade surpluses. Access to China as an export-base for global supply is, of
course, a very plausible option for MNEs. However, by contrast with the
earlier export-oriented successes of very much smaller economies (notably
the first and second waves of 'Asian tigers') the size and growth of China's
own market inevitably impinges on the strategic options addressed by
MNE subsidiaries. Approaching this in a manner that embeds the evolution of their operations into the processes of development and change
necessary for China's sustained growth and competitive progress then
becomes a further crucial strategic opportunity for MNEs.

For the outward expansion of Chinese MNEs we may discern two very
different sets of priorities that can influence their international operations
and determine the types of host-country characteristics that they respond
to. Firstly, we can distinguish a form of home-base exploiting behaviour
in which subsidiaries of these MNEs operate to expand profitability from
in-place sources of competitiveness. These may be the forms of firm-
level attributes familiar in MNE theorising (ownership advantages) or
sources of competitiveness endowed on the firms from state support (for
example, preferential access to capital). Secondly, Chinese MNEs may
be motivated towards home-base augmenting behaviour. One variant of
this may remain internal to the firm, which seeks to enhance its sources
of competitiveness through, for example, international learning processes (knowledge or strategic-asset seeking). An alternative variant then
sees Chinese MNEs targeting the alleviation of perceived weaknesses in
China's economic growth by securing, for example, improved and secure
access to raw material and energy sources.

The third set of issues relate to how the behaviour of MNEs may interact with the longer-term sustainable development of the Chinese economy. Inevitably the massive rates of economic growth achieved by, and targeted for, China have built into them equally extensive changes in terms of the needs to be met and the sources of competitiveness available. Whether, and how, MNEs interact with these developmental reconfigurations of the Chinese economy are implicit concerns of this study.

In effect the persisting development of the Chinese economy will change those location advantages that have, in the past, attracted MNEs to set up operations there. It will also reconfigure the factors that MNEs need to be considering when evaluating potential new operations in China. This should not, of course, imply lower rates of MNE entry into China, or even closure of existing facilities. What it does imply, and what becomes central to several chapters here, is a vital change in emphasis of what MNE operations in China will aim to do. Thus we can set up, as a working hypothesis for MNE operations in China, a move away from cost-effective production using mature group technologies towards more dynamic creative processes that evolve new sources of competitiveness. A decisive strand in this may be innovation of new products that are targeted specifically to improve MNEs' responsiveness to the evolving needs and tastes of the Chinese market. Beyond this, however, MNEs may perceive potentials in the Chinese science-base and creative human capital that can be built into innovation programmes for global competitiveness. Here we will aim to assess the extent, and the purpose, of embeddedness of MNE subsidiaries in the development of the Chinese economy and, especially, in its emerging national system of innovation.

In a complementary manner we can also speculate on the interdependence between China's economic development and the progress of its own MNEs. Here alternative possibilities can be offered according to the two broad types, or motivations, suggested earlier. For home-base exploiting operations the expanding knowledge-base and creativity in China itself may allow those firms to generate improved firm-level sources of competitiveness. This may simply provide them with an enhanced scope to extend international operations as sources of profitability. For home-base augmenting Chinese MNEs the sustained growth of the home economy may extend the range of resource and knowledge needs pursued.

As the United Nations Conference on Trade and Development (UNCTAD) data presented in Table 1.1 shows, the stock of FDI in China in 2009 was estimated to be 22.86 times what it had been in 1990. Taken over the whole period this massive rise in fact derives from two sources. Firstly, it occurs during a period when FDI grew at an enormous rate globally, the total stock in 2009 being 8.52 times its level of 1990. Secondly, China had increased its relative importance as a destination during this

China and the multinationals

Table 1.1   Foreign direct investment inward stock, 1990, 2000 and 2009

	Value of stock (billion $)			Percentage share		
	2009	2000	1990	2009	2000	1990
World	17,743.0	7,442.5	2,081.8	100.00	100.00	100.0
Developed countries	12,352.5	5,653.2	1,557.2	69.6	75.9	74.9
Developing countries	4,893.5	1,728.5	524.5	27.6	23.2	25.2
Asia	2,893.8	1,067.7	349.6	16.3	14.3	16.8
China	473.1	193.3	20.7*	2.7	2.6	1.0
Hong Kong	912.2	455.5	201.7*	5.1	6.1	9.7
S. Korea	110.8	38.1	5.2	0.62	0.51	0.25
Taiwan	48.3	19.5	9.7*	0.27	0.26	0.47
India	163.9	16.3	1.7*	0.92	0.21	0.08
Indonesia	72.8*	25.1*	8.7*	0.41	0.33	0.42
Malaysia	74.6*	52.7*	10.3	0.42	0.71	0.49
Singapore	343.6*	110.6	30.5	1.9	1.5	1.5
Thailand	99.0	29.9	8.2	0.56	0.40	0.39
Vietnam	52.8*	20.6	1.7*	0.30	0.28	0.08

Note: * UNCTAD estimates.

Source: UNCTAD *World Investment Report* (2010), annex table 2.

period of absolute growth, accounting for 2.7 per cent of inward stock in 2009 compared to 1.0 per cent in 1990. However, it then becomes clear that it was during the earlier years of this period that China asserted itself most distinctively as a host to FDI. Thus in the 1990s FDI stock in China grew 9.34 times compared to 3.57 times globally, so that China's share rose from 1.0 per cent to 2.6 per cent. By contrast from 2000 to 2009 the stock in China only rose in line with the global increase (that is, 2.45 times compared to 2.38 globally) so that its increase in share was marginal over this period. In an alternative perspective the table shows that in 1990 China accounted for 5.9 per cent of FDI stock in Asian developing countries, with this rising to 18.1 per cent in 2000 before declining slightly to 16.3 per cent by 2009.

The UNCTAD data also provides an assessment of the relative status of FDI stocks in host economies by expressing these as a percentage of gross domestic product (GDP). Here again the figures, shown in Table 1.2, indicate the 1990s as being the period when FDI in China was at its most dynamic, its stock value rising from 5.1 per cent of GDP in 1990 to 16.3 per cent in 2000. Though, as we have seen, FDI inflows to China continued strongly after 2000 their rate of growth fell below that of the economy, so that FDI stock as a percentage of GDP fell from its 16.2 per cent in 2000

Table 1.2   *Foreign direct investment stocks as a percentage of gross domestic product, 1990, 2000 and 2009*

	Inward FDI			Outward FDI		
	1990	2000	2009	1990	2000	2009
World	9.8	23.3	30.7	10.0	25.2	33.2
Developed countries	9.0	23.0	31.5	11.2	28.8	40.8
Developing countries	13.6	25.0	29.1	4.1	12.9	16.5
Asia	15.8	25.2	25.8	3.3	14.8	17.6
China	5.1	16.2	10.1	1.1	2.3	4.9
Hong Kong	262.3	269.3	433.2	15.5	229.6	396.1
S. Korea	2.0	7.1	13.3	0.9	5.0	13.9
Taiwan	5.9	6.0	12.7	18.4	20.4	47.8
India	0.5	3.5	12.9	–	0.4	6.1
Indonesia	6.9	15.2	13.5	0.1	4.2	5.6
Malaysia	23.4	56.2	39.0	1.7	16.9	39.5
Singapore	82.6	119.3	194.0	21.2	61.2	120.3
Thailand	9.7	24.4	37.5	0.5	1.8	6.2

Source: UNCTAD *World Investment Report* 2010, annex table 7.

to 10.1 per cent in 2009. This was by no means reflective of a generalised pattern in developing Asia with other important host economies (notably, Hong Kong, S. Korea, Taiwan, India, Singapore and Thailand) reporting continued rises in 2000–09.

The UNCTAD figures for FDI inflows for 2007–09 (Table 1.3) suggest a degree of recovery in China's relative position in attracting FDI. This seems to reflect a smaller negative effect on FDI flows to Asia resulting from the global credit crisis and overall falls in FDI. Thus whilst FDI inflows worldwide in 2009 were only 53.1 per cent of their 2007 level, in Asia they remained at 89.5 per cent of the earlier level. Within this China increased its share of global inflows from 4.0 per cent in 2007 to 8.5 per cent in 2009. This asserted its position as the major recipient amongst the Asian developing economies, though other major recipients (notably Hong Kong and India) also increased their shares.

As the data on outward FDI stocks in Table 1.4 indicates, China, at the aggregate level, remains a minor participant as a direct investor, with a share of global stocks still only at 1.21 per cent in 2009. Once again, though, this share has risen during what has been a period of massive FDI expansion, so that China's outward FDI stock in 2000 was estimated at 6.15 times greater than in 1990 and by 2009 was 8.29 times greater than in 2000. Though quite a few other developing Asian economies reported in

China and the multinationals

Table 1.3   Foreign direct investment inflows, 2007–09

	Value of inflow (billion $)			Percentage share		
	2009	2008	2007	2009	2008	2007
World	1,114.2	1,770.9	2,099.9	100.0	100.0	100.0
Developed countries	565.9	1,018.3	1,444.1	50.8	57.5	68.8
Developing countries	478.3	630.0	564.9	42.9	35.6	26.9
Asia	301.4	372.7	336.9	27.1	21.0	16.0
China	95.0	108.3	83.5	8.5	6.1	4.0
Hong Kong	48.4	59.6	54.3	4.3	3.4	2.6
S. Korea	5.8	8.4	2.6	0.5	0.5	0.1
Taiwan	2.8	5.4	7.8	0.3	0.3	0.4
India	34.6	40.4	25.0	3.1	2.3	1.2
Indonesia	4.9	9.3	6.9	0.4	0.5	0.3
Malaysia	1.4	7.3	8.5	0.1	0.4	0.4
Singapore	16.8	10.9	35.8	1.5	0.6	1.7
Thailand	5.9	8.5	11.4	0.5	0.5	0.5

Source: UNCTAD *World Investment Report* 2010, annex table 1.

Table 1.4   Foreign direct investment outward stock, 1990, 2000 and 2009

	Value of stock (billion $)			Percentage share		
	2009	2000	1990	2009	2000	1990
World	18,982.1	7,967.5	2,086.8	100.00	100.0	100.0
Developed countries	16,010.8	7,083.5	1,941.6	84.3	88.9	93.0
Developing countries	2,691.4	862.6	145.2	14.2	10.8	6.9
Asia	1,946.0	614.1	67.7	10.3	7.7	3.2
China	229.6	27.7*	4.5*	1.21	0.35	0.22
Hong Kong	834.1	388.4	11.9*	4.4	4.9	0.57
S. Korea	115.6	26.8	2.3	0.61	0.34	0.11
Taiwan	181.0*	66.7	30.4*	0.95	0.84	1.5
India	77.2	1.8	0.1*	0.41	0.02	–
Indonesia	30.2*	6.9*	0.1*	0.16	0.09	–
Malaysia	75.6*	15.9*	0.8	0.40	0.20	0.04
Singapore	213.1*	56.8	7.8	1.1	0.71	0.37

Note: * UNCTAD estimates.

Source: UNCTAD *World Investment Report* (2010), annex table 2.

Table 1.5   Foreign direct investment outflows, 2007–09

	Value of outflow (billion $)			Percentage share		
	2009	2008	2007	2009	2008	2007
World	1,101.0	1,928.8	2,267.5	100.0	100.0	100.0
Developed countries	820.7	1,571.9	1,923.9	74.5	84.5	84.8
Developing countries	229.2	296.3	292.1	20.8	15.4	12.9
Asia	176.7	204.2	225.5	16.0	10.6	9.9
China	48.0	52.2	22.5	4.4	2.7	1.0
Hong Kong	52.3	50.6	61.1	4.8	2.6	2.7
S. Korea	10.6	18.9	15.6	1.0	1.0	0.7
Taiwan	5.9	10.3	11.1	0.5	0.5	0.5
India	14.9	18.5	17.2	1.4	1.0	0.8
Indonesia	2.9	5.9	4.7	0.3	0.3	0.2
Malaysia	8.0	15.0	11.3	0.7	0.8	0.5
Singapore	6.0	−8.5	27.6	0.5	−0.4	1.2

Source: UNCTAD *World Investment Report* 2010, annex table 1.

Table 1.4 also increased their share during the period covered, only Hong Kong had a larger outward FDI stock in 2009 than China. When the stocks are presented as shares of GDP in Table 1.3 the ratio for China's overall outward FDI, though predictably low compared to smaller Asian economies, grows persistently through the period. Thus the very high growth rates of China's GDP over these years had been consistently exceeded by its expansion of FDI overseas. The flow figure in Table 1.5 confirms the continued growth in China's outward FDI in the years of global downturn, with its position now matching that of Hong Kong amongst economies in developing Asia.

An alternative indicator of patterns of international business expansion, documented by UNCTAD in recent years, covers greenfield FDI projects. This measures discrete decisions about the expansion of a firm's international operations that are manifest in either a completely new project or a major strategic extension of one that is already in place. The data reported by UNCTAD covered both newly realised projects and announcements of intended new operations. Here China's position with regard to inward investment (Table 1.6) emerges as much more notable than in the figures for FDI stock or flow values. Thus through the period 2003–09 China is reported as the host for 11.1 per cent of the projects realised or announced. Only India attracted at all comparable levels of projects amongst developing Asian economies.

In terms of outward greenfield FDI projects Table 1.7 shows China to

Table 1.6   *Number of greenfield foreign direct investment projects, by host location, 2003–09*

	Number of projects						
	2009	2008	2007	2006	2005	2004	2003
World	13,727	16,147	12,210	12,248	10,551	10,242	9,450
Developed countries	6,249	7,386	6,337	6,138	5,135	4,677	4,133
Developing countries	6,646	7,595	5,095	5,333	4,509	4,856	4,513
Asia	4,734	5,603	3,889	4,296	3,479	3,757	3,371
China	1,143	1,515	1,214	1,406	1,255	1,545	1,324
Hong Kong	253	216	150	160	125	127	91
India	742	965	695	985	590	694	452
Malaysia	158	212	171	125	93	125	186
Singapore	309	295	251	195	158	179	154
Taiwan	87	87	63	68	70	84	115
Thailand	273	330	123	112	120	126	161
Vietnam	256	348	264	196	169	161	130
	Percentage share of projects						
	2009	2008	2007	2006	2005	2004	2003
World	100.0	100.0	100.0	100.0	100.0	100.0	100.0
Developed countries	45.5	45.7	51.9	50.1	48.7	46.7	43.7
Developing countries	48.4	47.0	41.7	43.5	42.7	47.4	47.7
Asia	34.5	34.7	31.9	35.1	33.0	36.7	35.7
China	8.3	9.4	9.9	11.5	11.9	15.1	14.0
Hong Kong	1.8	1.3	1.2	1.3	1.2	1.2	1.0
India	5.4	6.0	5.7	8.0	5.6	6.8	4.8
Malaysia	1.2	1.3	1.4	1.0	0.9	1.2	2.0
Singapore	2.3	1.8	2.1	1.6	1.5	1.7	1.6
Taiwan	0.6	0.5	0.5	0.6	0.7	0.8	1.2
Thailand	2.0	2.0	1.0	0.9	1.1	1.2	1.7
Vietnam	1.9	2.1	2.2	1.6	1.6	1.6	1.4

Note: Data covers new FDI projects and expansion of existing projects, both announced and realised.

Source: UNCTAD *World Investment Report*, 2010, annex table 18.

be an emerging but, so far, relatively minor source country. Its annual average number of projects for 2007–09 (253.7) is, indeed, 2.13 times greater than that for 2003–06 (119.3), but this to a considerable degree reflects China holding its share in a growing global expansion of projects. By comparison with its dominance for inward projects China operates at similar levels to several other developing Asian economies in terms of

Table 1.7   Number of greenfield direct investment projects, by origin of investment, 2003–09

| | Number of projects | | | | | | |
	2009	2008	2007	2006	2005	2004	2003
World	13,727	16,147	12,210	12,248	10,551	10,242	9,450
Developed countries	11,250	13,219	10,318	10,255	9,048	8,766	7,863
Developing countries	2,235	2,629	1,702	1,785	1,321	1,309	1,429
Asia	1,835	2,215	1,411	1,566	1,166	1,098	1,231
China	303	256	202	131	140	98	108
Hong Kong	133	170	120	119	100	101	127
India	260	359	218	296	191	204	173
S. Korea	215	252	198	219	185	171	182
Malaysia	112	134	73	71	73	79	83
Singapore	117	175	92	100	85	101	90
Taiwan	131	156	123	121	88	110	149
	Percentage shared projects						
	2009	2008	2007	2006	2005	2004	2003
World	100.0	100.0	100.0	100.0	100.0	100.0	100.0
Developed countries	82.0	81.9	84.5	83.7	85.8	85.6	83.3
Developing countries	16.3	16.3	13.9	14.6	12.5	12.8	15.2
Asia	13.4	13.7	11.6	12.8	11.1	10.7	13.0
China	2.2	1.6	1.7	1.1	1.3	0.9	1.1
Hong Kong	1.0	1.1	1.0	1.0	0.9	1.0	1.3
India	1.9	2.2	1.8	2.4	1.8	2.0	1.8
S. Korea	1.6	1.6	1.6	1.8	1.8	1.7	1.9
Malaysia	0.8	0.8	0.6	0.6	0.7	0.8	0.9
Singapore	0.8	1.1	0.8	0.8	0.8	1.0	1.0
Taiwan	1.0	1.0	1.0	1.0	0.8	1.1	1.6

Note: Data covers new FDI projects and expansion of existing projects, both announced and realised.

Source: UNCTAD *World Investment Report*, 2010, annex table 17.

creation of outward greenfield operations. Thus over the whole 2003–09 period India (1.37 times as many projects as China) and South Korea (1.15) were ahead, whilst Hong Kong (0.70), Taiwan (0.71) and Singapore (0.61) had mainly fallen behind only in the more recent years.

The next chapter, by Si Zhang and Robert Pearce, reports the results of an exploratory survey and interview analysis of 25 subsidiaries of manufacturing sector MNEs as they were operating in China in 2005. The core of this investigation is an attempt to discover how these subsidiaries were

positioned in terms of the perceived strategic diversity of the contemporary manufacturing MNE. Thus the early sections of the chapter outline
the strategic options that might be addressed in MNEs' implementation
of their operations in China and how these could be reflected in different
types of subsidiary roles.

In line with well-established delineations the chapter's analysis adopts
three broadly defined strategic motivations that have the potential to
drive MNE operations in China. Firstly, market seeking (MS) which
is perceived as using a subsidiary in a country to primarily supply the
market of that country. The traditional formulation of MS saw it as primarily a 'tariff-jumping' motivation operationalised during eras of high
trade restraints. In an analysis predicated on China's opening to a wider
global positioning, however, the investigation also provides for a more
contemporary variant of MS, in which the subsidiary role seeks a responsive embeddedness in the distinctive current and evolving taste patterns
of Chinese consumers. The second strategic motivation that is likely to
be addressed in MNEs' operations turns the focus on a host country's
supply-side conditions, in the form of efficiency seeking (ES). This would
see subsidiaries focusing on the cost-competitive production (usually
for extensive international markets) of the well-established parts of the
MNEs' mature product range. Routine understanding of the role of international competitiveness in China's economic progress clearly provides a
potential for MNEs' ES operations. Since both MS and ES relate to securing profitability from MNEs' current competitive scope the third strategic
motivation addresses the need to extend and revitalise this competitiveness. Thus knowledge seeking (KS) reflects MNEs' increasing propensity
to seek creative inputs (technology, science, inventive and exploratory
human capital) to innovation in decentralised international facilities (subsidiaries and/or laboratories). With Chinese policy now emphasising the
need to address the generation of knowledge-based forms of development
the potential for MNEs to pursue parts of their own KS needs there may
be an important emerging forward-looking priority.

The survey results provide two, complementary, impressions of the
dominant forces conditioning the strategic positioning of the MNE subsidiaries in China. Firstly, that it is the Chinese market itself that provides
the most pervasive competitive context for their operations. Secondly,
that this market is approached very proactively by the subsidiaries, with
extensive commitment to individualising their competitiveness in ways
that respond to its tastes and dynamics. Thus well over half of the subsidiaries can be seen to have adopted MS-oriented roles, with a dominant
prioritising of the building of a sustainable position within the developing
Chinese market. So whereas these MS subsidiaries may tend to assert their

initial bridgeheads in the Chinese market around their MNEs' already established competitive product lines, and the mature technologies they use, a key dynamic imperative quickly emerged in terms of the differentiation of such goods in ways that respond to distinctive consumer tastes and needs. The dominant mode of such responsive MS behaviour is to adapt the established products and technologies to this new competitive context. Much more limited, but of considerable indicative potential, is the emergence of subsidiaries that are, in a hybrid KS-MS manner, moving towards the development of new goods that are uniquely targeting (at least initially) Chinese consumers.

Though less prevalent than the variants of MS a number of the subsidiaries did see their positioning in ES terms, in the sense of being located to benefit from supply-side factors in terms of input availability, so as to underpin cost-effective production. Here again, however, the Chinese context provokes a variant of normal expectations for the role, since most of the ES subsidiaries targeted cost-effective supply of the Chinese (and other adjacent Asian) market itself. This then leads to the, perhaps counterintuitive, conclusion of very limited involvement of these subsidiaries in the more normal ES role of export-oriented supply to an MNE's wider international markets.

The forward projection of the patterns indicated in the Zhang and Pearce analysis can, speculatively, be seen to suggest a dominant role for product innovation in China by MNEs that aims to embed their operations in the evolution of Chinese consumers' demands. The capacity to do this responsively will also, it is thus implied, reflect the ability to source the creative inputs to such innovations in China. One of the important manifestations of this localised developmental impetus in MNEs will be their creation of research and development (R&D) laboratories. The next two chapters turn the focus on the ways in which MNEs are increasingly placing R&D at the centre of their positioning within the dynamics of Chinese economic progress. Both of these R&D chapters build on the most crucial premise in understanding the strategic positioning of dispersed subsidiaries in MNEs, that they can play distinctively different roles in support of the different strategic imperatives addressed within these companies' global operations.

The important role of R&D in deepening MNEs' competitiveness in China is strongly confirmed and elaborated in the survey results of Si Zhang reported in Chapter 3. Notably, 69 of the 129 subsidiaries covered by the survey already possessed in-house R&D facilities. In line with the decisively emerging perception of the dominance of the Chinese market in defining the roles of MNE subsidiaries the pervasive motivations reported in their R&D laboratories are to support this through adaptation and/or development work. In terms of the dynamics of MNE positioning in the evolution of the Chinese market it is then very significant that the contribution of laboratories towards subsidiary-level development of new goods for that market now matches the, logically earlier, preoccupation with adapting established MNE goods towards the new context. To a lesser degree support of innovation in Chinese subsidiaries for their parent companies' global markets can be discerned as emerging in these R&D units.

A further dimension of Zhang's results underlines the extent of the ambitions of MNEs and their subsidiaries to proactively embed their position in the development of the Chinese economy and its knowledge-base. This comprises an investigation of the subsidiaries that did not, at the time of the survey, yet possess in-house R&D capacity. Firstly, a significant number of these reported the intention to create a laboratory in the near future. Secondly, only a small number of the subsidiaries without laboratories suggested that this was because they could perceive no benefits that could accrue to them from such support. Thirdly, these subsidiaries reported a very strong propensity to access the R&D support they did need from other laboratories of their group including, to a very significant degree, laboratories of other subsidiaries in China. This not only reflects again the sense of technological dynamism prevailing in most MNE subsidiaries in China but also a parallel sense that this can be secured locally, through an emergent knowledge-diffusion network within their Chinese operations.

The perception, emerging clearly in the work of Si Zhang, that leading MNEs already approach R&D in China through a diversified range of laboratories that have the potential to operate as an interdependent and mutually supportive network is investigated in detail in the two cases discussed by Feng Zhang and Robert Pearce in Chapter 4. Here the case of Ericsson represents a long-established MNE, with a fully developed approach to globalised R&D, which can be seen to generate its operations in China in terms of informal, but specifically tailored, expansions of already established programmes and practices. Samsung can, perhaps, represent a younger and very fast-growing competitor, whose entry into China may be a very significant component of both its internationalisation per se and the development of its technology strategy and learning processes.

Though with differing degrees of extent and emphasis, reflecting both the age of parent companies and the length of their commitment to operating in China, both cases provide very persuasive illustrations of patterns of MNE behaviour described in earlier chapters and, indeed, prove amenable to classification within accepted typologies of subsidiaries, R&D laboratories and approaches to innovation. Thus, in a manner familiar from earlier studies of the role of R&D in the international expansion of

MNEs, the pioneering positioning of MNE laboratories in China in these two cases was to facilitate the building of a competitive bridgehead in the market for their already successful goods. A notable aspect of how such laboratories solidify this initial entry, especially for a quite distinctive host market, is adaptation (of product and/or process) of technology. This adaptation is very influential in these Chinese cases since it can be seen to indicate sources of the two crucial evolutionary impulsions that emerge as these high-tech consumer-oriented MNEs seek to deepen their R&D positioning.

The first of these impulsions is to greatly amplify subsidiaries' commitment to local market responsiveness by very quickly moving forward from the limited ambition of adaptation and acceding to the development of new goods that aim to embed their competitiveness within the quantitative and qualitative growth of the Chinese market. That MNEs already mandate their subsidiaries in China to play this role to an extensive degree then points to the second impulsion. This is a growing supply-side responsiveness in terms of awareness of the capacity to derive knowledge-related inputs into competitive enhancement from the emerging Chinese national system of innovation itself. Indeed the study indicates that this ability to generate new knowledge and creative competences through their Chinese operations is increasingly spilling over beyond local market innovation. Thus the Ericsson case (reflecting its longer involvement with R&D in China) suggests both a commitment to innovations that can enter the company's wider international markets and the presence of laboratories and collaborations that target pre-competitive basic research of a purely scientific nature.

Two key factors that emerge from the preceding chapters are that MNEs are increasingly committed to develop new products explicitly for the Chinese market and that, at the subsidiary level, in-house R&D is very important in achieving this. The study reported in Chapter 5, by Feng Zhang, makes an important extension to this by analysing the sources of the technologies drawn into patented knowledge and product breakthroughs achieved by MNEs' operations in China. This adds importantly to our understanding of how MNEs deepen their competitiveness in China, but also provides an addition to our understanding of subsidiary-level development in MNEs. Thus, in a way that had not been considered likely in previous cases of subsidiary innovation, the key driving feature is to develop goods specifically for the local, uniquely large and fast growing, host market. This market focus explains the location of these innovation processes in Chinese subsidiaries, but does not preclude accessing technology inputs from outside China. The issues raised in this regard are systematically addressed in Zhang's study.

The investigation uses patents granted to the world's largest firms for inventions attributable to their subsidiaries in China between 1996 and 2005. The considerable rate of growth of such patenting is an immediate result, which validates the broad interest in MNEs' commitment to innovation in China already noted here. The crucial and distinctive step in Zhang's analysis is to determine the sources of the antecedent patents cited in the applications for the new patents granted to MNEs' Chinese subsidiaries. This provided a total of 3,845 pairs of citing and cited patents.

The first result provided in the analysis is that considerably more of the patents cited in the new patents secured by the subsidiaries derived from sources outside the parent MNE group, rather than from antecedent discoveries within the group itself. As the author suggests, innovation by MNEs' subsidiaries in China is likely to be an innately evolutionary process, so that it builds from a platform of mature group technologies already transferred from established group operations. Such mature intra-group knowledge foundations of subsidiaries' operations may be derived from gradual assimilation and integration of many earlier group innovations and not now be attributable to specific group patents, but still provide important bases from which the Chinese subsidiaries' innovations are developed.[1] It is then the new external patented knowledge sources that allow the subsidiary to generate the particular distinctive attributes that provide the patentable core of the new products targeting the local market.

A second key result of Zhang's analysis emerges as supportive of the interpretation of the innovations as distinctively evolutionary, with primary drivers in the local market. The patent data clearly validates the author's expectation that 'because of the limited absorptive capacity of Chinese subsidiaries, their knowledge accumulation activities might be largely limited to incremental innovations; namely, knowledge accumulation within the same technological area'. Thus consistently more of the cited patents derive from within the citing subsidiary's 'home' technology field, so that only a minority are inter-field and thus likely to drive more radical innovations. In line with this Zhang's empirical tests show that where a patent is cited from another field (that is, inter-technology, rather than intra-technology, citation) it is more likely to derive from an origin outside the group.

The third knowledge-sourcing dichotomy tested in the study is whether cited patents had originated inside or outside China. The general case for a disproportionate tendency to cite local patents would be that an innovation-oriented subsidiary is likely to generate learning roots (for example, scientific collaborations) in the host national system of innovation and, therefore, become strongly aware of potentially valuable external local knowledge that is already patented. In the Chinese case Zhang's evidence shows that, in the early stages of MNE innovation there, only a limited number of cited patents had been secured locally. Furthermore, a second facet of this result is that regression tests showed that where patents were cited for inventions in China these were more likely to be internal to the group; that is, the result of previous discoveries of the MNE in China, including by the citing subsidiary. This may reflect a limited amount of relevant patented knowledge by local operations so far in the relatively early stage of the Chinese NSI. It may also reflect a reluctance, due to intellectual property rights concerns, of MNEs to explore so far the contents of local science and R&D potentials through external collaborative arrangements. Overall, Zhang concludes that 'instead of accessing external knowledge from geographically local sources, [MNEs' Chinese] subsidiaries tend to access external knowledge from geographically distant locations and integrate such external knowledge with internally accumulated knowledge within the subsidiary'. In line with earlier chapters' analysis this 'internal knowledge [may be] generated through in-house R&D'.

As a valuable supplement to its main themes Zhang's study also elucidates some aspects of the absorptive capacity and ability to assimilate knowledge in the Chinese subsidiaries of MNEs. The first aspect of this shows that the more recent patents taken out by the subsidiaries tend to cite patents that themselves represent more recent discoveries. This can be interpreted to indicate an ever improving absorptive capacity in these operations, sharpening their ability to access and utilise more complex recent technological discoveries. Secondly, it is shown that cited patents from external sources are significantly older than those cited from internal sources. One cause of this could be that, due to their limited absorptive capacity, foreign-owned subsidiaries in China 'may only be able to understand and integrate older knowledge from external sources'. However, a more positive scenario is compatible with the strategic deepening of MNE subsidiary evolution of competitiveness for the Chinese market. This would see the market-targeting impulsion of subsidiary-level innovation deriving from 'newly generated knowledge through in-house R&D' which then secures competitive distinctiveness through the integration of 'external knowledge, which is well established and requires less further development'.

An important subtext of this introduction, and of several of the separate chapters, is of the various dimensions of heterogeneity that need to be invoked in understanding the operations of the contemporary MNE when seen, in broad terms, as a dynamic differentiated network. Thus the complex competitive agendas of individual MNEs are increasingly pursued through carefully articulated international networks of diversified operations. The crucial manifestation of this strategic heterogeneity emerges in the range of specific roles and motivations addressed by particular subsidiaries and R&D units. This, in turn, feeds off the distinctive and differentiating characteristics of the chosen locations for parts of MNEs' global networks. Clearly the characteristics that influence the choice of MS, ES or KS roles for MNE subsidiaries (or the status of R&D laboratories) will most predominantly reflect aspects of a country's current real economy, in terms of income levels and demand patterns, inputs to immediate supply operations and the state of progress of a national system of innovation.

But the availability and accessibility of such host-economy characteristics to MNEs will also reflect government policies and the institutions governing enterprise in the economy. A very significant aspect of this will be the mode of operation permitted to subsidiaries, most notably in terms of collaborations and interdependencies with local enterprises. The often institution-driven choice of such modes provides another important aspect of subsidiary heterogeneity, and one that has proved a vital feature of MNEs' operations in China and, indeed, in the forms taken by emerging Chinese enterprises and, ultimately, MNEs. In Chapter 6 Simon Collinson and Yanxue Sun provide valuable insights into these issues by introducing two variants of 'hybrid' enterprises in China that reflect both the institutional factors influencing modes of firm operations and how the behaviour of hybrids can be reflected in enterprises' progress in China. The authors aptly summarise the aim of their chapter as an examination of 'the complex and changing relationship between the state . . . and enterprise in China', introducing issues that feed forward into the concerns of several of the subsequent chapters on the emergence and international commitment of Chinese MNEs.

Based on material from two major studies (using survey, interviews and case study approaches) Collinson and Sun analyse, as their first hybrid form of operation in China, the international joint venture (IJV) involving large globally active MNEs and local state-owned enterprises (SOE). It is noted that the organisational challenges of securing competitive performance and development within such IJVs involves both internal and external interfaces that provoke 'contests and challenges'. Thus in the definition of 'internal' practices and procedures to be adopted in IJVs in China varying degrees of influence from the two parents can emerge. Collinson and Sun note that often this results in internal operational forms that 'can differ from both parent systems' so that they can 'represent more appropriate and effective adaptations to the specific organisational context in which' they are applied. They are, in effect, 'hybrids' in themselves. In their analysis of the management of the 'external' interface for IJVs Collinson and

Sun validate the logical expectation that it would be the Chinese partner that would be able to leverage local influence to articulate beneficial relationships 'with suppliers and customers and with government agencies'. But the authors are then able to go beyond this and show how through the content of this external interface the foreign MNE can often influence how the institutional 'rules of the game' are applied to the IJV.

A theme that runs through this chapter is the importance, in defining the policy context of MNE operations in China, of science and technology at the core of the long-term developmental strategy for the economy and reorientation of its international competitiveness. The analysis indicates two dimensions of this within the IJV. Firstly, an emphasis of technology transfer and training towards the SOEs from foreign partners. Secondly, the establishment within IJVs (especially in aerospace and automobiles) of technical centres and R&D units that can endow them with more distinctive competitive potentials. In this way the IJV cases analysed by Collinson and Sun again underpin the importance of innovation and creative activity amongst MNEs' operations in China, even when activated within IJVs.

The second type of hybrid investigated in Collinson and Sun's studies emerges through the widening of the competitive scope of SOEs. These are perceived as increasingly not only continuing to be controlled by state agencies in order to fulfil public sector contracts but as also moving into private sector operations where they buy and sell in formal and informal markets. Though these hybrids do not include an international firm element they do parallel the IJVs in that they also involve a significant reformulation and repositioning of SOEs. This again represents a major facet of the competitive development, and ultimately often internationalisation, of Chinese enterprise. Thus, in line with ideas provided in subsequent chapters, we can suggest that such hybrid SOEs may possess two key attributes valuable to emergent Chinese MNEs; access to official support and resources (for example, capital) and growing familiarity with the needs and behaviour patterns of open markets.

In their analysis in Chapter 7, Peter Buckley, Heinrich Voss, Adam Cross and Jeremy Clegg suggest that though established modes of International Business analysis certainly contribute to an understanding of outward FDI (OFDI) from emerging economies there are often important context-specific dimensions which also need to be drawn in to augment this theorising. Here they 'assert that the institutional environment of the home country is an important explanatory factor'. Their generation of this line of argument from the case of Chinese MNEs serves two purposes. Firstly, it draws out in detail ways in which specific aspects of China as a home country have conditioned the forms taken by its MNEs. Secondly, by doing this it then puts into place the components of an analytical methodology that can be used to discern and evaluate similarities and differences in MNEs that are emerging from other developing countries. From a careful review of the existing literature on inward FDI (IFDI) and institutions in China, Buckley et al. extract four dimensions around which to structure their assessment of the institutional regime from which Chinese MNEs emerge. These four dimensions then allow the derivation of nine propositions which reflect, to some degree, an 'interpretation' of the Chinese case and then provide generalisable 'criteria' for assessment of the OFDI context of other emerging economies.

The first of the four dimensions is distinguished by the authors as 'domestic institutions and government administration'. These represent the direct manifestation of economic policies and regulatory frameworks whose ultimate aim is to advance the economic development of the national/domestic economy. Even when not explicitly articulated to do so policies with this domestic economy focus may, in effect, compromise OFDI and the internationalisation of firms that are developing competitive advantages in home-market sectors. In their discussions of the case of Chinese MNEs Buckley et al. derive two propositions that reflect the origins of such firms from within the complex institutional and regulatory environment of China's development and industrialisation policies.

Firstly, it is indicated that once the Chinese government began to perceive the ways in which 'international' operations of its firms could generate specific benefits in support of sustained 'domestic' development, it adopted proactive OFDI policies to, in some degree, offset implications of earlier restrictive measures. Thus the 'go global' policy of 1999 is seen to represent 'a strong public commitment to the adoption of an institutional environment that encourages and fosters (both financially and administratively) the outbound investments of Chinese firms'.[2] Secondly, it is suggested that Chinese firms will have developed particular attitudes and skills from their experience in operating under the 'opaque and idiosyncratic arrangements' of their home economy. This may condition an 'idiosyncratic reaction to risk not observed [in the] behaviour of industrialised country firms' that encourages location and strategy decisions less amenable to more established MNEs.

The second institutional dimension evaluated by Buckley et al. comprises 'domestic government business networks', and their potential to influence the internationalisation of business. The content of such network relationships are perceived as structural and endemic market imperfections that can generate exploitable advantages for favoured firms. Applying their conceptualisation to the 'relation-based' governance system of China (with its innate potential for regulating capital and adverse selection problems) Buckley et al. document such imperfection in firms' access to external capital and technology as sources of competitive advantage leveraged in international expansion. From a careful review of studies of funding institutions and mechanisms operating in China they derive the strong proposition that 'Chinese MNEs utilise domestic capital market imperfections to support them in funding international investments'. Their review also provides them with a second proposition which asserts that SOEs and large private firms are better positioned than others to exploit such imperfections in the domestic capital market in China.

As indicated in several of the 'inward' chapters Chinese policy and institutional arrangements now place a strong priority on generation and access to technology as an element in building a National System of Innovation (NSI). These policies are seen here as both providing opportunities for Chinese MNEs and helping define their roles. Thus a proposition offered by Buckley et al. is that when Chinese firms participate in nationally funded technology and innovation schemes they are more likely to secure the resources and capabilities to internationalise through OFDI. Also it is proposed that where Chinese firms are part of an international technology and knowledge exchange agreement they will also have the 'resources, capabilities and mindset' to internationalise.

The two remaining dimensions of institution arrangements that condition the emergence of Chinese MNEs' move into the international context itself. The first of these does still retain participation of the Chinese government, since it comprises the international institutional agreements that increasingly reflect China's external economic relationships. The overriding intention of such arrangements is seen to be to reduce structural and endemic market imperfections relating to potential host countries in order to lower transaction costs of investors. China's extensive recent commitments to 'bilateral' arrangements such as investment treaties, double taxation treaties, trade agreements and aid programmes lead to the proposition that this provides a stability in potential host economies that has a positive influence on the international investment behaviour of Chinese MNEs. In a similar vein a complementary proposition argued that China's accession to 'multilateral' trade and investment agreements (most conspicuously the World Trade Organization (WTO)) benefits Chinese MNEs by securing access to regulations and standards that take better account of their needs and objectives. A third, much more ad hoc approach described by Buckley et al., within their international institution dimension, has involved the Chinese government and leading SOEs helping to facilitate the international expansion of small and medium-sized enterprises through the establishment of Special Economic Zones and Trade Hubs in overseas locations. It is proposed that such facilities would 'provide a familiar or facilitating institutional environment that encourages first time investors and SMEs from China to expand there'.

The fourth dimension of the institutional environment distinguished by Buckley et al. as affecting the expansion of Chinese MNEs is their 'access to international social or business networks'. The associated proposition suggests that where Chinese firms are positioned in one or more of those international networks this provides them with lower transactions costs in accessing information and identifying new business opportunities abroad. The authors discern and illustrate four types of such networks that have influenced the international expansion of Chinese firms. Firstly, overseas Chinese communities. Secondly, established foreign trade (for example, buyer-supplier) relationships and ongoing contract work for foreign MNEs. Thirdly, access to international business facilitators in the form of investment promotion agencies (such as the UK's regional development agencies), trade promotion organisations and consultancies. Finally, an established foreign business collaboration (for example, an IJV partner in China).

The central themes of particular institutional and policy bases in the international expansion of Chinese enterprise are given a precise context in the exploratory investigation of Yuxuan Tang and Robert Pearce in Chapter 8. Here the expansion of Chinese infrastructure MNEs into Africa is analysed with the aim of drawing out distinctive aspects of both infrastructure MNEs per se and the developmental roots of Chinese MNEs operating in those sectors. It is, of course, well understood that the ability of firms to expand as MNEs (their country-specific and firm-specific advantages) is likely to reflect the degree and formats of their home-country's development. However, the unprecedented pace of Chinese growth can be seen to place structural pressures and potentials in this development that then condition the emergence of Chinese MNEs to a very unusual degree. The precise forms taken by the influencing forces, internal to China's development, often determine specific relationships with host locations. Africa has emerged as a very important example of this.

Thus the chapter begins with an attempt to formalise the broad parameters of infrastructure MNEs (derived within established modes of International Business analysis) and applies aspects of this to discussion of Chinese FDI in the construction and information and communications technology (ICT) sectors in Africa. From this background it is suggested that, in effect, Chinese infrastructure MNEs expanding into Africa are serving to mediate between the needs and potentials of two differently based and differently phased processes of economic development. At the macro level Chinese economic growth has generated notable surpluses of capital and foreign exchange, which are being leveraged to support, inter alia, the internationalisation of Chinese business. But aspects of this international expansion target policy objectives that have specific roots in the sustainability of China's own growth and development. A very significant and familiar component of this is shortages of the energy and raw materials needed to secure continued industrial growth as a core of China's development.

From the African perspective, it is the presence of these resources in various countries that represents their most immediately accessible bases to initiate and drive growth and industrialisation. But the ability to leverage these resource-based potentials had been limited by the bottlenecks innate to early development; here shortages of capital and infrastructure restraints. It has become clear, China's need for such (African) resources is matched by its ability to provide capital and, specifically, to apply this capital to projects generating infrastructure capacity that, amongst other developmental benefits, helps secure the (export-oriented) realisation of African resource potentials.

But another aspect of infrastructure-related developmental bottlenecks resides in lack of expertise in the technologies and skills (essentially firm-specific attributes) needed to implement major infrastructure projects. Here, at the more micro level, it is Chinese firms that have tended to support the presence of Chinese capital by carrying out significant infrastructure projects. Though, as argued in other chapters, one facet of this can certainly reflect imperfections in the Chinese capital market Tang and Pearce also suggest that the Chinese MNEs may indeed possess very particular technologies and practices that are distinctively appropriate to the initiation of infrastructure capacities in emergent economies. The roots of these firm-level competences will have been learnt within the needs and conditions of earlier phases of China's development. This may render them more appropriate and viable as a basis for infrastructure creation in Africa than would comparable attributes of infrastructure MNEs from more developed economies.

As suggested in previous chapters much of the early expansion of Chinese FDI has been significantly related to the needs of the country's economic development, so that many investments are very strongly context (often project) specific. Nevertheless, the sense of Chinese MNEs emerging with an increasingly global strategic consciousness should not be undervalued. Thus, in Chapter 9, Bersant Hobdari, Evis Sinani, Marina Papanastassiou and Robert Pearce investigate the location, industry and strategic orientation of 297 subsidiaries of 147 Chinese parent companies as reported in the 2008 edition of *Lexis Nexis Corporate Affiliates Directory*.

To determine the positioning of subsidiaries in their parent groups a four part classification scheme is applied. Here a subsidiary is classified as 'horizontally integrated' if it operates in the same core or related industry as the parent. This is expected to correlate to MS, with the subsidiary applying core technologies of the parent group towards supply of the local market. This accounted for 129 of the 297 subsidiaries (43.3 per cent) and has comparable presence in the major developed markets (that is, 37.8 per cent of the subsidiaries in Asia-Pacific; 51.2 per cent in Europe; 38.0 per cent in North America). 'lateral integration' aims to capture the essence of ES, with a subsidiary allocated to this category if its operations take place in a different stage of the value chain from that of the parent. This emerges as, marginally, the least prevalent status for subsidiaries with 51 (17.2 per cent) of the cases. It was somewhat most prevalent (19.5 per cent) in Asia-Pacific and least so in North America (16.1 per cent). The presence in Asia-Pacific, in particular, could provide a very tentative indication of an emerging propensity for Chinese firms to 'offshore' some cost-sensitive production to other regional economies.

'Vertical integration' is defined to represent resource seeking, with a subsidiary being thus allocated if its operations take place in natural resource-based sectors. This matched lateral integration in overall relevance with 54 cases (18.2 per cent of the total) and again is most significant in Asia-Pacific (20.7 per cent), but is also strongly asserted amongst subsidiaries in North America (19.4 per cent). The final classification is designated by Hobdari et al. as 'risk diversification' and represents subsidiaries that operate in an industry that is unrelated to that of its parent company. The potentially exploratory and speculative aspects of these operations may then carry an element of KS. These subsidiaries emerged as the second most important with 63 (21.2 per cent) of the 297 cases. They were slightly most strongly represented amongst subsidiaries in North America (25.0 per cent), followed by Asia-Pacific (22.0 per cent) and least prevalent in Europe (16.7 per cent).

Overall the results of Hobdari et al. demonstrate an extensive geographic scope and strategic diversity in Chinese MNEs that may indicate an emerging resemblance to the global competitive postures of longer-established Western firms. Taken with the patterns described in the previous two chapters this may return us to a central analytical tension in understanding and interpreting the expansion of Chinese MNEs. Are they increasingly driven by firm-level competitive imperatives, reflecting their own firm-specific advantages and addressing a coherent and integrated global strategic agenda? Or will they remain institutionally positioned within needs and potentials that are more integral to their home-country's economic development? The chapters in this section of the book offer important facets of an analytical agenda to untangle this dichotomy.

NOTES

1. The argument here is that the technologies transferred to the Chinese subsidiary, from which it has built its initial bridgehead in the Chinese market, have derived from a range of earlier patented innovations but have now become assimilated into a broad body of essentially tacit knowledge that is, to some degree, treated as a public good within the group. This then, however, formed a basis for subsidiary-level innovation.
2. An interesting insight offered in the context of the 'go global' strategy may reflect earlier government attempts to organise the structure of industries in China (Buckley et al. discuss the telecommunications industry). Thus it is suggested that part of OFDI policy is to minimise competition between Chinese MNEs as they expand abroad 'by introducing measures to coordinate the international dispersion of Chinese firms' so that they do not compete with each other 'in the same industries in the same countries'.

2. The opening of China and the strategic expansion of multinationals: an analysis of subsidiary motivation and roles

Si Zhang and Robert Pearce

INTRODUCTION

The twin trends of the high growth of the Chinese economy and its pronounced ability to attract foreign direct investment (FDI) remains strong. Central to both of these phenomena is the opening of the Chinese economy and its emerging positioning within the processes of globalization. The most visible (and, indeed, to some countries and industries, stressful) current manifestation of China's economic opening is its export performance. Somewhat less obvious (certainly less present in current polemics and debates) is the immense importance of the growing Chinese market and, therefore, the concomitant trade role of imports. Understanding how the inward FDI, and its significance to multinational enterprises' (MNEs) strategies, relates to both sides of the trade performance equation is thus a very important issue.

With China's increased participation in the global economy, eventually exemplified by its membership of the World Trade Organization (WTO), access to foreign markets became more and more influential in the development of Chinese industry. This then allowed the emergence of export-oriented sectors that could build on current sources of low-cost inputs (that is, static comparative advantage). Participation of MNEs in this derives a clear logic from two directions. Firstly, for many MNEs, the efficiency-oriented input potentials offered by China could represent precisely those that are continuously sought to underpin competitive production of their existing product range for the global marketplace. Secondly, the ability of MNEs to activate these resources for international competition may derive from their possession of abilities (for example, technology, established access to global market networks) not yet available to domestic Chinese enterprise.

24

The sheer size and sustained growth of the Chinese market make it of inevitable importance to virtually all globally competing firms. However, the opening of the Chinese economy removes any suggestion of an immutable link between its growth and inward FDI, since lowering of trade barriers increases the potential for MNEs to supply the market from other parts of their established global-supply network. On the other hand the size (geographical as well as economic) of the Chinese market, its ongoing growth potential and, often, its distinctiveness can suggest that strategically adept MNEs can designate it as a separate competitive context that can benefit from individualized local supply. Thus FDI in China can also take the form of a more proactive and competitively positive form of import-substituting production.

The export-oriented and import-substituting modes of industrialization, and of MNE strategic motivation, are clearly the most relevant broad contexts to understanding current FDI in China. One further issue, of concern to both countries and firms, needs to enter, in a more speculative manner, into our analysis, however. Thus sustained competitive progress needs to move forward from current cost-effective inputs (for a developing country like China) and from a current product range (for MNEs). It is now well understood that, in pursuit of their own competitive regeneration, MNEs systematically internationalize their learning and creative programmes. Given China's strong commitment to education and science it is realistic to look, even now, for elements of MNEs' activity there to become oriented towards, for example, collaborative research and development (R&D) and localized product 'development' operations.

This chapter seeks to investigate the motivations for MNE entry into the growing and opening Chinese economy against the competitive context and strategic options suggested above. It is based on a survey carried out during the summer of 2005. In the next section we formalize the understanding of the strategic options likely to drive MNE entry and evolution in China, and the ways in which these can be manifest in a range of different types of subsidiaries. The following section describes the survey and its implementation. The subsequent four sections then provide the core of the results in terms of the analysis of the motivations of subsidiaries, the roles they play, the sources of technology they use and their degree of autonomy. The final section draws out conclusions.

BACKGROUND

As we have suggested the opening of the Chinese economy has provided enormous opportunities to MNEs that are themselves seeking to expand their competitive horizons and capabilities. We have also indicated that the ways in which MNEs activate their initial operations can address a number of different potentials and strategic imperatives. As a basis for this we use a variant of a familiar approach (Behrman, 1984; Dunning, 1993; Manea and Pearce, 2004, 2006) to categorization of MNEs' strategic motivation.

The first of the three motivations we use here is 'market seeking' (MS). This represents the extension of an MNE's production and distribution activity into a new country or region specifically to supply its local market.[1] The traditional context for MS was seen as innately defensive, in that it was usually considered as a second-best mode of supplying a market that was closed to imports by high levels of trade restraints (that is, tariff-jumping investment). But here we are dealing with a wave of FDI into China that coincides with the progressive removal of import barriers. Nevertheless more contemporary perceptions of an increasingly proactive (aggressive) MS motivation can be considered as potentially relevant. Thus an objective for MS operations in economies that are in the process of opening up and of implementing early stages of marketization can be active local responsiveness, in terms of adapting products and/or processes to local circumstances and generally securing early-mover experiences of conditions in such new and perhaps not fully defined or evolved market spaces.[2]

In the second motivation, 'efficiency seeking' (ES) MNEs relocate the production of established goods to a particular country (or region) in order to improve the competitiveness of an existing supply network. Thus the newly selected location is expected to provide the inputs to a standardized production process in a more cost-effective manner than a previous location in the network whose supply responsibility it then either usurps or supplements. Most of an ES facility's output is then exported to well-established markets for the MNE's goods, where the more competitive supply now allows the group to defend or enhance their existing market shares. Thus whilst MS complements existing production capacity (and thereby secures a wider market geographically), ES substitutes for parts of it (to deepen the supply of existing markets). It has been routinely hypothesized that newly emerging (or transition) economies will, on their opening to international competition, be revealed as having underutilized availabilities of the types of inputs that could support the pursuit of the optimized supply networks exemplified by the ES motivation in MNEs.

The MS and ES motivations address the need of MNEs to maximize the profitability they derive from the worldwide use of mature sources of competitiveness (products, processes and their associated technologies and practices). The remaining motivation then moves beyond the application of current capabilities in order to pursue the derivation of future sources of competitiveness. Thus 'knowledge seeking' (KS) reflects the acknowledgement in contemporary MNEs of a need to use dispersed facilities (subsidiaries and/or scientific laboratories or research collaborations) to support the longer-term regenerational aspects of strategic competitiveness (Papanastassiou and Pearce, 1999; Pearce, 1999). Such KS means the pursuit by MNEs of new technological capabilities, scientific capacity (research units) and creative expertise (market research, inventive engineers) from particular host countries, so as to extend the global competences (product range and core technology) of the group. The potential for emerging transition economies, such as China, to offer KS attributes to MNEs may be greater than might be initially considered. Thus commitment to advanced scientific research and extensive training in science and engineering may have put into place innovation-supporting capacities that were not properly realized under centrally planned environments. The potential to draw these into practical activation that emerges with marketization and opening to global competition may, at least initially, be most plausibly realized through the KS imperatives of MNEs.

In the contemporary MNE the diverse range of strategic imperatives is considered to be operationalized through different types of subsidiary. For our analysis we adopt a three-role variant of the scope typology (White and Poynter, 1984; D'Cruz, 1986; Pearce, 1989, 2001; Papanastassiou and Pearce, 1999, pp. 21–33) for categorization of subsidiaries. This typology considers three dimensions of subsidiary scope. Firstly, 'product' scope, which takes account of the extent of the product range to be supplied. Secondly, 'market' scope, where the basic distinction is between MS supply of a limited host-country (or some closely defined 'local') market (that is, essentially import-substitution) or ES access to much more extensive geographic markets (that is, export oriented). Finally, 'value-added (or functional)' scope, covering how many of the functions of what might be considered a 'complete' value chain the subsidiary operation encompasses.[3]

The first type of subsidiary in our variant of the scope typology is designated as a 'truncated miniature replica' (TMR). The traditional TMR positioning was seen as being the MS supply of important markets that could not be reached through trade.[4] This often involved supply of extensive parts of the MNE group's existing range of goods (thus the characterization as a 'miniature replica' of the parent company) so that product scope could be extensive. However, the protected market context implied a narrow market scope. In this traditional context the functional scope would be clearly 'truncated', with just some allowance for adaptation to products or processes (limited R&D) and for localized marketing of the goods (not logically extending to more development-oriented market research). Our view of contemporary modes of MS can allow for a more modern type of TMR, exploring local market potentials for a MNE's existing goods in newly open economies. This can somewhat extend functional scope, perhaps allowing for investigation of local technology and science (more committed R&D) and more ambitious market research. Taken with allowance for more ambitious attitudes in local management, the forward-looking capacities of this extended TMR scope can provide for evolution of such subsidiaries' status in their MNE groups.

The evolution of the global economy into an increasingly free-trade environment removed the protection barriers that underpinned the strategic logic and survival of TMRs. It also allowed MNEs to then build on the logic of free trade by focusing the production of particular goods in their product range in locations whose inputs optimized the cost-effectiveness of the production process. This provided the genesis of 'rationalised product subsidiaries' (RPSs). By comparison with TMRs, therefore, this type of subsidiary would reflect the 'rationalization' of the MNE's international supply profile into a network of specialized units, each focusing on highly efficient manufacture of a small subset of the group's products. In addition to building on a host-country's sources of comparative advantage, RPSs can enhance efficiency through realization of economies of scale (export-oriented access to the extended markets of the group) and through removal of X-inefficiency (which may have been endemic to the protected TMRs) due to a need to assert competitiveness within an ever evolving group supply network. From this description we can see that RPSs will have narrow product scope but extensive market scope (reversing the positioning of TMRs). The dependency of this routine and networked supply responsibility would mean an even more innately limited functional scope than TMRs.

Finally, 'product mandate' (PM) subsidiaries provide a very precise manifestation of KS in MNEs' global operations, by allowing individual (mandated) affiliates the scope to take localized initiatives in order to secure the development of specific new products that will represent unique extensions to the group's competitive range. This can build on creative attributes of the local economy (dynamic comparative advantage or created assets). Thus the PM's functional scope will here be extensive and normally include significant R&D, ambitious market research, creative engineering units and entrepreneurial subsidiary management. Since a PM's new products will be unique to the group they would normally be expected to have access to major segments of the global market (that is, wide market scope). The product scope of PMs is not definitionally determined, but would normally be expected to focus around the development and sustained competitive evolution of a relatively small group of products reflecting their distinctive core capabilities.

THE SURVEY

The study of the roles of MNE subsidiaries in China is based on the analysis of a questionnaire survey carried out between March and August 2005.[5] The initial population of 40 manufacturing subsidiaries was selected based on information provided by the Foreign Corporation Administration of China (FCAC). From a list of the largest foreign subsidiaries located in China, 40 were selected that had employment levels of at least 2,300 personnel. The 40 questionnaires were delivered to managing directors of foreign subsidiaries, either by post or in person. In the latter cases the survey was supplemented by an interview, which frequently yielded additional insights and perceptions that are reflected in the discussion of subsequent sections.

Ultimately 25 complete and useable replies were secured. By home country of parent MNE eight were German, two French, two more from elsewhere in Europe, five from the USA, six from Japan and two Korean. Machinery was the most strongly represented sector with nine subsidiaries, followed by six in electronics, five from telecommunications, three in motor vehicles and two others.

PRIMARY MOTIVATIONS OF SUBSIDIARIES IN CHINA

Respondents to the questionnaire were asked to indicate which of eight possible motivations best represented their predominant reason for setting up a subsidiary in China. Two of these motivations were not considered to be a primary reason for any of the subsidiaries. The first of these was entry into China 'after the MNE's rivals had entered [so as] to protect a position there'. Though this need not mean that such an oligopolistic response to strategic moves by rivals did not ever lead firms to initiate (or bring forward with greater alacrity) consideration of Chinese operations, it does seem that once such an operation was *in situ* its motivation was quite clearly defined in a more positive fashion. The second of these rejected motives was seen as 'to acquire knowledge or expertise from particular local scientific institutions'. Again this need not mean that this particularly ambitious variant of KS may not already be viable in China, but suggests that MNEs would not expect it to be implemented as a primary motivation of subsidiaries (at least at an early stage of their development).

Table 2.1   Motivations of MNE subsidiaries in China

	Motivation						
	A	B	C	D	E	F	Total
Sector							
Machinery	5	2	1	0	1	0	9
Electronics	4	0	0	1	0	1	6
Telecommunications	2	0	0	2	1	0	5
Automobiles	0	0	2	1	0	0	3
Other	0	0	1	1	0	0	2
Total	11	2	4	5	2	1	25

Notes:
Motivation
A – to expand the market for the MNE group's existing products.
B – to avoid costs of trade (for example, trade restraints and tariff barriers).
C – to make use of local technological and market knowledge to adapt the MNE group's established products for supply to local market.
D – to produce in China to make use of cheap labour, raw materials and natural resources.
E – to use local technological and market knowledge to develop new products for the Chinese market or for China's neighbour countries in Asia.
F – to use local science capacity to innovate new technology and products for the MNE group.
Two other motivations were tested but were not acknowledged by any respondents. These were (i) to enter the market after the MNE's rivals had entered to protect a position there; and (ii) to acquire knowledge or expertise from a particular local scientific institution.

The most strongly supported motivation in Table 2.1 then emerges as basic MS behaviour, in the form of 'to expand the market for the MNE group's existing products'. Thus nine of the 25 respondents saw the inherent need for firms to expand the demand for their established products, taken with the very obvious potential of the Chinese market in this regard, as providing an adequate explanation for the initiation of their operations. Here the sheer driving imperative of the size and growth of the Chinese market appears to render as secondary the question as to why that market is supplied by local production rather than through trade. However six other, still essentially MS, respondents did see their motivation as involving clear response to the 'local-supply' question. That only two of these (both in the machinery sector) endorsed the more traditional source of MS behaviour, in the form of 'to avoid costs of trade (for example, trade restraints and tariff barriers)', underlines the perception that MNE expansion into China correlates to a positive response to the opening of that economy. The four remaining MS subsidiaries then responded to the more contemporary proactive motivation, by setting out 'to make use of local technologies and market knowledge to adapt the MNE group's established products for supply to the local market'. This suggests that in the modern, differentiated and networked MNEs when a local market does assert itself as significantly strategically important it will do so (along with its size and growth potential) by manifesting distinctive tastes and conditions and the capacity to support (with technological and marketing expertise and insights) subsidiary-level adaptation to meet them. It may then be the case that some of these subsidiaries, whose initial MS motivation merely reflects the more obvious quantitative potentials of a market, will deepen their behaviour and capacities to respond to the more idiosyncratic potentials differentiating it.

The strategic motivation of ES was represented in the survey by the supply-side-driven decision 'to produce in China to make use of cheap labour, raw materials and natural resources'. This recognizes the potentials for Chinese inputs to enhance the competitive position of MNEs' current supply as a key strategic priority. Nevertheless only five respondents (dispersed over all industry sectors except machinery) saw this as the predominant motivation. Though the strategic significance of the Chinese market is an obvious factor in limiting the relative emphasis on an ES priority here, this result does also resemble other evidence for smaller host countries, that also refute the initially theorized use of local inputs as a dominant attraction to early MNE operations in transition economies (see note 2). It can be suggested that this may relate to the fact that the performance of an ES subsidiary has implications (including reliability and reputation) in a wider component of the MNE's competitive environment (Manea and Pearce, 2004, 2006). If a new ES subsidiary in a (potentially lower-cost) newly open location substitutes for a higher-cost, but reliable, established subsidiary and then proves less effective than predicted (due to infrastructural or institutional failures or limitations, for example) the knock-on competitive effects could be considerable. It could then be suggested that MS supply of a local market (even one less substantial and strategic than China's) is a useful, lower risk, way of learning about a country's economic conditions, and thereby facilitating a more informed basis for an extension to ES priorities.

As would be expected, KS was sparse as a dominant motivation in these early MNE entrants to China. Yet two of the three KS variants did receive some recognition. Thus two respondents endorsed 'to use local technological and market knowledge to develop new products for the Chinese market or for China's neighbour countries in Asia'. This could be seen as an evolutionary upgrading of the third MS motivation, extending from the use of local expertise to adapt existing MNE goods into a more complete localized new product development process targeting the specific needs of Asian markets. One subsidiary endorsed its commitment 'to use local science capacity to innovate new technology and products for the MNE group'. This would represent much more radical innovation, deriving from locally originated new technology to add to the overall competitive scope of the parent MNE group.

ROLES OF SUBSIDIARIES IN CHINA

An alternative reflection on the strategic positioning of MNE subsidiaries in China derives from a question that asked them to specify their main role from five options (Table 2.2) derived within the parameters of the scope typology outlined earlier.

Two of the descriptions of subsidiary roles provided are broadly of the TMR type, in that they focus on supply of the Chinese market and allow for local production of all relevant parts of the MNE group's existing product range. This is then also MS behaviour in that it predominantly sees local production substituting for supply through trade (that is, the subsidiaries are strategically outside of global-network supply programmes). The first of these is the most routine type of MS[6] in the form of 'to produce the MNE group's established product range for the Chinese

Table 2.2   Roles of subsidiaries of MNEs in China

	Role of subsidiary					
	A	B	C	D	E	Total
Sector						
Machinery	3	3	3	0	0	9
Electronics	1	2	1	1	1	6
Telecommunications	0	1	2	1	1	5
Automobiles	0	2	1	0	0	3
Other	0	1	1	0	0	2
Total	4	9	8	2	2	25

Notes:
Subsidiary roles
A – to produce the MNE group's established product range for the Chinese market.
B – to produce the MNE group's established product range for the Chinese market, with adaptation of products or production processes to suit local demand and conditions.
C – to produce a specialized part of the MNE group's established product range to supply Chinese and nearby Asian country markets.
D – to produce a specialized part of the MNE group's established product range, or component parts for assembly, as part of the MNE group's world-wide supply network.
E – to develop and produce products that are new for the MNE group.

market'. That only four respondents endorsed this role rates it much lower than the basic form of MS in Table 2.1. More significant then, with nine replies, is the second variant of TMR[7] 'to produce the MNE group's established product range for the Chinese market, with adaptation of products or production processes to suit local demand and conditions'. By comparison to the evaluation of motivations in Table 2.1 this suggests greater prevalence of the more contemporary form of MS, involving a significant commitment to adjusting the sources of current MNE competitiveness used to meet local conditions.

Again by comparison with the assessment of broad motivation in Table 2.1 this evaluation of subsidiary roles suggests a greater status for ES activity. Thus the second most prevalent role overall (eight replies) is 'to produce a specialized part of the MNE group's established product range to supply Chinese and nearby Asian country markets'. We see this as a RPS emphasis since the subsidiary focuses on a specialized part of the product range and is allocated a market scope that is not constrained to the host-country market. Here again the contrasting results may reflect the unique characteristics of China as a host-country market. In normal analysis of the RPS positioning this ES priority is routinely correlated with export orientation. However, the market for RPS supply does normally encompass the host country on a non-preferred basis (that is, by contrast with TMR supply). Usually this means that the local market represents a small (almost always minority) share that does not impinge in any particular way on subsidiaries' views of their role. The vast Chinese market may change these dimensions here. Thus some subsidiaries that saw their role as most adequately defined in this way ('C' in Table 2.2) may view the importance of the newly available Chinese market as best defining their motivation.

The limited response to the two remaining roles in Table 2.2 again reinforces the view that the early entry of MNE subsidiaries into China predominantly represents very localized context-specific behaviour. Thus these roles (each endorsed by one electronics and one telecommunications subsidiary) would assert a position in the wider supply or creative concerns of the MNE group. The first would be to claim a more distinct and powerful globalized ES status, in the form of 'to produce a specialized part of the MNE group's established product range or component parts for assembly, as a part of the MNE group's world-wide supply network'. As suggested earlier, such a positioning in the supply of an MNE's more significant established market areas (and, therefore, with the potential to compromise reputation there) might emerge more strongly once quality and reliability has been demonstrated in less strategically defined 'local' markets (for example, first three roles). Similarly, the essentially PM role of 'to develop and produce products that are new for the MNE group' should have the potential to evolve from experience and knowledge gained in the more adaptive versions of MS (for example, 'B' in Table 2.2).

SOURCES OF TECHNOLOGY

The survey asked the respondents to evaluate the importance of five sources or types of technology that might be utilized in their operations. By asking respondents to not only indicate their predominant or primary source of technology but also (where appropriate) a secondary source, it was hoped to not only obtain further insights on the initial positioning and competitive basis of subsidiaries but also how any technological diversity might indicate the presence of possible dynamic or evolutionary scopes. In fact all of the seven subsidiaries that did not nominate a secondary source were of the TMR type. The interesting corollary of this is that all the ES RPS facilities did operate from more than one technology source. This initially confounds the expectation that RPS operations would be expected to apply an MNE's existing technology in an undifferentiated form so as to increase the efficiency of supply of well-established products. We will comment further on this below.

Two of the five sources evaluated in Table 2.3 recognized that, in some way, MNEs' initial operations in China would be established around the groups' mature and commercially successful technologies. However, by far the most predominant of these options was 'MNE group's existing technology from which subsidiaries adapt products for the Chinese market or create new products', thus allowing scope for considerable adaptation and differentiation in localizing a subsidiary's operations even when positioned within its group's staple competences. Thus 16 (64 per cent) of respondents rated this as their primary technology source and four (16 per cent) more applied it on a secondary basis. The undifferentiated acceptance of mature sources of parent-company competitiveness in the form of 'MNE group's existing technology embodied in established products' was then limited to seven (28 per cent) cases as a primary type and seven more secondary ones.

Three ways in which distinctively local sources of technology might be part of the differentiation of subsidiaries' operations in China were offered for the evaluation of respondents. Here some degree of adoption of 'established local Chinese technology' was already beginning to emerge in subsidiaries, with eight (32 per cent) acknowledging its use (two as a primary source and six in a secondary capacity). However, whilst subsidiaries often seemed to have been able to pick up local technologies of established

Table 2.3   Sources of technology used by subsidiaries in China, by role of subsidiary

| | Subsidiary Type | | | | | | | |
| | TMR | | RPS | | PM | | Total | |
	Prim.	Sec.	Prim.	Sec.	Prim.	Sec.	Prim.	Sec.
Sources of technology								
A	4	4	3	3	0	0	7	7
B	9	0	7	3	0	1	16	4
C	0	2	0	4	2	0	2	6
D	0	0	0	0	0	1	0	1
E	0	0	0	0	0	0	0	0
Total	13	6	10	10	2	2	25	18

Notes:
Prim. = Primary source. Sec = Secondary source.
Subsidiary types
TMR – truncated miniature replica.
RPS – rationalized product subsidiary.
PM – product mandate.

Sources of technology
A – MNE group's existing technology embodied in established products.
B – MNE group's existing technology from which subsidiaries adapt products for the
    Chinese market or create new products.
C – established local Chinese technology.
D – new technology derived by the Chinese subsidiary itself.
E –technology created for the subsidiary by local scientific institutions or local companies.

effectiveness the generation of new technology, either within their operations or through external collaborations, was not yet having significant
effect. Thus 'new technology derived by the Chinese subsidiary itself' was
rated a secondary source by one subsidiary, but no respondent yet felt that
'technology created for the subsidiary by local scientific institutions or
local companies' was part of their currently operative scope.[8]
   By types of subsidiary it is not surprising that nine (69.2 per cent) of
TMRs used adapted versions of their groups' existing technologies as their
primary source, as this role's prioritizing of the local market as a distinct
competitive environment can logically allow for responsive changes to the
products and processes through which initial entry is secured. The remaining four TMRs used unadapted established group technology as their
primary (and only) source. In terms of secondary sources four of the nine
TMRs that designated adapted established technology as their primary

source (that is, in the majority part of the product range they supplied to the Chinese market) did also use the unchanged variant in some of their goods. In addition two TMRs used established Chinese technologies as an input to their adaptation activities.[9]

In terms of primary technology the ten RPSs are proportionately very similar to the TMRs, with seven using the adapted and three the unaltered versions of the group's established technologies. As already noted the surprising fact about RPSs here is the deviation from the normal expectations of routine cost-effective use of existing technologies to secure competitive supply of particular limited parts of the product range. The normally anticipated source of this ES capability is then expected to derive from the availability of low-cost local inputs, rather than any adjustments to the technology. This is confounded here in two ways. Firstly, that a majority of the RPSs acknowledge adaptation within their primary technology. Secondly, that all ten designate a secondary, differentiating, technology somewhere within their scope. In fact this does indicate that three of the seven subsidiaries that mainly adapt technologies do, nevertheless, supply a minority part of their range using unaltered technology: whilst each of those three whose main supply responsibility involved unchanged goods also do apply secondary technologies in a limited part of their operations. It is very interesting that four of these RPSs recognized established local Chinese technology as the most significant secondary source in adapting and differentiating their supply capabilities. From this we can hypothesize, in line with earlier discussion of these RPSs, that the unusual dominance of one market (that is, the Chinese) can generate adjustment to their performance of the role. Thus whilst the defining motivation remains cost-efficiency in production of a focused part of the group's established range, the choice of China as the location for the supply of a wider geographical market may provoke minor adjustments to the routine technology to be used. This could involve changes to the products to reflect the needs of Chinese customers (even if these changes do not similarly improve marketability of the good in the other parts of the RPS's market space) or changes to the process to better use Chinese inputs.

The two PM subsidiaries both indicated that the primary technology source for their innovation success was established Chinese technology. This may suggest an evolutionary process, in which MNE subsidiaries in China that originally brought local technologies into their operations so as to enrich their initial scope on entry then found that these products and/ or processes actually provided such a distinctive and individualized character to their competitiveness that it asserted a unique PM status within the group. In one of these cases the local technology was supported by use of adapted elements of the MNE's existing technology. In the other, existing local technology was enhanced, in a supporting manner, by new technology derived within the subsidiary itself. The survey also addresses another aspect of the technology scope and evolutionary potential of subsidiaries in China, in terms of their current and future commitment to R&D (Von Zedtwitz, 2004). In fact only two of the subsidiaries (both with the KS motivation as characterized in Table 2.1) had R&D laboratories contributing to their current capabilities. One of these was responsible for the generation of new products that specifically targeted (at least initially) the Chinese market. Its subsidiary was thus concerned mainly with selling new products in high-income areas, such as Beijing, Shanghai and Macau. The other laboratory takes responsibility for innovation for the entire MNE group. It develops technology for new goods and production processes and also undertakes some of the marketing of its new products. Its new technology needed to be validated by HQ, which then allowed it to be used in other subsidiaries. Of the respondents that did not yet have R&D units 11 (47.8 per cent) said they expected to have one in the future. Thus one subsidiary was planning to build its R&D unit during 2006; six more anticipated that they would have a laboratory within five years and four more within ten years.

AUTONOMY IN MNE SUBSIDIARIES IN CHINA

The varied roles, responsibilities and capacities of subsidiaries reviewed in previous sections are likely to have different implications for the extent of managerial autonomy allowed to these facilities. This was assessed by requesting respondents to indicate which of three levels of autonomy best described their own status.

Here 'high' autonomy was available where a subsidiary's Chinese management could make decisions on not only day-to-day operations but also on strategic marketing and development. Thus they include the autonomy to do technological research and to develop new products, perhaps for the MNE group as well as their own markets. Five respondents felt that their managerial autonomy had attained this high level, allowing them scope to take essentially strategic decisions about their own competitive development. Although all five considered that they were allowed autonomy to do technological R&D of new products, only two felt they were so far fulfilling this potential. The other three respondents explained that they were not yet fully prepared to achieve this degree of technological individualism. But all these were considering having subsidiary-level R&D centres in order to move towards realization of the competitive scope allowed by high autonomy.

Next 'moderate' autonomy allowed subsidiaries that were essentially constrained technologically to the supply of established MNE group products to take the initiative to adapt these to meet local conditions and demand of the market. Sixteen of the respondents felt this was the level of autonomy allowed them by their parent MNE. Sometimes autonomy in altering product characteristics was constrained by a refusal to allow changes to manufacturing technology. MNE parents of subsidiaries operating at this level of autonomy often decided on the hiring of the important managerial personnel who would exercise this moderate discretion. In some cases this still included sending top management from HQ.

Finally, 'low' autonomy constrained management to day-to-day decisions that, in effect, limited their responsibility to routine production of products delegated to them by the parent company for a fixed local market. These managements would have no scope at all to alter the essentials of their own competitive capacities, let alone any dimension of the group's scope. However, only four of the 25 subsidiaries felt they were still held at this ineffective and inactive level of managerial discretion.

CONCLUSIONS

Overall the results confirm that it is the local market that provides the most decisive impetus to the formulation of the initial positioning of MNEs' subsidiaries in China. In somewhat differently nuanced ways this emerges clearly from both the categorization of motivations (Table 2.1) and of subsidiary roles (Table 2.2). The evidence, especially that from subsidiary roles, then indicates quite strongly that this represents the more strategically updated version of MS, with a strong commitment to adaptive responsiveness to local conditions and needs and little acknowledgement of the more traditional tariff-jumping. This pattern is further confirmed in the information on technologies used. Thus whilst all 13 TMRs, as would be inevitable, used established technologies of the MNE group as their primary source nine of these said they needed to adapt it to respond to local needs and potentials.

Ten of the subsidiaries emerged as being of the RPS type, with all except two of these focusing on regional supply to China and neighbouring Asian markets. Two facts from elsewhere in the analysis can be related to this. Firstly, only five subsidiaries in Table 2.1 endorsed the logical core of ES motivation in the form of use of low-cost inputs. Secondly, seven of the ten RPSs adapted the established technology they used (Table 2.3), which would not normally be expected in the fulfilment of the pure ES-supply role. As we have argued this may reflect a further influence of the Chinese market. Thus whilst the RPS has been allocated a wider market scope than just China, the fact that China is both its location and the clear largest part of its market may provoke MS-style adaptation as a strong characteristic of its behaviour.

In terms of the expectations, in wider analysis of MNEs' evolution, that ES/RPS activity would supersede MS/TMR positioning the limited status of ES here may be surprising (though we have observed that the same result has been found in European transition economies). Three possible influences can be indicated. The particular force of the exceptional characteristics of the Chinese market have already been noted. By contrast, though there is a strong a priori view of the ES potentials in China, these are not (unlike the market) categorically different from other locations. Indeed like comparable locations (for example, export processing zones) the ES potentials in China are focused in a clearly and institutionally defined area (the coastal provinces).[10] Secondly, ES performance in one location has external benefits and costs throughout a MNE supply network. Whatever the apparent low-cost potentials may appear to be, MNEs may wait to co-opt them until they gain confidence in the reliability of the wider institutional and infrastructural environment. Thirdly, as noted earlier, a new RPS will divert supply responsibility from an established facility elsewhere in the network. A more politically experienced and adept management in the threatened subsidiary may then be able to use network connections and influence to slow such relocation, retarding ES expansion into new and unfamiliar locations.

As would clearly be anticipated at this early stage, KS motivation and the localized product development of PM subsidiaries only claim very marginal status amongst the primary activities of the respondents so far. However, elements in the current status of subsidiaries can be seen to have quite promising evolutionary potentials. Notably the fact that established Chinese technology is the primary source for both of the PMs and is also a secondary source in four of the ten RPSs (as well as two TMRs) suggests MNEs can already see this as a developmental potential. Further, the clearly asserted desire to adapt MNEs' existing competences to reflect local conditions and capabilities in TMRs and RPSs can always possess logical potential to deepen into more fully localized and wider-targeted innovations.

NOTES

1. An MNE that used MS subsidiaries as its predominant mode of operation would be adopting what Porter (1986) termed a 'multidomestic' strategy. By considering MS as

one among a number of options we here see it more as a potential facet of the scope of firms with more evolved global strategies.

2. Several survey studies (Rojec and Svetlicic, 1993; Donges and Wieners, 1994; Rojec, 1994; Lankes and Venables, 1996; Mutinelli and Piscitello, 1997; Meyer, 1998; Manea and Pearce, 2004, 2006) of MNEs' operations in the transitional economies of Europe in the 1990s found MS to be the leading motivation.
3. To some extent this is likely to correlate to another aspect of product scope; in terms of whether the subsidiary's products have already been generated elsewhere in the group (so that its value-added scope only extends to the ability to assimilate and operationalize established technologies transferred to it) or are the results of its own innovative activities (therefore requiring many more of the creative aspects of the value chain).
4. In industrialized countries TMRs may have emerged initially during the protectionism of the interwar years. In developing countries the main context was the import-substitution strategies of the 1950s and 1960s.
5. The survey was carried out by Si Zhang as part of the preparation of an MSc dissertation at Reading University. The research has since been extended in doctoral studies.
6. The 'adopter' variant of miniature replica described by White and Poynter (1984).
7. The 'adapter' variant of miniature replica described by White and Poynter (1984).
8. Interviewed managers suggested that it was hard to find a match between the technologies needed by subsidiaries in order to move forward from their current operations and aims and the research carried out by local scientific institutions or other Chinese firms.
9. In an interview the manager of one of these TMRs indicated that its use of local technology in its operations only took place after investigation and validation of this Chinese technology at headquarters.
10. For data and analysis of the geographical location and performance of FDI in China see Henley et al. (1999), Buckley et al. (2002) and Li (2004). Ge (1999) provides discussion and analysis of Special Economic Zones.

REFERENCES

Behrman, J.N. (1984), *Industrial Policies: Industrial Restructuring and Transnationals*, Lexington, MA: Lexington Books.
Buckley, P.J., J. Clegg, C. Wang and A.R. Cross (2002), 'FDI, regional differences and economic growth: panel data evidence from China', *Transnational Corporations*, **11**(1), 1–28.
D'Cruz, J. (1986), 'Strategic management of subsidiaries', in H. Etemad and L.S. Dulude (eds), *Managing the Multinational Subsidiary*, London: Croom Helm, pp. 75–89.
Donges, J.B. and J. Wieners (1994), 'Foreign investment in the transformation process of Eastern Europe', *International Trade Journal*, **VIII**, 163–91.
Dunning, J.H. (1993), *Multinational Enterprises and the Global Economy*, Wokingham: Addison Wesley.
Ge, W. (1999), 'Special Economic Zones and the opening of the Chinese economy: some lessons for economic liberalisation', *World Development*, **27**(7), 1267–85.
Henley, J., C. Kirkpatrick and G. Wilde (1999). 'Foreign direct investment in China: recent trends and current policy issues', *The World Economy*, **22**(2), 223–43.
Lankes, H.P. and A.J. Venables (1996), 'Foreign direct investment in economic transition: the changing pattern of investment', *Economics of Transition*, **4**, 331–47.

Li, S. (2004), 'Location and performance of foreign firms in China', *Management International Review*, **44**(2), 151–70.

Manea, J. and R. Pearce (2004), *Multinationals and Transition*, Basingstoke: Palgrave Macmillan.

Manea, J. and R. Pearce (2006), 'MNEs' strategies in Central and Eastern Europe: key elements of subsidiary behaviour', *Management International Review*, **46**(2), 235–55.

Meyer, K.E. (1998), *Direct Investment in Economies in Transition*, Cheltenham, UK and Lyme, NH, USA: Edward Elgar Publishing.

Mutinelli, M. and L. Piscitello (1997), 'Differences in the strategic orientation of Italian MNEs in Central and Eastern Europe: the influence of firm-specific factors', *International Business Review*, **6**, 185–205.

Papanastassiou, M. and R. Pearce (1999), *Multinationals, Technology and National Competitiveness*, Cheltenham, UK and Northampton, MA, USA: Edward Elgar Publishing.

Pearce, R. (1989), *The Internationalisation of Research and Development by Multinational Enterprises*, London: Macmillan.

Pearce, R. (1999), 'The evolution of technology in multinational enterprises: the role of creative subsidiaries', *International Business Review*, **8**, 125–48.

Pearce, R. (2001), 'Multinationals and industrialisation: the bases of inward investment policy', *International Journal of the Economics of Business*, **8**(11), 51–73.

Porter, M.E. (1986), 'Competition in global industries: a conceptual framework', in M.E. Porter (ed.), *Competition in Global Industries*, New York: Free Press, pp. 15–60.

Rojec, M. (1994) 'Foreign direct investment in the transformation process', *Development and International Cooperation*, **X,** 5–26.

Rojec, M. and M. Svetlicic (1993), 'Foreign direct investment in Slovenia', *Transnational Corporations*, **2**, 135–51.

Von Zedtivitz, M. (2004), 'Managing foreign R&D laboratories in China', *R&D Management*, **34**(4), 439–52.

White, R.E. and T.A. Poynter (1984), 'Strategies for foreign-owned subsidiaries in Canada', *Business Quarterly*, **9**, 59–69.

3. Multinationals' R&D in China and its implications for China's national system of innovation

Si Zhang

INTRODUCTION

China has been bearing the title of 'the World's factory' for the last three decades, while, however, the potential of the country's ability to sustain and deepen multinational enterprises (MNEs) competitiveness, within or outside the nation, has been overlooked. The chapter seeks to examine the growing research and development (R&D) of MNEs in China, and its implications for China's National System of Innovation (NSI), by documenting and analysing the extent and the strategic roles and motivations of these laboratories. Thus, a quite remarkable fact in the recent extensive entry of MNEs into China has been the quickness with which a majority of these firms have established R&D laboratories there.

The chapter elaborates an analysis of results from a questionnaire survey conducted in 2005 to examine, firstly, the existence of MNE overseas R&D in China by the six industrial sectors involved in the survey (including automobiles, electronics and electrical equipment, food and drink, IT hardware and software, personal care and pharmaceuticals and chemicals). In the research, technology-intensive industries, such as telecommunications electronics and pharmaceuticals, tend to receive more attention and investment in R&D projects and to enjoy a rapid development in research capacity. Surprisingly, however, companies in some industries that are often considered as middle- or low-tech sectors, such as food and drink and personal care, also have R&D facilities quickly established in China. Thus one aim of the chapter will be developed by looking into how the roles of R&D labs are different in each of the six manufacturing sectors.

Overall, R&D activities in China mainly focus on better serving the Chinese market, either by adapting existing group technology or by generating new technology and new products suitable for the local market. However, research activities within certain R&D units are found to be targeting not just the host-country market but aiming to actually become parts of MNEs' wider global innovation regimes, such as developing new technology and production techniques for markets elsewhere in the world or even engaging in pure scientific research that is not immediately applicable to current production technologies and supply activities. These types of research units largely belong to MNEs from particular regions, notably Europe and the USA. Also, the sustainability of MNEs' commitment to an economy, as it undergoes the competitive reformulations of development, depends on how they react to the changes in location advantages (LAs) and the content of those that emerge (Pearce and Zhang, 2010). Therefore, the chapter will proceed to discuss the roles of MNEs' R&D in China by their home-country origins, as well as by the specific economic regions they are located in in China. The three focal economic zones are Jing-Jin-Yi Economic Circle (JEC), Pearl River Delta (PRD) and Yangtze River Delta economic zone (YRD). These three 'circle' economies have the closest connections to foreign capital. They account for 6.3 per cent of China's land and 24 per cent of the population, whilst contributing around 48 per cent of the country's gross domestic product (GDP) and over 80 per cent and 70 per cent of the international trade balance and of actual use of foreign investments, respectively. The research aims to look at the performance of MNE subsidiaries in terms of higher-value-adding development activities in the special economic environments.

What is also equally interesting at this stage are the reasons that respondents gave for not having R&D operations established in China. The result shows that the main explanation is that the majority of such subsidiaries are currently technically supported by R&D units of other subsidiaries within the group. Such high level of interdependency was usually found in mature multinational global networks where some subsidiaries have succeeded in decentralization and have come to the stage of both increasing their individualized identification among the group and improving competitiveness in host countries. However, in China, while subsidiaries are still largely relying on mature centrally generated technology, a high tendency of intragroup interdependency has already appeared with wide scope. This suggests how special the Chinese market is to fulfilling successful multinational business operations. The chapter will thus dedicate a large section to elaborating this important issue.

DATA

The chapter uses results from a questionnaire survey of MNEs' subsidiaries in China. The respondents were chief executive officers (CEOs) of subsidiaries of manufacturing multinational companies on the Fortune 500 list of 2005. Overall 134 subsidiaries responded to the survey but five were unusable due to incomplete information, which left 129 valid observations, one fourth of which were conducted as face-to-face interviews. Apart from subsidiaries' general information, questions were also asked about their motivation, strategic roles in China and their competitive evolution and R&D activities. The overall research project received generous help from the National Bureau of Statistics of China and from the Ministry of Commerce of the People's Republic of China, these being the bridge connecting to the companies and providing valuable statistics.

THE PRESENCE OF MNE R&D LABORATORIES IN CHINA

The results show that 69 (53 per cent) of the subsidiaries have established their own R&D labs in China. It is also worth noticing that 20 (that is, 33 per cent out of 60) of the subsidiaries that have not yet set up R&D labs indicated in the survey that they will, or are already planning to, establish their own R&D unit within five years.

Table 3.1 shows the establishment of MNE R&D labs in China by the sector of MNEs. The highest percentage of subsidiaries is found in both IT and personal care industries. In electronics, pharmaceuticals and food and drink, there are also over half of the subsidiaries that have set up labs. In the automobile industry, however, only 35 per cent of subsidiaries have R&D labs, which is a reflection of the fact that central group technology, viewed as MNEs' core competence, is still mainly developed outside of China, probably in places that are considered to be long-standing key locations in the development of the automobile industry. In the table it also seems that the decision of whether or not to build subsidiary-level R&D labs in China are differently made by MNEs from different home countries. Subsidiaries from western countries are more likely to have their own firm-level R&D labs established in China compared to Asian companies. Thus over 60 per cent of European and US MNEs set up R&D operations, while, respectively, 50 per cent and only 26 per cent of Korean and Japanese firms do so. This tends to confirm Japanese MNEs' conservative view towards decentralized R&D (Cantwell, 1995). By geographical location in China, the differences in the distribution of MNE R&D labs across the three economic circles are not extensive. However, Table 3.1 does show that subsidiaries located outside any of the three designated zones have a significantly smaller density of R&D labs.

Table 3.1   MNE R&D labs by industry, region of origin and regions in China

Industry	Without		With		Total	
	count	%	count	%	count	%
Auto & parts	13	65.00	7	35.00	20	100
Electronics	30	49.18	31	50.82	61	100
Food & drink	3	50.00	3	50.00	6	100
IT	3	25.00	9	75.00	12	100
Personal care	3	25.00	9	75.00	12	100
Pharmaceutical & chemical	8	44.44	10	55.56	18	100
Total	60	46.51	69	53.49	129	100
Pearson Chi-Square	7.447					

Region of origin	Without		With		Total	
	count	%	count	%	count	%
USA	17	37.78	28	62.22	45	100
Europe	20	40.00	30	60.00	50	100
Japan	19	73.08	7	26.92	26	100
Korea	4	50.00	4	50.00	8	100
Total	60	46.51	69	53.49	129	100
Pearson Chi-Square	9.646**					

Region in China	Without		With		Total	
	count	%	count	%	count	%
JEC	18	14.0	24	86.0	42	100
PRD	7	43.75	9	56.25	16	100
YRD	24	26.0	33	74.0	57	100
OUT	11	43.0	3	57.0	14	100
Total	60	63	69	37	129	100
Pearson Chi-Square	6.503*					

Note: $*p < 0.1$; $**p < 0.05$; $***p < 0.01$. OUT – Labs outside JEC, PRD and YRD.

REASONS FOR NOT HAVING R&D

There are 60 subsidiaries in the survey that do not have R&D units in China. Such respondents mainly gave three possible reasons to explain why they have no subsidiary-level R&D units. They are (i) it is not necessary to have research and development as it is not needed to support our current position; (ii) our subsidiary is supported by HQ labs where all our production techniques and technology came from; (iii) our subsidiary is supported by labs of other subsidiaries of our MNE in China, including regional R&D centres. Thirty-nine respondents specified the reasons for not having R&D, among whom only five stated the reason as being 'not necessary', 15 (38.5 per cent) indicated that they are supported by HQ and 19 (48.7 per cent) are supported by the MNEs' other Chinese labs.

By home regions (Table 3.2), US and Japanese firms rely on both HQ knowledge transfer and knowledge flows from other subsidiary labs inside China. European subsidiaries show the highest response to other labs of the group as the reason that they do not require R&D activities of their own. Korean firms are most likely to be sticking to their central technology sources. There could be three possible interpretations for this: (i) it means that European MNE subsidiaries are building up an integrated China-specific network, with a better understanding of the Chinese market; (ii) it means more autonomy from the HQ side; (iii) it reflects China's National System of Innovation by suggesting that it incorporates R&D resources, such as research personnel and infrastructure that can well sustain MNEs' R&D there, so that the cost of knowledge transfer from HQ is reduced. MNEs benefit from more cost-effective R&D and improved efficiency in R&D in response to the local market and, by doing so, their competitiveness in China is improved.

From the subsidiary perspectives this may also be due to the fact that the size of these operations is not yet big enough to justify labs of their own. However, this arrangement is more reasonably understood as largely a part of MNEs' strategies in China. The labs of those subsidiaries that are actually sharing their resources and technical outputs with other subsidiaries in China can be seen as regional R&D centres. For example, respondents mentioned that they are supported by Beijing or Shanghai subsidiary-level R&D of other subsidiaries that have the budget and ability to run a large R&D base. In this case, capital resources and human resources are centralized in one subsidiary in an advanced location in China, such as Beijing, Shanghai and Guangzhou, so that the R&D centre can reach a certain scale that is strong enough to modify and transfer, or create and transfer, technology to other subsidiaries in order to achieve economies of scale. Thus an R&D centre often takes care of several other subsidiaries apart from the one they actually belong to. So here MNEs are seemingly adopting new strategic approaches in gaining competitiveness in China. R&D activities are decentralized away from HQ but then centralized when they come to China. The establishment of such regional R&D centres is a mature and unique strategy of MNEs in China, because it reflects their understanding of the country's large market scale and their perception of the fact that the provincial markets are hugely dispersed, so that excessive decentralization of their R&D activities to provincial units in order to better serve each province or city may drive up the cost and lower efficiency.

Table 3.2 also presents the results by industries. Over half of subsidiaries in automobiles, electronics and food and drink industries indicate that they receive technical support from other subsidiaries of the group elsewhere in China. IT and pharmaceutical subsidiaries tend to be technically sustained by their own HQs. By economic circles, in JEC and YRD, subsidiaries without their own labs inclined slightly towards seeking support from HQs, while subsidiaries in PRD and outside any circles are more likely to get support from other labs within the group. All in all, only a small number of respondents (12.8 per cent) considered a lab in their own operation to be an unnecessary step, again emphasizing the pervasive importance of technological development to MNEs' subsidiaries in China.

ROLES OF MNE R&D LABS IN CHINA

Based on the typology developed by Papanastassiou and Pearce (1999) the questionnaire survey addressed the roles of MNEs' Chinese labs. The respondents were asked to evaluate each of the four possible roles that their subsidiary-level R&D may adopt in China, the result of which is shown in Table 3.3. Respondents evaluated the dominance of each of the four roles as 4 points if it is their 'only' role, 3 for a 'major' role, 2 for a 'secondary' role and 1 for 'not' being part of their lab's responsibility.

The first role optioned in the survey was that of adapting existing technology of the MNE group to suit local markets, which is the Support Laboratory (SL) role in the typology. The major responsibility for such R&D units is to apply adapted central technology and production processes into local production. What is different in China from the earlier applications of the typology is that subsidiaries completed the evolution from SL to more ambitious, Locally Integrated Laboratory (LIL), types of role in a considerably shorter period of time, often involving an almost immediate transformation. Chinese labs initially help their subsidiaries to supply a substantial mature product range to the host-country market and at the same time help to adjust production in a more cost-efficient manner. They adapt technology and production techniques for a short period of time, but soon look for the potential for rationalization and development. Basically SL activity often soon begins to function as just a supplementary task within more ambitious LIL labs. Thus, in this chapter, the support laboratory role is defined as 'to adapt existing technology of the MNE

Table 3.2   Reasons for not having subsidiary-R&D labs

Industry	Not necessary		Supported by HQ R&D		Supported by labs of other subsidiaries in China		Total	
	Count	%	Count	%	Count	%	Count	%
Auto & parts	2.00	33.33	1	16.67	3	50.00	6	100
Electronics	1	4.76	7	33.33	13	61.90	21	100
Food & drink	1.00	50.00	0	0.00	1	50.00	2	100
IT	0	0.00	2	0	0	0.00	2	100
Personal care	1.00	33.33	1	33.33	1	33.33	3	100
Pharmaceutical & chemical	0.000	0.00	4	80.00	1	20.00	5	100
Total	5	12.82	15	38.46	19	48.72	39	100
Pearson Chi-Square	15.677							

Home region	Not necessary		Supported by HQ R&D		Supported by labs of other subsidiaries in China		Total	
	Count	%	Count	%	Count	%	Count	%
USA	2.00	20.00	4	40.00	4	40.00	10	100
Europe	1	6.67	3	20.00	11	73.33	15	100
Japan	1.00	10.00	5	50.00	4	40.00	10	100
Korea	1	25.00	3	75.00	0	0.00	4	100
Total	5.00	12.82	15	38.46	19	48.72	39	100
Pearson Chi-Square	8.566							

Circles	Not necessary		Supported by HQ R&D		Supported by labs of other subsidiaries in China		Total	
	Count	%	Count	%	Count	%	Count	%
JEC	3.00	33.33	4	44.44	2	22.22	9	100
PRD	0	0.00	2	33.33	4	66.67	6	100
YRD	0.00	0.00	9	56.25	7	43.75	16	100
OUT	2	25.00	0	0.00	6	75.00	8	100
Total	5.00	12.82	15	38.46	19	48.72	39	100
Pearson Chi-Square	14.127**							

Note: OUT – Labs outside JEC, PRD and YRD.

Table 3.3   Roles of MNE R&D in China

	ADAPT-MNETECH		LOCAL-DEVELOP		GLOBAL-DEVELOP		INNOVA-TION	
	Mean	Std dev.	Mean	Std dev.	Mean	Std dev.	Mean	Std dev.
JEC	2.52	0.814	2.82	0.395	2.20	0.894	1.35	0.671
PRD	3.00	0.535	2.75	0.463	1.25	0.707	1.00	0.000
YRD	2.88	0.492	2.81	0.397	1.56	0.840	1.31	0.644
OUT	2.67	1.528	2.33	1.155	2.33	1.155	1.33	0.577
Total	2.77	0.684	2.78	0.450	1.76	0.911	1.29	0.607
Chi-Square	4.23		0.91		10.151**		2.47	
df	3.00		3.00		3.00		3.00	
Auto & parts	3.00	0.000	2.43	0.535	1.00	0.000	1.00	0.000
Electronics	2.67	0.679	2.70	0.542	2.00	0.938	1.23	0.514
Food & drink	3.33	0.577	3.00	0.000	1.67	1.155	1.33	0.577
IT	2.22	1.093	2.89	0.333	2.33	0.866	1.44	0.726
Personal care	3.11	0.333	2.89	0.333	1.56	0.882	1.22	0.667
Pharma-ceutical	2.90	0.316	3.00	0.000	1.30	0.675	1.50	0.850
Chi-Square	10.847*		10.390*		13.043**		3.66	
df	5.00		5.00		5.00		5.00	
Total	2.77	0.684	2.78	0.450	1.76	0.911	1.29	0.607
USA	2.85	0.675	2.88	0.326	1.69	0.928	1.42	0.703
Europe	2.70	0.669	2.75	0.441	1.77	0.908	1.19	0.491
Japan	3.00	0.577	2.57	0.787	1.71	0.951	1.29	0.756
Korea	2.25	0.957	2.75	0.500	2.25	0.957	1.00	0.000
Total	2.77	0.684	2.78	0.450	1.76	0.911	1.29	0.607
Chi-Square	3.66		2.13		1.47		3.16	
df	3.00		3.00		3.00		3.00	

Note: * is significant at 10%; ** is significant at 5%.

group to suit local markets' (ADAPTMNETECH). In the survey (Table 3.3) this role emerges as the equal strongest among the MNE labs in China.

Evidence has also, as suggested above, supported a strong presence of the second type of lab role, which is the LIL. In the survey, LIL is divided into two sub-types:(i) 'To develop new technology and products for local markets' (LOCALDEVELOP) and (ii) 'To develop new technology and products for the MNE global market' (GLOBALDEVELOP). The rationale for this is to emphasize the understanding of the implications of the Chinese market in MNEs' global innovation strategy (Papanastassiou and Pearce, 2009), so that we separate China from the global market. Forty-four R&D labs evaluated developing for the Chinese market (LOCALDEVELOP) as one of their major roles, while 11 also claimed developing for a wider global market (GLOBALDEVELOP) as another major role at the same time. An interesting fact is that all the labs that develop for their MNE's world market, or specific markets elsewhere, also conduct R&D for the Chinese market. However, the predominance of role GLOBALDEVELOP, with an overall average score of 1.76, is considerably weaker than the 2.78 of LOCALDEVELOP, which clearly confirms that serving the Chinese market and improving MNEs' competitive status there is the primary role of LILs.

The fourth type of role involves labs playing a part in their group's global innovation programme, in a way that is not directly related to current technology and production processes, and to seek to generate new knowledge and technology that is not immediately targeting new products (INNOVATION). This is the Internationally Interdependent Laboratory (IIL) in the typology. According to Papanastassiou and Pearce (1999), IILs mostly require the creation of independent (stand-alone) R&D units by MNEs, which has been verified by the survey. Among the labs that perform such a role as one of their major roles, they are either regional/central labs that support many other subsidiaries in China, or major labs with the largest amount of investment and directly supported by HQ. The overall predominance of the role is not significant here, with only four respondents indicating it as their major role and three as a secondary one. So we conclude that the largest proportion of subsidiary-level R&D is there to serve the Chinese market, compared to that with wider value-added objectives of the MNEs. However, we see the potential for it to grow among MNEs' China-based labs. Adaptation and development for the local market thus appear to be the two most important responsibilities for MNEs' China-based labs. Therefore, in general, R&D labs in China are locally oriented, mainly working on product improvement, cost-efficiency enhancement and new product development facing the Chinese market. Developing for the Chinese market now appears to be as relevant as adaptation, so that we can therefore conclude that MNE R&D in China is mainly local market-oriented and its main role is to significantly increase and deepen local competitiveness. To create new technology and new products for a wider global market is not yet of great strategic importance on average. However, judging by the fact that, in the survey responses, three points were already awarded to the global LIL and IIL roles by several respondents, some subsidiaries have already taken up these two broader innovation roles as one of their main commitments.

Adaptation and development for the local market are then pervasively the main roles across all industries. However, in some industries such as electronics, IT and pharmaceuticals, developing for the local market is now clearly more important than adaptation. In electronics and IT industries MNE R&D has also already started to commit to developing new technology for the market outside China. In the food and drink industry, due to the fact that the Chinese people have quite distinct preferences and traditions when it comes to eating and drinking, foreign companies often find that slight adjustments to, for example, flavours may not be enough for them to succeed in competition. More changes need to be made to the products, such as ingredients, processing methods and so on, which may then entail new production lines and so new products. This is when they need R&D to be involved and to be closely working with market research personnel and local marketing experts. Therefore, developing new products for the Chinese market appeared to be a more dominant responsibility than merely improving in product and production efficiency within this particular industry. Automobile MNEs' labs in China are restricted to strong adaptation. Development for the Chinese automobile market is weaker and basically no R&D is of wider concept.

By home-country origins, US and European labs generally focus more or less equally on locally oriented adaptation and development for the local market. Japanese R&D concentrates more decisively on adaptation and less so on local development. Korean R&D then is the most likely to develop for the global market, as well as for China.

By the economic circles in China the labs that are located in PRD units take a strong responsibility towards adaptation and towards development for the Chinese market, but have very limited commitment towards global development or innovation, by comparison with JEC or YRD. This suggests that, from the R&D point of view, PRD is most likely to provide basic value-adding inputs for the improvement or evolution of MNEs' extant technology and products for local competitiveness. In YRD the same local focus again predominates, but here commitment to the more outward-oriented roles is emerging. In JEC R&D is again taking up a strong local market position, though now more development than adaptation oriented, but also has the strongest focus on development for MNE group markets. Certainly it seems that MNE focus in the JEC area are rather more knowledge-seeking oriented compared to those in the Coastal states.

Though based on a small number of units the results for labs outside the three circles (OUT) emerge with a notably strong development focus. This may be indicative of policies towards the Western regions of China. Thus the Western areas are known as the less developed regions of China. However, as a result of China's Western development programme, the region is developing quickly in terms of both economy and science. Western provinces adopted foreign investment policies in quick succession during the past decade, in favour of both foreign investors and of local sustainable development, and thus successfully attract a large amount of foreign direct investment (FDI) flowing into the region. In terms of R&D, the Western region is now showing its capacities for scientific innovation by the incredibly large number of professional research personnel and the amount spent by the Western province governments to support R&D. Taking the poorest province in China, Guizhou, as an example, in 2005 GDP per capita was only 6,742 RMB (around $US 963) while the government spent 1.45 billion RMB on R&D projects, which was 64 per cent of GDP. There were 11,000 full-time research personnel, given that the population of the province was 39.04 million. The survey has confirmed that MNE subsidiaries have been taking notice of the rapid development in the Western region and have acted on it as well as other benefits related to policies. Developing new technology and products for both the local market and for MNEs' global market are above average as secondary roles among MNE R&D in the Western areas which comes very close to their major role, SL adaptation.

ROLES OF MNE SUBSIDIARIES IN CHINA

Evidence is found from the survey supporting the fact that MNEs' Chinese subsidiaries are expanding their roles from market seeking and efficiency seeking to knowledge seeking. Table 3.4 shows the average response to the relevance of the six subsidiary roles defined in the questionnaire survey at three different points in time, which shows the changing importance of each role. Responding subsidiaries were asked to evaluate the importance of the roles by awarding 4 points to a role if they think it is their only role, 3 points for a major role, 2 for a secondary role and 1 for not relevant. In the analysis, the six roles that were defined in the questionnaires were then labelled as MS (market seeking) 1 and MS2; ES (efficiency seeking) 1 and ES2; KS (knowledge seeking) 1 and KS2. The numbers, 1 and 2, indicate two levels in which '2' is wider scope in terms of subsidiary roles compared to '1'. For instance, subsidiaries with KS2 roles are developing wider concept and new technology for the global market while KS1 subsidiaries are only developing new products

Table 3.4 Evolution of roles of subsidiaries

Role	Past[a]	2005/06	2010[b]
MS1	2.47	2.43	2.41
MS2	1.61	2.10	2.16
ES1	1.52	1.81	1.86
ES2	1.31	1.38	1.48
KS1	1.57	2.11	2.27
KS2	1.19	1.30	1.53

Notes:
MS1 – Produce MNE's established products for the Chinese market.
MS2 – Produce MNE's established products to serve China with adaptation.
ES1 – Produce a specialized part of the MNE's established product range to supply China and nearby countries.
ES2 – Produce a specialized part of the MNE's established product range/component parts as a part of the MNE's world supply network.
KS1 – Develop and produce products that are new for the Chinese market.
KS2 – Develop and produce new products that are expected to supply global market.
a. Respondents were asked to evaluate the roles at the very beginning of the subsidiary's history.
b. Evaluation of predicted roles for 2010.

and technology for the local Chinese market. Detailed definition of the labels are listed under Table 3.4. In general, among subsidiaries of all home regions, to produce MNEs' well-established products for the Chinese market (MS1) is the most predominant role. The second most dominant role is then to 'develop' and produce new products for the Chinese market (KS1), which appears to become very marginally more important than to produce established product range with 'adaptation' (MS2). It suggests that MNE subsidiaries in China are local-market oriented with an increasing value-adding motivation. They seek to improve their competitiveness within the Chinese market. By home regions, European subsidiaries are more active in developing new technology and producing new products for the local market (KS1). The role is also valued as an above average secondary role by subsidiaries of all other home regions, except among Japanese firms where the development for China is the least relevant role. The tendency for Japanese companies to have less innovation in China is also confirmed by the smaller percentage of R&D labs amongst Japanese subsidiaries, the analysis of which is noted in the earlier sections. Generally speaking, being part of MNEs' global innovation strategy by carrying out research and developing new technology (KS2) that may not be immediately applied to current production operations is not a dominant role. However, Korean companies have valued this subsidiary role (the highest score compared with that given by subsidiaries from all other home origins), as an average secondary role. It is also worth noticing that Korean companies have the smallest score in the original market-seeking role (MS1) (which is just to produce for the Chinese market) and has comparatively higher scores in adaptation and innovation. It implies that Korean subsidiaries are more likely to establish R&D labs that are dealing with both adaptation and innovation and that they have the strongest knowledge-seeking motivation among subsidiaries of all other nationalities.

The importance of traditional market-seeking roles (MS1) reduces over time as that of MS2 is gradually picking up. Efficient-seeking operations remain as less important roles throughout the years into the future predicted by subsidiaries. The focus of the chapter is on the improvement of knowledge-seeking motivations, which is evident in Table 3.4. KS1 role increased to 2.11 by 2005 while it was predicted to grow in dominance in five years time until 2010. KS2 role has a similar general trend only with less absolute significance. The results indicate that MNEs' Chinese subsidiaries are putting more effort into increasing competitiveness locally by engaging in new product and knowledge development, which would suggest a increase in the intensity of R&D activities in China.

Paired-sample t-tests were performed in order to diagnose whether the changes in subsidiary roles are significant and not due to random factors. The results shown in Table 3.5 suggest that the evolution of roles from past year through to 2010 that we have discussed earlier are generally statistically significant apart from changes in the MS1 role, which is not significant at all times, and the predictions for the evolving possibilities for MS2 and ES1. However, if the age of each subsidiary is taken into account, it may be possible to further refine the results. The survey was launched in China from the summer in 2006. The 'youngest' firms invited to fill in the questionnaire were only set up at the beginning of 2006. In that case, when they evaluate the past roles of their subsidiaries, they were thinking about the past six months. This may reduce the overall difference between the subsidiary roles in the past and in year 2005/06 and make it less significant.

Roles of subsidiaries respectively orient the responsibilities of their R&D units once established in the host country. A regression test (Table 3.6) confirmed a few significant connections between the two sides. Traditional market expanding role reduces the likelihood of their R&D units, if any, taking up an adaptation role but increases the possibility of a world development role. As mentioned earlier, subsidiaries' MS1 type of role evolves rapidly into a more advanced form in the Chinese market

Table 3.5   *Paired-samples t-test of roles of MNE Chinese subsidiaries*

	Mean[a]	Std Dev.	t
MS1 past – MS1 2005/06	0.039	0.861	0.512
MS2 past – MS2 2005/06	−0.488***	0.830	−6.681
ES1 past – ES1 2005/06	−0.295***	0.700	−4.776
ES2 past – ES2 2005/06	−0.070**	0.358	−2.216
KS1 past – KS1 2005/06	−0.531***	0.963	−6.239
KS2 past – KS2 2005/06	−0.109***	0.419	−2.941
MS1 2005/06 – MS1 2010	0.023	0.441	0.599
MS2 2005/06 – MS2 2010	-0.054	0.563	−1.094
ES1 2005/06 – ES1 2010	−0.047	0.557	−0.948
ES2 2005/06 – ES2 2010	−0.101**	0.528	−2.168
KS1 2005/06 – KS1 2010	−0.163**	0.758	−2.439
KS2 2005/06 – KS2 2010	−0.225***	0.640	−3.988
MS1 past – MS12010	0.062	0.966	0.729
MS2 past – MS2 2010	−0.543***	0.866	−7.116
ES1 past – ES1 2010	−0.341***	0.734	−5.277
ES2 past – ES2 2010	−0.171***	0.614	−3.155
KS1 past – KS1 2010	−0.695***	1.000	−7.863
KS2 past – KS2 2010	−0.333***	0.774	−4.892

Note: a.   The mean is the average value of past roles minus current roles or future roles.
* $p < 0.1$;** $p < 0.05$; *** $p < 0.01$.

as soon as they take in information and see the development potential of China. In this case, subsidiaries originally established for the purpose of exploring the market are more likely to establish their own R&D units aiming at developing new technology and products for the MNE world market, possibly at a later stage of their operations in China. R&D labs of ES2 subsidiaries are found to be positively associated with the development of new technology for the global market, which suggests subsidiaries aiming at improving world productive efficiency are more likely to have R&D labs for the further improvement of an MNE's global competitiveness by creating new technology and products. A positive connection between KS2 and GLOBALDEVELOP R&D labs is verified by the regression test. As expected, a KS subsidiary located in China motivated by the competitiveness of the wider world market will have a GLOBALDEVELOP type of R&D lab to realize its knowledge-seeking goal.

Table 3.6 Regression for roles of MNE R&D in China

	ADAPTMNETECH		LOCALDEVELOP		GLOBALDEVELOP		INNOVATION	
	B	S.E	B	S.E	B	S.E	B	S.E
(Constant)	4.465***	0.566	2.414***	0.415	-0.648	0.611	0.598	0.559
MS1	-0.535***	0.141	0.149	0.104	0.446***	0.152	0.084	0.139
MS2	-0.002	0.142	-0.056	0.104	-0.101	0.153	-0.047	0.140
ES1	-0.139	0.115	-0.038	0.084	0.159	0.127	0.094	0.116
ES2	-0.192	0.137	-0.025	0.101	0.007	0.154	0.335**	0.141
KS1	-0.029	0.123	0.132	0.091	-0.002	0.133	0.086	0.122
KS2	0.212	0.134	0.087	0.099	0.718***	0.157	0.003	0.144
Control Variables								
Auto	-0.038	0.328	-0.536**	0.234	-0.037	0.354	-0.513	0.324
Electronics	-0.040	0.273	-0.159	0.202	0.361	0.299	-0.445	0.274
Food & drink	0.701	0.448	-0.117	0.330	0.304	0.483	-0.318	0.442
IT	-0.422	0.352	-0.057	0.259	0.543	0.379	-0.278	0.347
Personal care	0.096	0.284	-0.085	0.210	0.253	0.306	-0.281	0.280
USA	0.021	0.201	0.079	0.147	0.015	0.219	0.262	0.200
Japan	0.214	0.277	-0.104	0.202	-0.588*	0.305	0.075	0.279
Korea	-0.495	0.370	-0.036	0.271	-0.560	0.419	-0.145	0.384
JEC	-0.196	0.218	-0.054	0.156	0.267	0.240	-0.040	0.220
PRD	-0.210	0.265	-0.035	0.194	-0.305	0.285	-0.198	0.261
OUT	-0.327	0.437	-0.548*	0.323	-0.044	0.474	-0.127	0.434
R Square	0.438		0.288		0.635		0.310	
Sum of Squares	12.913**		3.745		32.639***		7.087	

Note: *$p < 0.1$; **$p < 0.05$; ***$p < 0.01$.

CONCLUSION

R&D orientation of subsidiaries presented regional and industrial differences which are also influenced by their home origins. Adaptation and development for the local market appeared to be the two most common roles for R&D labs in most Chinese regions, but in the JEC area a generally stronger role of developing new products for the global market is found, which is likely to be a result of higher R&D potential, rich human resources and favourable government policy. In terms of cutting-edge scientific research, R&D units in all Chinese regions appear to be less active, but a trend has shown that some R&D labs have already turned their attention towards this. By industries, the IT industry, followed by electronics, showed stronger interest in developing new technology and products for the MNE global market, which could be a direct influence of the recent improvement in China's IT and electronic technology and higher education standards in both fields. MNEs' origin has not played a significant role in the formation of R&D roles. However, Korean R&D labs do seem to have the edge in terms of new technology development.

The chapter, using survey data, elaborated the fact that over 50 per cent of subsidiaries (69 out of 129) have established R&D labs in China. Although adaptation to the established product range is still the dominant role for MNE Chinese labs, developing new technology and improving global competitiveness have become more relevant to both MNE subsidiaries and their R&D units. The roles of MNE subsidiaries are shifting away from solely providing for the Chinese market and producing for the MNE world wide market to increasing value-adding production and development in China for the market both inside and outside of China. Thus the aim is to increase subsidiaries' own competitiveness in China and also within the MNE group. The importance of SL roles is not as large as expected compared to the presence of LIL and IIL. It is thus obvious that China's strategic importance to MNEs has increased. MNEs have gradually realized that apart from a large population and market and a cost-effective production base, China possesses value-adding competitiveness with which MNEs are able to compete more effectively within and outside of it.

REFERENCES

Cantwell, J.A. (1995), 'The globalization of technology: what remains of the product cycle model?', *Cambridge Journal of Economics,* **19,** 155–74.
Papanastassiou, M. and R. Pearce (1999), *Multinationals, Technology and National*

Competitiveness, Cheltenham, UK and Northampton, MA, USA: Edward Elgar puublishing.
Papanastassiou, M. and R. Pearce (2009), *The Strategic Development of Multinationals*, Basingstoke: Palgrave Macmillan.
Pearce, R. and S. Zhang (2010), 'Multinationals' strategies for global competitiveness and the sustainability of development in national economies', *Asian Business and Management*, **9**(4), 481–98.

4. The growth and strategic orientation of multinationals' R&D in China

Feng Zhang and Robert Pearce

INTRODUCTION

In a now familiar aphorism Terpstra (1977, p. 25) stated that 'the last activity of the firm to be organised on an international basis – if it is at all – is R&D'. In fact by the mid-1970s both the extent of, and academic interest in,[1] overseas research and development (R&D) in mature multinational enterprises (MNEs) was becoming significant. Subsequent investigation of MNE R&D soon suggested that, far from being a belated ad hoc add-on to the scope of their international operations, dispersed R&D had become part of carefully articulated technology strategies and programmes. As new firms embarked on strategic internationalisation, or when mature MNEs entered newly open economies for the first time, incorporation of R&D facilities early in their expansion profiles became a matter of routine consideration. A classic example of this speeding up of the functional sequencing implied by Terpstra has been the alacrity with which localised R&D has become part of the competitive scope of MNEs entering China (Von Zedtwitz, 2004; Zhou, 2005). This chapter seeks to provide some insights on this phenomenon.

In the next section we provide some of the evidence on the extent of foreign firms' R&D in China as it has emerged over the past decade. In the following two sections we then interpret website information on two leading MNEs with significant R&D in China, to review the ways this has been built into the early strategic positioning of these firms' scope in this emergent environment. Here Ericsson serves as an illustration of a long-established MNE with well-honed attitudes to internationalisation of R&D and innovation. Then Samsung works as a contrasting case of a fast-growing international competitor whose entry into China is in some way codeterminate with formalisation of aspects of its global policies, including technology strategy.

THE GROWTH OF MULTINATIONALS' R&D IN CHINA

One important element of the macro-context facilitating the growth of MNE R&D in China has been the massive overall growth in R&D spending in that economy. Thus the World Investment Report, 2005 (UNCTAD, 2005, table 111.1, p. 105) indicates that gross domestic expenditure on R&D (GERD) in China rose from $4.9 billion in 1996 to $15.6 billion in 2002. This placed China firmly in the ten leading R&D spending economies in 2002 (at number 6; one place ahead of South Korea, the only other developing country in the top ten).[2] Though figures for Business Expenditure on R&D (BERD) in China in 1996 are not available this too had become prominent by 2002; its value of $9.5 billion ranking it seventh in the world (here one place behind South Korea).[3] Overall these UNCTAD (2005, table A111.2) figures suggest a strong assertion of business R&D in total R&D in China. Thus BERD in China was 61.2 per cent of GERD in 2002, compared with 55.7 per cent in all developing countries and 66.5 per cent worldwide.

A second macro-context for the growth of MNE R&D in China is dramatically exemplified in UNCTAD's (2005, pp. 130–2) analysis of data compiled by OCO Consulting on location of greenfield foreign direct investment (FDI) projects between 2002 and 2004. This dataset distinguished 1,773 projects involving R&D, either as its 'key' business function[4] or as an 'additional' function. Overall 1,053 of these projects were in developing countries[5] (that is, 59.4 per cent). UNCTAD (2005, table IV.9, p.132) then usefully extends its analysis of this data using Von Zedtwitz's (2005, pp. 120–23) four-part typology of R&D internationalisation based on developmental levels of home and host countries.

This designates as 'traditional' R&D projects from advanced home countries into advanced host countries. This accounted for 612 of the 1,773 cases (that is, 34.5 per cent). Then 'modern' R&D projects are those from advanced home countries into developing host countries. With 993 cases[6] (that is, 56.0 per cent of the total) this was the most prevalent case. The remaining two segments of the typology then reflect another emerging trend in MNE R&D location; that of firms from developing countries. The first of these was described by Von Zedtwitz (2005, p. 122) as 'catch-up', reflecting R&D from developing countries into advanced countries, 'attracted to using developed countries as R&D bases, partly in order to acquire local technology and science, and partly in order to support local product development'. The 1,773 projects analysed by UNCTAD included only 66 (that is, 3.7 per cent) of the catch-up type. Finally, 'expansionary' R&D was that from developing home countries into other developing countries as hosts. This may be to support 'second-generation technology transfer (when the earlier recipient of technology transfers [it] on to an even less developed country) or, to support other local business activities' (Von Zedtwitz, 2005, p.122). The data found 102 cases of such expansionary R&D (that is, 5.8 per cent).[7]

We can note two reasons why, by comparison with more familiar expenditure data,[8] the greenfield project-based data quoted above is likely to overemphasise the undoubted trend towards MNE R&D in developing countries. Firstly, routine growth in established R&D units is likely to represent a major component of MNEs' overall R&D expansion, which is likely to be much more significant in mature developed country laboratories (and not reflected in 'new project' data). Secondly, expansion of MNE R&D capacity in developed countries can occur through (or be a motivation for) mergers and acquisitions in a way that is less feasible in developing countries (where emerging technological potentials are less likely to be already embodied in commercially successful enterprises). Nevertheless the data does suggest a very significant reorientation of MNEs' R&D strategies to encompass location in less-advanced economies. This willingness, taken with the massive increase in commitment to R&D in its growing scientific potential, can be seen to underpin the growth of MNEs' R&D in China.

UNCTAD calculations (UNCTAD, 2005, annex table A.1V.1) indicate foreign affiliates' R&D expenditure in China in 2003 of $2,748 million. This was estimated to be 23.7 per cent of business expenditure on R&D in China in that year, a ratio that had risen steadily from 18.0 per cent in 1998. These data clearly suggest that foreign R&D expenditure had very quickly established above average importance in total business R&D in China. Thus the ratio of 22.0 per cent of total BERD in China in 2002 compares with UNCTAD estimates of 15.9 per cent for world total (all host countries), 17.7 per cent for all developing countries and 15.7 per cent for all developed countries (2003 aggregates were not available for these groupings). The Chinese ratio of 18.0 per cent for 1998 compared with 13.3 per cent for all hosts, 4.1 per cent for all developing countries[9] and 13.6 per cent for all developed countries.

Information on the R&D expenditures of majority-owned affiliates of US MNEs (UNCTAD, 2005, table IV.6, p. 129) again reflect, through data on a dominant source, the growth in importance of China as a host to foreign corporate R&D. Thus US MNE R&D expenditure in China only totalled $132 million between 1994 and 1998, before rising to $319 million in 1999, $506 million in 2000 and an estimated $646 million in 2002.[10] This meant that China accounted for 0.19 per cent of all overseas R&D expenditure of US MNEs between 1994 and 1998 (and for 2.82 per cent of that in developing countries). From 1999 to 2002 (excluding 2001) China's share rose to 2.46 per cent of the total (and to 19.55 per cent of that in developing countries).

Reporting data compiled by the Japanese Bank for International Cooperation, UNCTAD (2005, table IV.8, p.131) trace a very significant role for operations in China in the expansion of overseas 'R&D bases' of Japanese manufacturing companies between 2000 and 2004. In 2000 the Japanese companies had 13 R&D bases in China in a total of 177 such facilities overseas (that is, 7.3 per cent in China). By 2004 67 such R&D bases were in China (a growth of 415.4 per cent) out of a total of 310 (growth of 75.1 per cent). Thus in 2004 China accounted for 21.6 per cent of all overseas R&D bases of Japanese manufacturing companies. The distinctiveness of this level and growth can be additionally emphasised by comparison of the 67 R&D units in China in 2004 with 25 in the original four newly industrialising countries (NICs)[11] (up from 16 in 2000, a growth of 56.3 per cent) and 29 in the ASEAN-4[12] (up from ten in 2000, growth of 190.0 per cent).

ERICSSON IN CHINA

The first of the two subsections surveys broad dimensions of the expansion and strategic deepening of Ericsson's commitment to its Chinese operations over, mainly, the past two decades. Against this background the second subsection then reviews the prompt emergence and diverse scope of R&D in the functional competence of Ericsson's Chinese operations.

The Emergence and Strategic Positioning of Ericsson's Chinese Operations

'Prehistory' (1892–1987)

If we see the start of Ericsson's commitment to strategically coherent value-adding operations in China as occurring in 1988 it is useful to acknowledge that this, and its immediate quantitative and qualitative expansion, benefited from a long and satisfactory 'prehistory' of cooperation between the firm and the country. As shown in Table 4.1 Ericsson accepted its first order from China in 1892, as a result of which Shanghai imported 2,000 telephone sets in 1894. The first manual telephone exchange appliance was put into use in 1900, followed by the first automatic exchange in 1924. Ericsson then introduced the first vertical and horizontal exchange equipment in China in 1961. 1981 then saw Ericsson's first order for numeric telephone sets from Beijing and, crucially, the first mobile phone system was put into use in Qinhuangdao in 1987.

Table 4.1   Ericsson's biggest events in China

DS	IA	Year	The biggest events
The long satisfactory cooperation history with China		1892	Ericsson signed the first order form with China
		1894	Shanghai imported 2,000 telephone sets
		1900	The first manual telephone exchange appliance put into use
		1924	The first automatic telephone exchange appliance put into use
		1961	Introduced the first vertical and horizontal telephone exchange appliance to China
		1981	The first order for numeric telephone sets from Beijing
		1985	Ericsson Beijing Office set up
		1987	The first set of mobile phone system put into use in Qinhuangdao
The Preliminary Stage	With no official R&D facilities, and implemented SL function	1988	Licensed technology to 738 factory to manufacture PABX MD110
		1989	Ericsson Guangzhou Office and Shanghai Office set up
		1990	Provide equipment to Shanghai International Communication Bureau
The Development Stage		1992	Set up joint ventures to produce AXE-10 mobile phones and exchange equipments
		1994	Set up Ericsson China Ltd
		1995	China became the third biggest market globally of Ericsson
		1996	Became the first company in China to pass the ISO 9001 qualification
			China became the second biggest market globally of Ericsson
The Advanced Stage (to be cont.)	Local-for-Local and Globally Linked	1997	Shanghai Research and Development (R&D) Centre and 'Ericsson Academe' Beijing Subsection came into existence
		1998	China became the biggest market globally of Ericsson
			Set up Chongqing Ericsson Science and Technology Ltd
		1999	Established Ericsson Management Consulting Ltd (Shanghai)
			Set up Ericsson Mobile Multi Media Open Laboratory in Zhongguan Village, Beijing
		2000	Completion of China's first WCDMA evaluation system testing and report
		2001	Fulfilment of China's first WCDMA terminal call on its trial system
		2002	Realised global first communication of commercial terminal's Multi-Media Message (MMS) among different operators

Table 4.1 (continued)

DS	IA	Year	The biggest events
The Advanced Stage	Local-for-local and Globally Linked		The establishment of Ericsson Chief Academy of Research & Development (China) Ericsson Panda Communication Ltd (Nanjing) became the supply hinge of Ericsson group and the logistic centre of Asia-Pacific market of Ericsson
		2003	The worldwide release of the first generation of 3G/WCDMA base station product – RBS3402 which was researched and developed by Ericsson China Ericsson Putian Telecommunication Co., Ltd (Beijing) took over the products analyses and R&D duties for Ericsson's Asia-Pacific market region
		2004	The release of CDMA2000 1X omni-bearing cellular wireless base station – RBS1143, which aimed at Chinese market and clients Set up Ericsson Wireless Technology Co., Ltd (Chengdu), a R&D centre in charge of developing the wireless base station products based on GSM, CDMA, WCDMA and other technologies
		2005	Set up Ericsson Data Application Technology Research and Development Centre in Guangzhou for business solution's research for the Chinese market Set up Ericsson TD-SCDMA Research and Development Centre in Nanjing, and declare Ericsson China's cooperation with ZTE (a leading Chinese telecommunication enterprise) on TD-SCDMA technology Ericsson China declare its cooperation with Shanghai Research Centre for Wireless Technologies for future telecommunication technologies' research Set up cooperative R&D centre with Beijing Telecommunication University for future networking technologies' research

Notes: DS = Development Stages; IA = Innovation Approaches. The chronicle part is translated from Ericsson China's web Pages 'The biggest event in China'.

Ericsson's long-term involvement with key stages in the evolution of China's telephone and communications infrastructure clearly pointed towards a strong commitment when the economy opened to foreign business. Thus 1985 saw the setting up of Ericsson's Beijing office, the start of a process that, by August 2003, had resulted in 26 representative offices, 16 joint ventures (JVs) and four wholly owned companies in China.

The preliminary stage (1988–92)

The first step in Ericsson's move towards value-adding operations in China was the licensing of the technology and production right of PABXMD110 to 738 factory in 1988, its initial cooperation with Chinese enterprise. This was quite promptly followed by the next stage in localised commitment with, in 1992, the establishment of JVs to manufacture AEX-10 mobile telephones and transfer equipment.[13] The initial aim of these JVs was the efficiency-seeking (Behrman, 1984; Dunning, 1993; Manea and Pearce, 2004) aim of using low input-cost factors in China to supply the markets of other Ericsson subsidiaries overseas. Thus, in terms of the scope typology for roles of subsidiaries,[14] Ericsson would have seen these early JVs as rationalised product subsidiaries (RPSs).[15] RPSs are normally considered to have a limited 'product' scope, focusing on the manufacture of closely defined parts of the MNE's established product range (here the AEX-10 mobiles), but an extensive 'market' scope (normally considered to be achieved through export orientation). They are also expected to have a very limited 'functional' scope, due to constraint to a specialised supply role in an existing group network.

The development stage (1992–96)

By the mid-1990s the strong growth of the Chinese economy led to the emergence of a high-income consumer group large enough to constitute a major market for mobile phone services, such that in 1995 China became Ericsson's third biggest market globally. In response to this the establishment in 1994 of Ericsson China, as a wholly owned subsidiary, reflected the need to take a more holistic view of Ericsson's operations there, including a distinctive commitment to the local market.

With the decisive acknowledgement of a market-seeking (MS) element in the strategic orientation of Ericsson China, the traditional logic of the scope typology would be to categorise it as a truncated miniature replica (TMR). These MS subsidiaries can now be seen to have historically been most prevalent in the multidomestic strategies (Porter, 1986) of an era in which high trade restraints fragmented markets. Thus they were then assumed to have narrow market scope (the, usually relatively small, markets of individual national economies) but wide 'product' scope (all those parts of an MNE's range relevant to local consumers). This strategically dependent status would also imply very narrow 'functional' scope, limited to securing the most effective application of already mature products and technologies in local conditions. We can immediately see that the MS positioning of Ericsson China refocused several aspects of the TMR as the subsidiary pursuing this motivation.

A key element of this is that the MS imperative of Ericsson China did not mainly derive (in a negative manner) from trade restraint, but rather (in a more positive fashion) from the immediate size and growth potential of the Chinese market. This opens up the possibility of stronger functional scope (both R&D and market research) to secure adaptation of products to local conditions.[16] However, this was not initially necessary as the SIM card used in China was the same as that used in Europe (along with the USA, one of Ericsson's two largest established markets), so that no R&D was necessary to change products to meet local technological needs. The only change needed to Ericsson's product in China, compared to its products in the European Union (EU), was the language in the systems.

Furthermore Ericsson China was unlikely to succumb to the inefficiencies imputed to traditional TMRs. There the small local markets and protection from import competition had been seen as likely to make efficient production difficult (lack of economies of scale) and unnecessary (X-inefficiency due to market power). The sheer size of the Chinese market, and the competitive imperative of building a secure position in it, should negate these concerns in Ericsson China.[17] Indeed, in a perhaps unexpected and unplanned way, the level of efficiency in the supply of some of Ericsson China's products[18] may lead to parts of its output entering Ericsson's global supply programmes in an RPS manner (alongside the continuing export role of the earlier JVs).[19]

Finally, the earlier MS TMRs were presumed to be strategically dependent, so that the scope of management was routine and devoid of creative or evolutionary capacities. By contrast, the management of Ericsson China immediately acquired responsibility for the strategic maintenance and development of what, in 1996, became Ericsson's second largest market worldwide.

The advanced stage (1997–2003)

If the development stage ended with Ericsson's operations in China constituting a somewhat amorphous mixture of MS and efficiency-seeking (ES) objectives, we can see the defining imperative of the subsequent 'advanced' stage as knowledge seeking (Manea and Pearce, 2004; Pearce, 2006) or strategic asset seeking (Dunning, 1993, 2000). At the core of this was the commencement of innovation in Ericsson China's strategic priorities and, with this, its increasing acquisition of the characteristics of a product mandate (PM) subsidiary. As understood within the viewpoints of contemporary views of the MNE,[20] the PM receives from its parent company full authorisation to take complete responsibility for the origination and subsequent competitive development of unique and distinctive extensions to the MNE group's product range. One essential element of accession to

PM status is progress away from the technological dependency of the RPS and TMR, with a concomitant enriching of functional scope, especially in terms of localised knowledge creation and application. This, we will see, was at the core of the evolution of Ericsson China during the advanced stage of its development.

The initiation of innovation in Ericsson China seems to have derived from the perceived value of a more locally individualised response to the Chinese market. One element of this was that in 1998 China completed its swift progress to the position of Ericsson's largest market. In addition the mobile phone market in China was reaching a level of maturity and familiarity where customers were beginning to demand products and services that were more distinctively responsive to local needs, tastes and conditions. One source of this was that the strong marketing units of Ericsson China, set up within the TMR role to market established goods, were capable of picking up emerging trends and tastes in China that could drive the motivation to create new products.

Another source of the evolution was that by the second half of the 1990s China was capable of not only indicating new consumer needs (demand-side factors) but also of providing distinctive local technology competences that would serve as key inputs into the product development process (supply-side factors). A long-term commitment to scientific education and research had provided China with a strong science-base (that is, local universities, independent laboratories, state-owned research facilities) with unique elements of research capacities and programmes, and distinctive competences in creative human capital (talented scientists, inventive engineers, innovative marketing personnel, ambitious management). From this conjunction of influences we can suggest that the foundation stages of innovation in Ericsson China reflected Bartlett and Ghoshal's (1989, 1990) traditional local-for-local approach in which 'national subsidiaries of MNCs [use] their own resources and capabilities to create innovations that respond to the needs of their own environments' (Bartlett and Ghoshal, 1990, p. 217). As shown in Table 4.1 the early years of the advanced stage saw the creation of several of the units through which Ericsson China tapped into China's emerging science-base. Thus 1997 saw the creation of the Shanghai Research and Development Centre and 'Ericsson Academy' Beijing Subsection, with Chongqing Ericsson Science and Technology Ltd following in the next year. In 1999 the Ericsson Mobile Multi Media Open Laboratory was established in Zhongguan Village, Beijing and Ericsson Management Consulting Ltd (Shanghai) was set up.

Whilst the local-for-local approach to innovation clearly provides a very effective context for learning about the potentials of a newly emerging economy it has obvious limitations from the wider strategic viewpoints of a dynamic and globally competing MNE such as Ericsson. Thus where such a company accesses strong creative competences, initially manifest in a local-for-local focus, it is likely to promptly seek their application to wider markets. Bartlett and Ghoshal thus detected two 'transnational' approaches to innovation, in which creative resources in a specific location work for a group's global competitiveness. Very plausible here would be the possibility that some of the goods developed for the Chinese market would in fact achieve levels of originality that secure them much wider international markets, thus, in effect, encompassing what Bartlett and Ghoshal term a 'locally-leveraged' approach to innovation.[21] Perhaps more intriguing, however, are the early signs of Ericsson's creative work in China playing a role in a 'globally linked' approach to innovation which 'pools the resources and capabilities of many different components of the MNC – at both headquarters and the subsidiary level – to create and implement an innovation jointly' (Bartlett and Ghoshal, 1990, p. 217).

A pioneer example of Ericsson's Chinese operations being brought into its global innovation network occurred in 1999, with the initiation of cooperation between Ericsson Panda Communication Ltd (Nanjing) and Ericsson Wireless Communication Ltd (USA) to develop a CDMA R&D project to be carried out in China. This started Ericsson China's collaboration with Ericsson parent and other overseas R&D facilities, and signifies the entry of Ericsson's Chinese units into globally linked innovation programmes. In 2002 Ericsson Panda Communications Ltd (Nanjing) became the supply hinge and logistic centre of Ericsson's Pacific market. In a similar manner in 2003 Ericsson Putian Telecommunications (Beijing) took over product analysis responsibilities and R&D duties for the Asia-Pacific market region. Also in 2003 Ericsson China released to worldwide markets its RB53402 (a first generation of 3G/WCDMA base station) product, which had been researched and developed in China.

A more general and less formalised manifestation of involvement with globally linked innovation may be seen in the emergence in China of pre-competitive basic/applied research, whose results (somewhat in the manner of a public good within the firm) is likely to be available to any part of the group to which it may be seen to be relevant, rather than having any a priori one-to-one link to any Ericsson innovation project in China. Sources of this were the 'Ericsson Academy' Beijing Subsection, part of the work of the Ericsson R&D Centre (Shanghai) and collaborative work with Chinese institutions such as Tsinghua University, China Science and Technology University and Beijing Telecommunications University.

Ericsson R&D in China

Introduction

The competitive deepening of Ericsson's operations in China during the 'advanced' stage, we have already indicated, incorporated a very significant commitment to local R&D facilities. This not only reflected the aim of developing new products to secure a more responsive position in the vast and increasingly mature Chinese market for mobile phones and associated products, but also the desire to tap into emerging Chinese technological and research capacities to generate new products and scientific knowledge to support Ericsson's globalised innovation perspectives. This section elaborates some aspects of the emerging R&D network of Ericsson's laboratories in China. In line with wider understandings of R&D in MNEs Ericsson's Chinese operations, more or less from their initiation, embodied a range of diverse strategic orientations. Thus we adopt a three-part typology of laboratories (Haug et al., 1983; Pearce, 1989, 1999; Papanastassiou and Pearce, 1999, 2005) that reflects the ways in which MNE R&D units can help facilitate different aspects of these firms' strategic competitiveness (Pearce, 1999). Table 4.2 lists the main R&D facilities of Ericsson China and relates their roles to the typology. Figure 4.1 then emphasises the way in which the different facilities and collaborations amount to an interdependent and powerful R&D system in China that is, in turn, linked into Ericsson's global innovation network.

The Ericsson Chief Academy of R&D (China) was founded in 2002 in order to provide a coordinating overview of all of Ericsson China's established and emerging laboratories, collaborations and projects. The operating level below the Chief Academy can be seen to comprise nine components. Six of these are Ericsson's own Centres (that is, Ericsson and China Telecommunications Science and Technology, Academe R&D Centre; Ericsson R&D Centre (Shanghai); Ericsson Mobility World China Subsection; Ericsson Academy Beijing Subsection; Ericsson Wireless Technology Co. Ltd (Chengdu); Ericsson Data Applications Technology R&D Centre (Guangzhou). The three other parts of the system are R&D projects of Ericsson's Chinese JVs, cooperation projects between Ericsson and Chinese universities and cooperation projects and indigenous firms (coordinated by Ericsson TD-SCDMA R&D Centre of Nanjing).

Support laboratories

In the typology the *support laboratory* (SL) essentially plays the role of facilitating technology transfer in the MNE. The more traditional variant of support laboratory (SL1) facilitates inward technology transfer, by assisting a subsidiary in which it is located (TMR or RPS) in assimilating

Table 4.2   Laboratory roles of Ericsson China's research and development facilities

R&D Facilities of Ericsson China	IIL	For domestic market		For global market	
		SL1	LIL	SL2	LIL
Ericsson Chief Academy of R&D (China)					
Ericsson and China Telecommunications Scientific Technology Academe R&D Centre			✓		✓
Ericsson R&D Centre (Shanghai)	✓	✓	✓	✓	✓
Ericsson Mobility World China Subsection					
Ericsson Mobile Multimedia Open Laboratory					
Beijing Laboratory			✓		
Chengdu Laboratory		✓	✓		
Zhuhai Laboratory		✓			
Ericsson Mobile Internet Application and Testing Centre (Shenzhen)		✓			
Ericsson Mobile Internet Application and Exploring Centre (Shanghai)		✓			
Ericsson Wireless Technology Co., Ltd (Chengdu)			✓		✓
Ericsson Data Application Technology Research and Development Centre (Guangzhou)			✓		
Ericsson TD-SCDMA Research and Development Centre (Nanjing)			✓		
Cooperation projects of Ericsson and indegenous firms					
Cooperation projects of Ericsson and universities or institutions	✓				
R&D projects of Ericsson joint ventures		✓	✓		
Ericsson Panda Communication Ltd R&D Centre (Nanjing)				✓	✓
Ericsson Mobile Communication Ltd R&D Centre (Beijing)		✓	✓	✓	✓
Ericsson Putian Telecommunication Co., Ltd	✓				

and, if necessary, adapting the technology to host-country needs or conditions. A more recently emergent variant (SL2) involves itself in a form of outward technology transfer, by assisting and advising other units of the MNE in the use of established knowledge of the group.[22] In terms of SL1, in particular, ad hoc support laboratory type activity may have been

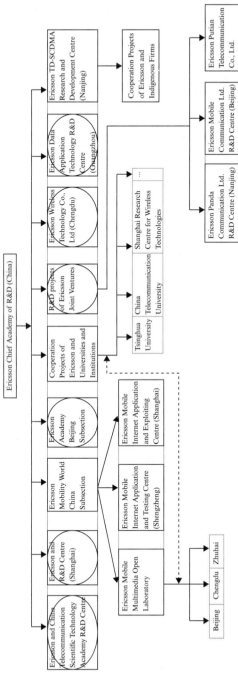

Note: The R&D centres with circles are directly linked with Ericsson's global innovation network.

Figure 4.1   The R&D system of Ericsson China

present in Ericsson China's preliminary and development stages before the establishment of formally constituted labs. However, higher-profile SL type work can then also be found in some of the units in the R&D system that later emerged.

Ericsson R&D Centre (Shanghai) has wide-ranging responsibilities, as part of Ericsson's global R&D network, in the areas of communication software. Amongst its more advanced commitments and capabilities the centre also retains significant SL responsibilities. Thus one of the Shanghai Centre's functions is to help Ericsson China in inward transfer and application of technologies from the parent company (SL1), and also providing related technical support for Chinese (SL1) and foreign (SL2) customers in the receiving net, mobile systems and consumables, 3G and broadband areas.

Ericsson Mobility World is a project established to construct a mobile internet application R&D network in major countries, and the China Subsection includes provision of support services for in-house and external-collaborative R&D projects in the mobile multimedia area in China. Here one of the subsection's second-level subordinates, Ericsson Mobile Internet Application and Testing Centre (Shenzhen), provides advice to other parts of Ericsson China and collaborators in the areas of multimedia application and mobile internet technologies (and their testing). Another second-level subordinate, Ericsson Mobile Internet Application and Exploiting Centre (Shanghai), assists the development of mobile internet application in China's market by providing GPRS application testing environment (GATE) to software exploiting companies in Shanghai. Finally, the third subordinate of the China Subsection of Ericsson Mobility World, the Ericsson Mobile Multimedia Open Laboratory, comprises three third-level facilities. Two of these, the Changdu Laboratory and the Zhuhai laboratory, include SL1 responsibilities. Some of this, in turn, integrates into Ericsson's cooperation with local universities (Figure 4.1).

The R&D projects of Ericsson JVs also included some SL work, though always in support of more ambitious laboratory roles. Thus the Panda R&D Centre (Nanjing) and Putian Telecommunications Co. involved SL1s, whilst the latter also include SL2 as did the Mobile Communications Ltd Centre (Beijing).

Locally integrated laboratories
Whilst SLs merely facilitate the transfer and improved application of existing technologies (already embodied in goods and services) the two remaining types of laboratory play roles in creating new technologies and sources of competitiveness. Here the locally integrated laboratory (LIL)

is a MNE R&D unit, in a particular country, that works in a closely integrated manner with other functions of a subsidiary there (logically a PM) to develop a distinctive product which can be supplied to local, regional or even global markets. Thus a LIL and its subsidiary not only extends the competitiveness of an MNE but places the initial manifestation of this in a location that can supply the relevant creative (including R&D) inputs.

Ericsson R&D Centre (Shanghai), Ericsson Mobile World China Subsection, Ericsson Wireless Technology Ltd (Changdu), Ericsson Data Application Technology R&D Centre (Guangzhou), Ericsson TD-SCDMA R&D Centre (Nanjing) as well as R&D projects of Ericsson's JVs in China all include LIL-type functions. To take R&D projects of the JVs as examples, we find significant LIL output in both Ericsson Panda Communication Ltd R&D Centre (Nanjing) (ENC) and Ericsson Mobile Communication Ltd Centre (Beijing) (BMC). ENC committed itself to the R&D of second generation GSM mobile communication systems and CDMA systems. Now it is responsible for R&D of GSM AC-A systems and GSM CAN systems of Ericsson's global markets, and for the GSM exchange system, CDMA systems and receiving system (ADSL, ADC, PSTM) for the Chinese market. BMC showed strong input to global operations, with responsibility for accessory products of communication systems successfully exploited in the MMC exchange implement for Vodafone (Australia) and helped in the simplification of its range of mobile phones. Also Ericsson and China Telecommunications Scientific Technology Academy R&D Centre includes LIL work for the Chinese market (products of WCDMA) and for the global market (research of 3G for future mobile communication systems and the WCDMA FDD wireless receiving net).

Internationally interdependent laboratories
The third type of R&D facility that has emerged in MNEs pursues the longer-term enrichment of technology potentials by tapping into distinctive scientific (pre-competitive) research agendas and knowledge stocks of particular countries' NSIs. Thus the internationally interdependent laboratory (IIL) carries out basic or applied research, separately from the current commercial activities of an MNE, but interdependently with similar units internationally. An IIL network therefore seeks to articulate a range of separate pre-competitive projects in several countries (each building on distinctive attributes of its host national system of innovation (NSI)), but to also encourage communication between them so that potentially significant synergies in their results can be detected and, hopefully, built into subsequent innovation programmes. Thus IILs can be components (along with LILs) in globally linked approaches to innovation, and

we have already noted that the emergence of this type of work in China may imply its growing positioning in Ericsson's creative programmes and perspectives.

Since IIL-type work depends on top quality local capacities in scientific research it is not surprising to find that it is the defining content of Ericsson's cooperative projects with Chinese universities. In 1999 Ericsson sponsored an acoustics laboratory in Beijing Science and Engineering University to carry out research in disciplines relevant to its evolving commercial priorities. It also cooperated with multiversities, such as Tsinghua University and China Science and Technology University, and with Professional Universities such as Beijing and Zhengzhou Telecommunications Engineering School and Beijing Telecommunications University, for research projects and to organise conferences to help Ericsson to identify potentially important directions for future basic or applied investigation.

The Ericsson Academy Beijing Subsection was established in 1999 and has recruited large numbers of high-quality Masters and Doctoral level personnel. It mainly deals with fields of wireless technology research that can feed into many of Ericsson's product and service categories. Though not predominantly focused on such work the multifaceted Ericsson R&D centre (Shanghai) does also address aspects of IIL research, alongside the SL and LIL discussed earlier.

SAMSUNG IN CHINA

Development of Samsung's Chinese Operations

As Table 4.3 shows, Samsung implemented its first significant operations in China in 1992, the same year as the establishment of diplomatic relations between South Korea and the People's Republic of China. This comprised a JV in Tianjin to produce VCRs and the setting up of Samsung (Huizhou) Electronic Ltd to manufacture music centres, family movie theatres, MP3 and so on. The predominant market for this output would have been the global supply network of the parent company (that is, mainly RPS activity as described earlier). This preliminary stage of Samsung's expansion into China then proceeded (1993/94) with further JVs (producing electronic exchange equipment and, in Tianjin, general consumer electronics products), Tongguang Samsung Electronics Ltd (also in Tianjin, to produce TVs) and Samsung (Suzhou) Electronic Ltd to produce household electronic goods (washing machines, fridges, air conditioners).

This quite extensive and diverse set of pioneering entries led Samsung to formalise its Chinese operations by setting up headquarters organisations

Table 4.3   Samsung's biggest events in China

DS	IA	Year	The biggest events	Major business
Previous Coopera- tion		1970s	Samsung imports coal from mainland China through Hong Kong	N/A
		1992	Set up the first joint venture in Tianjin, China to produce VCR before establishing the diplomatic relationship between PRC and South Korea	VCR
			PRC and South Korea established diplomatic relationship	N/A
			Set up Samsung (Huizhou) Electronic Ltd	Music centre, family movie theatre, MP3, etc.
The Preliminary Stage	With no official R&D facilities, but had some SL functions	1993	Set up Samsung (Tianjin) Electronic Ltd	DVD, video, camera, digital video or camera
			Set up the first joint venture for electronic exchange equipment in China	No information
		1994	Set up the joint venture in Tianjin for general electronic products	No information
			Set up Tongguang Samsung Electronic Ltd in Tianjin	Various kinds of television
			Set up Samsung (Suzhou) Electronic Ltd	Fridge, air conditioner, washing machine, etc.
The Developed Stage		1995	Set up Samsung China headquarters, and Samsung (China) Investment Ltd established in Beijing	Headquarters
		1997	Set up Samsung (Suzhou) Washing Machine Ltd	No information
			Set up Samsung (Tianjin) Electronic Display Ltd	LCD, CDT display
		1999	The first supplier of CDMA equipments in China	N/A
The Advanced Stage	Local-for-Local and Globally Linked	2000	Samsung Communication Technology Research Centre established in Beijing, China	Research on technologies of mobile communication systems and terminals

Table 4.3 (continued)

DS	IA	Year	The biggest events	Major business
		2001	Protocol with China Unicom and supply of the first Samsung and Unicom CDMA mobile equipments	N/A
			Set up Samsung (Tianjin) Communication Technology Ltd	GSM mobile phone
			Set up Shanghai Bell and Samsung Mobile Communication Technology Ltd	CDMA systems' research, production and sales
		2002	Set up Samsung Kejian Mobile Communication Technology Ltd	CDMA Mobile Phone
		2003	Shanghai, Beijing and Guangzhou Distribution Ltd established	N/A
The Advanced Stage	Local-for-Local and Globally Linked	2004	Samsung Semiconductor Technology Research Centre established in Suzhou, China	Research on software and hardware for electronic components and integrated circuits, and product solutions
			Chengdu and Shenyang Distribution Ltd established	N/A
			WCDMA joint venture established	No information
		2005	Ranked as the best foreign investor in China and won the best performance award	N/A
		2006	Currently, Samsung China is a group with 28 production factories, 30 distribution companies and 4 research and development centres	N/A
			Samsung was elected as the most valuable consumable brand in China, the most respected enterprise in China, the best contributor among foreign enterprises in China	N/A

Note: DS = Development Stages; IA = Innovation Approaches. The chronicle part is translated and summarized from Samsung China's web pages 'Samsung China development history'.

in 1995, initiating its developed stage (lasting for perhaps the rest of the 1990s). This comprised the establishment in Beijing of Samsung China Headquarters and Samsung (China) Investment Ltd. In addition the supply scope of Samsung's Chinese operations extended further, in 1997, with the creation of Samsung (Suzhou) Washing Machine Ltd and Samsung (Tianjin) Electronic Display Ltd (LDC, CDT display). In 1999 Samsung became the first supplier of CDMA equipment in China. This period is likely to have seen a growing commitment of, at least parts of, Samsung's Chinese production to the supply of the local market. In the main it would seem likely that in the stages of building its bridgehead in China Samsung was able to depend on the use of its already established product scope, with little localised technological activity beyond some SL-type work within production units.

The ongoing advanced stage of Samsung's commitment to China can be exemplified by the emerging presence of R&D and localised creative activity. This will be reviewed in the next section. The mainstream expansion of Samsung's Chinese operations also continued at a significant pace, so that by 2006 the group had 28 production facilities, 30 distribution companies and four main R&D centres. Samsung was also rated as the most valued consumer brand in China, the most respected enterprise there and the best contributor among foreign enterprises in China.

Samsung R&D in China

Within the R&D system of Samsung China, depicted in Figure 4.2, two units reflect not only an increasing quantitative relevance of the local market but also a need to address it in a more individualised manner. Here the Samsung Economic Research Centre (Beijing Office) assesses the market potentials of the host economy, whilst the Samsung (China) Electronics Design and Research Institute operates (collaboratively with higher-level research units elsewhere in the system) to orientate products to local consumer preferences.

Two major R&D initiatives have been set up in Samsung's mobile communication division in China. Thus 2000 saw the creation, in Beijing, of Samsung (China) Communication Technology Research Centre, to investigate the technologies of mobile communication systems and terminals. Then the next year saw the setting up of Shanghai Bell and Samsung Mobile Communications Technology Ltd, with the product mandate scope of research, production and sales of CDMA systems.

In the Semiconductor Division the Samsung (China) Semiconductor Technology Research Centre was created in Suzhou in 2004. Along with its Integrated Circuit Subcentre this unit addresses research on software

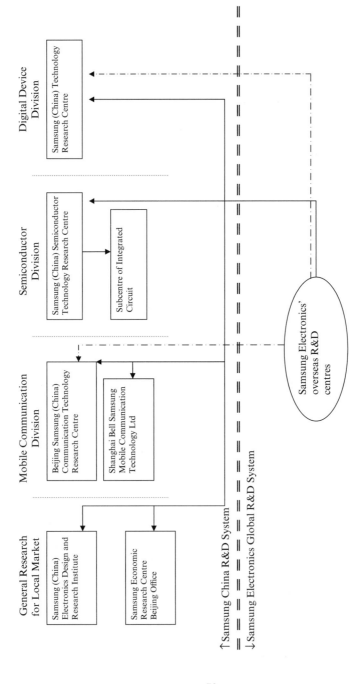

Note: ——▶ Presents the direct and frequent link;   ----▶ Presents the indirect or infrequent link.

Figure 4.2   The R&D system of Samsung China

and hardware for electronic components and integrated circuits. Finally, the Digital Device Division now has the support of its own Technology Research Centre.

So far it would seem that Samsung China's R&D system has quite limited interdependency (compared, for example, to Ericsson) with the wider international network of Samsung Electronics Ltd. Thus the only facility reported to have direct and frequent links to the wider network is the Semiconductor Division Technology Research Centre. Indirect or infrequent links are noted for the Samsung (China) Technology Research Centres of the mobile communication and digital device divisions.

CONCLUSION

The massive growth of MNEs' R&D operations in China can be seen to occur at the intersection of two significant phenomena. Firstly, the increasing focus of MNEs on R&D in developing countries, as an extension of their longer-standing commitment to triad countries.

Secondly, the vast expansion of R&D, scientific investigation and emergent innovation in China.[23] This can then be seen to relate to three separate components of MNE strategy, all of which may now be relevant to their activities in China.

Firstly, export-oriented efficiency-seeking supply units (notably in the Special Economic Zones of the Coastal states) represented an early motivation for MNE entry. Though this use of mature standardised technology is unlikely to generate significant need for R&D support, some adaptation to make better use of local inputs may occur. Secondly, the size and growth potential of the Chinese market quickly generated a market-seeking commitment. Indeed the cases reviewed here suggest that the long-term strategic potential of the Chinese market very promptly led R&D for localised responsiveness to go beyond mere adaptation of established goods and, instead, move into more ambitious development (a variant of Bartlett and Ghoshal's local-for-local innovation) targeting local needs and tastes.

Finally, the Ericsson case, at least, indicates an enthusiasm for participation in the longer-term orientations of scientific research potentials of the emerging Chinese national system of innovation. Questions can then be raised (Pearce and Papanastassiou, 2006) about the benefits and costs to a 'national' system of innovation from the selective involvement of components of a MNE's 'global' innovation strategy. Therefore the potential interdependencies of the technological progress of China and MNEs, introduced here in its early stages, becomes a major issue of academic concern and public policy.

NOTES

1. By the time of Terpstra's statement two major pioneering survey and case study analyses of MNE R&D were already underway. Thus Ronstadt (1977, 1978) was able to provide a typology of diverse roles for overseas laboratories in MNEs, in effect supplying the basis for the categorisation used here. Similarly Behrman and Fischer (1980a, 1980b) initiated an important mode of analysis, again reflected here, by drawing out the influence of wider strategic priorities in MNEs on the extent and role of dispersed R&D.
2. The growth rate of China's GERD from 1996 to 2002 was 218.4 per cent, compared with 17.5 per cent for all countries, 16.6 per cent for developed countries and 30.6 per cent for all developing countries (UNCTAD, 2005, table A.111.2). China's share of global GERD rose from 0.8 per cent in 1996 to 2.3 per cent in 2002, and from 12.3 per cent of that in developing countries in 1996 to 30.0 per cent in 2002.
3. Thus China accounted for 2.1 per cent of global BERD in 2002 and for 33.1 per cent of that in developing countries.
4. For 1,489 of the 1,773 cases R&D was the key business function of the project (UNCTAD, 2005, annex table A.1.3, p. 259). Over the 2002/04 period 939 of these R&D projects (63.1 per cent) were in developing countries (including Southeast Europe and the Commonwealth of Independent States (CIS)). Through the three years the most dramatic development was in R&D projects in Asia and Oceania. Here 155 projects were 46.8 per cent of the total in 2002, 291 represented 56.4 per cent of the total in 2003 and 405 were 63.1 per cent of the total in 2004.
5. As well as 42 in Southeast Europe and the CIS.
6. This figure includes 40 projects in Southeast Europe and the CIS.
7. Von Zedtwitz's (2005) application of his typology to his own survey data (Von Zedtwitz and Gassman, 2002) showed less dramatic divergence from prevalent expectations. Thus 496 of 776 cases were 'traditional' (64 per cent), only 194 (25 per cent) 'modern', 64 (8 per cent) 'catch-up' and 22 (3 per cent) expansionary. The likely reason for this was that the survey was carried out in the 1990s and covered *in situ* units created over a long period of time (rather than new projects in the UNCTAD/OCO data), thus reflecting earlier patterns and motivations.
8. For example, in UNCTAD's (2005, table IV.6, p. 129) presentation of US MNE overseas R&D expenditure, developing countries accounted for only 12.4 per cent of the total between 1998 and 2002.
9. The rise of this figure to 17.7 per cent by 2002 again endorses the view of a very strong relative (both compared to local developing country R&D expenditures and compared to MNE R&D expenditures in developed countries) growth of MNE R&D in developing countries in recent years.
10. The 2001 figure is suppressed in the data for reasons of disclosure.
11. Hong Kong, South Korea, Singapore and Taiwan.
12. Indonesia, Malaysia, the Philippines and Thailand.
13. The interim had seen the setting up of Ericsson Guangzhou and Ericsson Shanghai Offices in 1989 and the provision of equipment to Shanghai International Communication Bureau in 1990.
14. The original formulation of the scope typology derives from White and Poynter (1984) and D'Cruz (1986). For details of the three-part variant used here see Pearce (1989, 2001) and Papanastassiou and Pearce (1999, pp. 24–30).
15. In White and Poynter's (1984) version of the typology it would be a rationalised manufacturer and in D'Cruz's (1986) version a globally rationalised business.
16. Thus Ericsson China could have covered the adapter as well as the adopter variants of White and Poynter's (1984) miniature replica.
17. Indeed in 1996 Ericsson China became the first company in China to pass the ISO 9001 qualification.
18. Most plausibly those products whose established production technology makes strongest use of inputs that are most readily (cost-effectively) available in China.

19. Here, though, China alters some dimensions of the RPS role of these JVs. Thus the host-country market is always part of that supplied by an RPS, but usually a very small and neutral part with no scope to influence the subsidiary behaviour. Over time this is unlikely to remain true for a RPS-type operation in China.
20. Notably as a heterarchy (Hedlund, 1986; Hedlund and Rolander, 1990) or the transnational (Bartlett and Ghoshal, 1989, 1990).
21. Bartlett and Ghoshal (1990, p. 217) suggest the locally leveraged approach involves 'utilizing the resources of a national subsidiary to create innovations not only for the local market but also for exploitation on a world-wide basis'.
22. For elaboration of circumstances where this may occur see Papanastassiou and Pearce (2005).
23. There is, of course, no assumption of unidirectional causation here. The growth of MNEs' R&D in China is itself a major determinant of the two other phenomena.

REFERENCES

Bartlett, C.A. and S. Ghoshal (1989), *Managing Across Borders: The Transnational Solution*, London: Hutchinson Business Books.

Bartlett, C.A. and S. Ghoshal (1990), 'Managing innovation in the transnational corporation', in C.A. Bartlett, Y. Doz and G. Hedlund (eds), *Managing the Global Firm*, London: Routledge, pp. 215–55.

Behrman, J.N. (1984), *Industrial Policies: International Restructuring and Transnationals*, Lexington, MA: Lexington Books.

Behrman, J.N. and W.A. Fischer (1980a), *Overseas R&D Activities of Transnational Companies*, Cambridge, MA: Oelgeschlager, Gunn and Hain.

Behrman, J.N. and W.A. Fischer (1980b), 'Transnational corporations: market orientations and R&D abroad', *Colombia Journal of World Business*, **XV**, 55–60.

D'Cruz, J. (1986), 'Strategic management of subsidiaries', in H. Etemad and L. Séguin Dulude (eds), *Managing the Multinational Subsidiary*, London: Croom Helm, pp. 75–89.

Dunning, J.H. (1993), *Multinational Enterprises and the Global Economy*, Wokingham: Addison-Wesley.

Dunning, J.H. (2000), 'The eclectic paradigm as an envelope for economic and business theories of TNC activity', *International Business Review*, **9**(2), 163–90.

Haug, P., N. Hood and S. Young (1983), 'R&D intensity in the affiliates of US-owned electronics companies manufacturing in Scotland', *Regional Studies*, **17**, 383–92.

Hedlund, G. (1986), 'The hypermodern MNC – a heterarchy?', *Human Resource Management*, **25**, 9–35.

Hedlund, G. and D. Rolander (1990), 'Action in heterarchies – new approaches to managing the MNC', in C.A. Bartlett, Y. Doz and G. Hedlund (eds), *Managing the Global Firm*, London: Routledge, pp. 15–46.

Manea, J. and R. Pearce (2004), *Multinationals and Transition*, London: Palgrave Macmillan.

Papanastassiou, M. and R. Pearce (1999), *Multinationals, Technology and National Competitiveness*, Cheltenham, UK and Northampton, MA, USA: Edward Elgar Publishing.

Papanastassiou, M. and R. Pearce (2005), 'Funding sources and the strategic roles of decentralized R&D in multinationals', *R&D Management*, **35**(1), 89–100.

Pearce, R. (1989), *The Internationalization of Research and Development by Multinational Enterprises*, London: Macmillan.

Pearce, R. (1999), 'Decentralized R&D and strategic competitiveness: globalized approaches to generation and use of technology in multinational enterprises', *Research Policy*, **28**(2–3), 157–78.

Pearce, R. (2001), 'Multinationals and industrialization: the bases of inward investment policy', *International Journal of the Economics of Business*, **8**(1), 511–73.

Pearce, R. (2006), 'Globalization and development: an international business strategy approach', *Transnational Corporations*, **15**(1), 39–74.

Pearce, R. and M. Papanastassiou (2006), 'Multinationals and national systems of innovation: strategy and policy issues', in A.T. Tavares and A. Texeira (eds), *Multinationals, Clusters and Innovation*, Basingstoke: Palgrave Macmillan, pp. 289–307.

Porter, M.E. (1986), 'Competition in global industries: a conceptual framework', in M.E. Porter (ed.), *Competition in Global Industries*, Boston, MA: Harvard Business School Press, pp. 15–60.

Ronstadt, R.C. (1977), *Research and Development Abroad by US Multinationals*, New York: Praeger.

Ronstadt, R.C. (1978), 'International R&D: the establishment and evolution of R&D abroad in seven US multinationals', *Journal of International Business Studies*, **9**(1), 7–24.

Terpstra, V. (1977), 'International product policy: the role of foreign R&D', *Colombia Journal of World Business*, **12**(4), 24–32.

UNCTAD (2005), *World Investment Report, 2005*, New York and Geneva: United Nations.

Von Zedtwitz, M. (2004), 'Managing foreign R&D laboratories in China', *R&D Management*, **34**(4), 439–52.

Von Zedtwitz, M. (2005), 'International R&D strategies of TNCs from developing countries: the case of China', in UNCTAD (ed.), *Globalization of R&D and Developing Countries*, New York and Geneva: United Nations, pp. 117–40.

Von Zedtwitz, M. and O. Gassmann (2002), 'Market versus technology drive in R&D internationalization: four different patterns of managing research and development', *Research Policy*, **31**(4), 569–88

White, R.E. and T.A. Poynter (1984), 'Strategies for foreign-owned subsidiaries in Canada', *Business Quarterly*, Summer, 59–69.

Zhou, Y. (2005), 'Features and impacts of the internationalization of R&D by transnational corporations: China's case', in UNCTAD (ed.), *Globalization of R&D in Developing Countries*, New York and Geneva: United Nations, pp. 109–16.

5. Capability development of foreign-owned subsidiaries in China during their early evolution

Feng Zhang

INTRODUCTION

The fact that overseas subsidiaries could play strategic roles in the competence development of multinational corporations (MNCs) has attracted considerable attention from researchers in both strategic management and international business in the past three decades. Correspondingly, asset-augmenting, also known as strategic asset seeking (Dunning, 1998; Kuemmerle, 1999), emerged as an alternative motivation for foreign direct investment. Moreover, a large amount of effort has been given to subsidiary level analyses, generating revolutionary insights on the capability development of MNCs and their overseas subsidiaries. For instance, a decentralized control mechanism in some MNCs to encourage local initiatives of overseas subsidiaries has been documented since 1980s (Bartlett and Ghoshal, 1986) whereas host location conditions along with the formal and informal management mechanism within MNCs were later emphasized by much literature (Birkinshaw and Hood, 1998; Andersson, et al., 2002; Almeida and Phene, 2004). On top of these factors, a well-received wisdom is that internal and external embeddedness of an overseas subsidiary is crucial, and sometimes decisive (Andersson, et al., 2005), for its performance and capability development. This argument has been put forward recently with the notion of 'network MNCs' (Ghoshal and Nohria, 1989; Ghoshal and Bartlett, 1990; Andersson and Forsgren, 2000; Ernst and Kim, 2002); in other words, the subsidiary's capability is shaped by its embeddedness in both internal and external networks.

While the capability development of an overseas subsidiary may be represented by the performance in any supply chain activities (for example, innovation, engineering, production, marketing, financing, and so on), most studies chose to focus on technological innovations (Pearce and Paparastassiou, 1999; Andersson et al., 2002; Almeida and Phene, 2004;

83

Cantwell and Mudambi, 2005). Among other reasons, this choice could be explained by the belief that technological capability is an important indicator of international competitiveness of firms and even countries under the current knowledge economy. Technological innovations normally require the complementary inputs from both internal and external knowledge resources. On the one hand, firms specialize in the internal transfer of certain types of knowledge due to the imperfect knowledge market (Buckley and Casson, 2002), the tacit nature of knowledge (Nonaka and Takeuchi, 1998) and/or strategic considerations; on the other hand, firms increasingly rely on external resources in knowledge generation in response to both demand side and supply side factors; the former may include, to name a few, the sharing of soaring research and development (R&D) costs, the accessing of scientific knowledge and the search for technological opportunities; the latter denotes the capability improvements of host locations, for instance, the emergence of specialized/ general locational clusters and the capability upgrading of some developing locations. Consequently, previous literature has drawn upon internal and external environments (Bartlett and Ghoshal, 1986; Birkinshaw and Hood, 1998; Schulz, 2003; Almeida and Phene, 2004; Andersson et al., 2005), as well as the subsidiary-embeddedness in internal and external networks (Andersson and Forsgren, 2000; Andersson et al., 2002; Cantwell and Mudambi, 2005), in explaining the technological innovation performance of subsidiaries.

Whereas the capability development of overseas subsidiaries has been the focus of many previous studies, little attention has been given to the capability per se. In particular, we still miss precise knowledge of what kinds of knowledge from each network contribute to the capabilities developed in subsidiaries. This study seeks to shed some light on this issue by looking at the structure and components of technological knowledge attributable to internal and external knowledge sources, respectively.

The competence development of firms is a dynamic process. It is expected that the role of internal and external knowledge resources would change over the process. An ideal setting to investigate this process would be a host location, which has been actively upgrading its capabilities, and in which the strategy of foreign-owned firms has also evolved over time. China, as a strategically important market with locational advantages for production facilities of many MNCs around the world, has started to attract R&D affiliates of those firms over the last couple of decades. The accumulated R&D investment of MNCs in Mainland China (thereafter China) had reached approximately $4 billion by June 2004 (WIR, 2005). By 2005 there were reportedly as many as 750 foreign-invested R&D

centers in China (China Daily, 2005). In other words, China provides an ideal background for the purpose of this study.

Patents granted to the world's largest firms by the United States Patent and Trademark Office (USPTO) for inventions attributable to their subsidiaries in China between 1996 and 2005 were analysed in this study. Patent citations allow us to measure different technological knowledge components, in particular, knowledge across organizational, technological, and geographical boundaries. Given the costs of filing an international patent, we assume that technologies invented by foreign-owned subsidiaries in China must be strategically important for their individual parents to be allowed to apply for US patents. We are not suggesting that foreign-owned subsidiaries in China have developed technological capabilities that are comparable with those accumulated in some overseas subsidiaries in developed countries, but the technological innovations of foreign-owned subsidiaries in China may have started to contribute to the competence creation of their individual parents. While previous literature suggests that licensing would be a good indicator of basic technological capability development of firms in developing countries (Athreye and Cantwell, 2007), this study is interested instead in the more advanced level of technological capabilities of foreign-owned subsidiaries in China by focusing on their patents.

By investigating the technological knowledge components of patents invented by foreign-owned subsidiaries in China over the ten-year period, we found that the results are largely consistent with our overall argument that the technological capabilities of foreign-owned subsidiaries in China are developing. In particular, foreign-owned subsidiaries in China are increasingly involved in technological knowledge generation; for instance the annual number of patents invented by those subsidiaries has dramatically increased since 2000. Moreover, those subsidiaries have been able to access external sources for technologically complex knowledge, namely knowledge in different technological fields. We further found that foreign-owned subsidiaries in China are increasingly able to not only understand newer knowledge, but also integrate older external knowledge with newly generated knowledge through in-house R&D. However, contrary to our expectation, we found that external knowledge from geographically local sources, that is, knowledge from other firms/organizations in China, has played a much less important role in the capability development of foreign-owned subsidiaries in China. While using USPTO patent data in this study may partly contribute to this finding, it also could be that foreign-owned MNCs strategically avoided the knowledge exchange with other firms or organizations in the host environment because of their concerns about the intellectual property rights conditions in China. The findings of this study contribute to the better understanding of the knowledge accumulation pattern of foreign-owned subsidiaries in some developing countries, in particular, the accumulation of strategically important knowledge in their early phase of evolution.

The next section develops hypotheses based on descriptive statistics evidence, as well as previous literature. Empirical settings and the results of hypotheses tests are discussed in the following section. The final section discusses implications and concludes.

CONCEPTUAL DEVELOPMENT

Studies have shown that a high proportion of technology for innovations is generated within innovating firms themselves, while the acquisition of technological knowledge from other firms and institutes is always involved in the process (Pavitt, 1988). Evolutionary theory believes that firms exist because of their superior efficiency in knowledge creation, transfer and combination (Kogut and Zander, 1993); such a capability may also be relevant in explaining the heterogeneity of overseas subsidiaries. In the literature of subsidiary evolution, the profile of knowledge transferred from the parent company and that sourced from the host environment are generally implicit criteria in defining the capability of a subsidiary. A number of established subsidiary typologies, for instance, classify subsidiaries based on their dependence on parent knowledge and local creative initiatives (White and Poynter, 1984; Bartlett and Ghoshal, 1989; Pearce, 1999). Under the notion of network MNCs (Ghoshal and Nohria, 1989; Ghoshal and Bartlett, 1990; Andersson and Forsgren, 2000; Ernst and Kim, 2002), subsidiaries are, more explicitly, differentiated based on each subsidiary's unique and idiosyncratic patterns of internal and external network linkages (McEvily and Zaheer, 1999; Phene and Almeida, 2003).

Correspondingly, the internal management mechanism and the conditions in the external environment have been extensively studied during the last three decades in explaining subsidiary capability development. The former include internal control mechanisms in terms of decision making, incentives and local initiatives (Bartlett and Ghoshal, 1986; Birkinshaw et al., 1998; Pearce, 1999), the co-evolution of subsidiary capability development and charter change (Birkinshaw and Hood, 1998), organizational structure (Bartlett and Ghoshal, 1989), strategic concerns (Schulz, 2003), corporate culture and informal employee networks and so on. The latter, on the other hand, focuses on the supply side factors of host locations, for instance, host country technology competencies, capacities and heritage (Pearce, 1999), the technological richness and diversity of the local knowledge network (Almeida and Phene, 2004) and the presence of major competitors in host locations (Cantwell and Mudambi, 2005). Finally, the embeddedness of a subsidiary in its internal network (Pearce, 1999) and external network (Andersson et al., 2002) links the two categories of determinants sketched above, and influences the capability development of the subsidiary. In other words, subsidiary evolution has been explained by internal and external factors, interactively.

Whereas most of the previous studies use the scale or scope of technological innovation as a proxy for the level of subsidiary capability development, our knowledge is largely limited at the aggregated level of capability measurements, such as R&D expenditures (Cantwell and Mudambi, 2005), the number of patents (Almeida and Phene, 2004), the inflow of knowledge from parent and peer subsidiaries (Schulz, 2003), the possession of product development or international market development function (Andersson et al., 2002; Cantwell and Mudambi, 2005) and so on. Pearce and Papanastassiou's (1999) R&D laboratory typology indirectly provides a possible way to disaggregate the capability accumulated in a R&D subsidiary, that is, technological, marketing, engineering, management and scientific capabilities. Garcia-Pont et al. (2009) suggest disaggregating the embeddedness of a subsidiary into three categories, namely, operational, capability and strategic embeddedness, in response to different capability and strategic considerations of firms. However, on the one hand, it is well received that subsidiary evolution can be defined '*as the process of accumulation or depletion of resources/capabilities in the subsidiary over time*' (Birkinshaw and Hood, 1998 p. 773, emphasis added), and that the resources/capabilities per se could be complementarily acquired from internal and external sources; on the other hand, we still miss precise knowledge of which types of knowledge from each source contribute to the capabilities developed in the subsidiaries. This study aims to unfold this black box. Instead of interest in the mechanism, of which firms accumulate skills and capabilities, we focus on the pattern change of the structure and components of the resources/capabilities that are accumulated from internal and external sources over time, with a particular interest in the disaggregation of the technological knowledge accumulated by foreign-owned subsidiaries in China.

To operationalize this study, we used patents granted to the world's largest firms by the USPTO for inventions attributable to their subsidiaries in China between 1996 and 2005. During the ten-year period, 554 patents were invented by foreign-owned subsidiaries in China that are affiliates of 51 of the world's largest MNCs from 11 countries/regions and across 14 industries. With citing patents as the reference category, we examined the pattern of the patents they cite, as an indicator of the

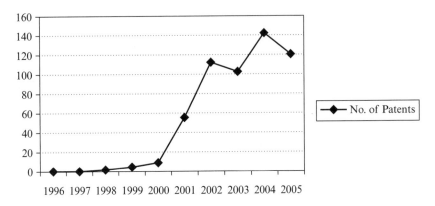

Figure 5.1   The growth of patenting between 1996 and 2005

technological knowledge sources on which they have drawn. The citation records of patents to earlier patents allow us to measure the knowledge structure and components of a patented technology. A total of 3,845 pairs of citing and cited patents were extracted.

There has been a historical discussion about the advantages and disadvantages of using patent and patent citation data (see Cantwell, 2006 for a detailed review). A concern relevant to the current study might be whether patent citations could represent real technological knowledge flows (Griliches, 1990; Alcacer and Gittelman, 2006). Several studies have shown that patent citations are a reasonable measurement for knowledge flows (Jaffe et al., 2000; Duguet and Macgarvie, 2005); moreover, the current study is interested in the types of internal and external technological knowledge that may contribute to the capability development of overseas subsidiaries (rather than knowledge flow). Even a citation added by patent examiners represents a legitimate component of the knowledge in the corresponding citing patent. More importantly, the examining procedures in the USPTO make patent citations a relatively objective method to measure the knowledge structure and components of citing patents.

Figure 5.1 illustrates the growth of patenting among foreign-owned subsidiaries in China (thereafter CN subsidiaries). The annual number of patents invented by CN subsidiaries started to pick up pace after the year 2000. In particular, a total of 19 patents were invented by CN subsidiaries from 1996 to 2000, whereas 143 patents were invented in the year 2004 alone.

Given the emerging status of CN subsidiaries in the knowledge accumulation networks of MNCs, one might expect that their early patents would rely heavily on current technological knowledge from their individual corporate groups, namely the headquarters and peer subsidiaries of

Table 5.1   Knowledge accumulation across organizational boundary

Organizational Boundary	1996	1997	1998	1999	2000	2001	2002	2003	2004	2005
Internal	0	0	3.7	18.52	13.85	20	25.5	23.1	24.25	20.7
External	100	100	96.3	81.48	86.15	80	74.5	77	75.75	79.3
Total	100	100	100	100	100	100	100	100	100	100

equivalent MNCs. Consequently, for each pair of citing and cited patents, we determined whether the citing patent draws upon knowledge within the innovating firm or from other firms or organizations by comparing the assignees of citing and cited patents. Internal knowledge accumulation is defined if the assignees of citing and cited patents are the same firm; and external knowledge accumulation, otherwise. Interestingly, Table 5.1 shows that CN subsidiaries almost exclusively rely on external knowledge in their early inventions, in particular in 1996 and 1997. This result suggests that the initial patenting activities of CN subsidiaries might be the results of experimental or accidental evens. Figure 5.2 further illustrates the pattern change of knowledge accumulation across organizational boundary over the ten-year period. Obviously, the two lines in Figure 5.2 are converging. From 2001 onwards, about 80percent of the knowledge in technological inventions of CN subsidiaries was from external knowledge sources. Such a knowledge structure was comparable with that of well-established overseas subsidiaries of MNCs in the 1990s (Cantwell et al., 2008). This result suggests the catching up of CN subsidiaries at least in terms of the knowledge accumulation across organizational boundary.

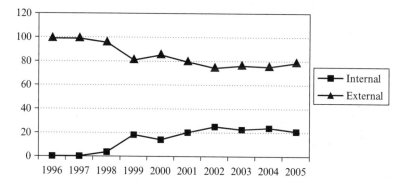

Figure 5.2   The pattern of knowledge accumulation across organizational boundary

Table 5.2   Knowledge accumulation across technological boundary

Technological Boundary	1996	1997	1998	1999	2000	2001	2002	2003	2004	2005
Intra-Tech Field	100	50	74.1	75.92	73.85	81.7	84.8	72.6	82.83	78.8
Inter-Tech Field	0	50	25.9	24.08	26.15	18.3	15.2	27.4	17.17	21.2
Total	100	100	100	100	100	100	100	100	100	100

Today, the number of technologies required per product is increasing in many industries, by, for example, the shift from mechanical to electro-mechanical to electronic systems in the automobile industry (Miller, 1994; Granstrand et al., 1997; Howells et al., 2003); in the pharmaceutical industry the rise of biotechnology and information and communication technology (ICT) applications has been critical, as well as the role of optics and laser technologies for medical instruments. In this context, companies increasingly have to deal with much more difficult and multidisciplinary technological problems. Another important factor that contributes to this process is the blurring of the boundary between science and technology. A great many antecedent examples can be found in the history of science and technology, including the cases of pharmaceutical, biotechnology and modern science of bacteriology.

However, because of the limited absorptive capacity of CN subsidiaries, their knowledge accumulation activities might be largely limited to incremental innovations, namely, knowledge accumulation within the same technological areas. By comparing the technological fields of each pair of citing and cited patents, we defined inter-technological field and intra-technological field knowledge accumulation. The 56 technological fields considered are derived from an appropriate combination of the classes and sub-classes of the US patent class system (Cantwell and Noonan, 2007). Table 5.2 shows that the CN subsidiaries still mainly draw upon intra-technological field knowledge. In other words, the ability of CN subsidiaries to integrate technological knowledge from different fields was still limited during the studied period. This result suggests that competence-exploiting activities, instead of competence-creating activities, might still dominate the innovative efforts of CN subsidiaries.

Although the line of 'inter-tech field' in Figure 5.3 is quite flat at the level of 20 percent from 1998 onwards, we expected that inter-technological field knowledge would more likely come from external knowledge sources. This is because of the increased technological complexity, as we discussed

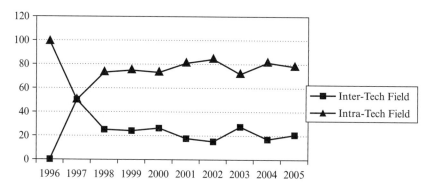

Figure 5.3   The pattern of knowledge accumulation across technological boundary

above; meanwhile the persistence of the specific profile of specialization of firms due to the path dependence and tacit nature of technologies makes firms have to search external knowledge sources for 'non-local search' (Rosenkopf and Almeida, 2003). The limited resources and capabilities of a single firm may encourage the firm to seek outside support to overcome internal technical limitations. This might be particularly true for CN subsidiaries that had just started to accumulate innovative capabilities.

Hypothesis 1: Knowledge crossing technological disciplines is more likely to come from external knowledge sources instead of internal knowledge sources.

Whereas the accumulation of internal knowledge, in general, becomes increasingly important for firms over time (Jaffe and Trajtenberg, 1999), local embeddedness has been emphasized by subsidiary evolution literature for over a decade (Birkinshaw et al., 1998; Andersson et al., 2002; Cantwell and Mudambi, 2005). Therefore, the current study is particularly interested in the knowledge accumulation from geographically local sources. Fortunately, patent citations allow us to incorporate the knowledge accumulation of CN subsidiaries across geographical boundary, in addition to organizational and technological boundaries. For each pair of citing and cited patents, we compared the geographical locations of the inventors of the citing and cited patents. Local knowledge accumulation is defined if the cited patent was invented in China; and international knowledge accumulation, otherwise. Table 5.3 and Figure 5.4 report the knowledge accumulation pattern across geographical boundary for CN subsidiaries over the studied period. Whereas the

Table 5.3   Knowledge accumulation across geographical boundary

Geographical Boundary	1996	1997	1998	1999	2000	2001	2002	2003	2004	2005
International	100	100	100	100	100	98.3	96.1	94.8	4.96	95.1
Local	0	0	0	0	0	1.71	3.91	5.19	5.04	4.89
Total	100	100	100	100	100	100	100	100	100	100

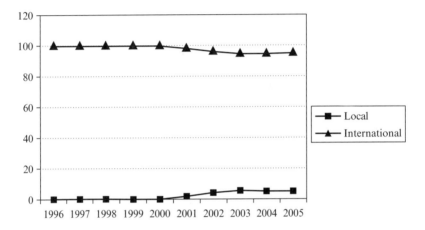

Figure 5.4   The pattern of knowledge accumulation across geographical boundary

two lines in Figure 5.4 are certainly converging, by 2005 local knowledge, that is, knowledge generated in China, only accounted for around 5 percent among all the knowledge upon which CN subsidiaries draw. In other words, CN subsidiaries relied almost exclusively on knowledge sources located in other countries outside of China. This result contradicts our expectation, given the importance of the Chinese market for many of the world's largest MNCs and the growing number of foreign-owned R&D centers in China. We further investigate this in hypotheses tests below.

Previous literature suggests that the access of geographically local external knowledge could be strategically important in the capability development of, as well as the internal charter competition of, a subsidiary (Birkinshaw and Hood, 1998). Whereas geographically local knowledge only contributes a small percentage in the overall knowledge accumulation of CN subsidiaries, we still expected that such local knowledge would come from external sources.

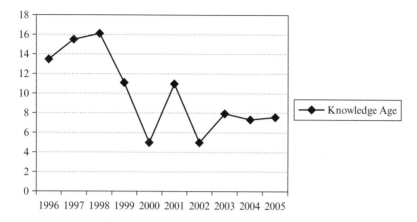

Figure 5.5   The pattern of knowledge age

Hypothesis 2: The local portion of the technological knowledge of a subsidiary is more likely to come from external knowledge sources instead of internal knowledge sources.

Figure 5.5 illustrates the age changes in knowledge, upon which CN subsidiaries draw. The age of knowledge was determined by subtracting the granting year of cited patent from the granting year of citing patent in each pair of citing and cited patents. While little comparable evidence could be found in previous literature, the pattern in Figure 5.5 shows that CN subsidiaries increasingly utilized newer knowledge, which might suggest the improved absorptive capability of CN subsidiaries.

Due to the path-dependent nature of technology, firms will seek to improve and to diversify their technology by searching in areas that enable them to build upon their existing technological base (Pavitt, 1988; Cantwell and Barrera, 1998). Many firms have employed niche applications of external sourced technological knowledge, for example, ICT technologies for pharmaceutical firms. In other words, external technological knowledge is complementary to the internal knowledge base and may be sourced largely for the purpose of application instead of further development. In contrast, open innovation literature argues that an equal weight should be given to external knowledge, in comparison to internal knowledge (Chesbrough, 2006). However, the latter argument might be more relevant for well-established overseas subsidiaries that have accumulated considerable absorptive capacities. Given the emerging status of CN subsidiaries, we expected that externally sourced technologies must be relatively established, which are ready for application and require minimum further development in their original technological areas. In other words, when CN subsidiaries integrate external and internal knowledge to generate new knowledge, the age of external knowledge might be significantly older than that of internal knowledge.

Hypothesis 3: Mature technological knowledge is more likely to come from external knowledge sources instead of internal knowledge sources.

HYPOTHESES TESTS

As we mentioned earlier, this study uses patents granted to the world's largest firms by the USPTO for inventions attributable to their subsidiaries in China between 1996 and 2005. A total of 554 citing patents and 3,845 patent citations were extracted. Our dependent variable (*EXT*) is an indicator of whether a patent citation (a pairwise combination of citing and cited patents) falls into the category of external knowledge accumulation. In other words, *EXT* equals one if the citing patent cites a cited patent assigned to another firm/organization; and zero, otherwise.

By utilizing the 56 technological fields, we measured the knowledge accumulation across technological boundary (Inter-Tech) by pairwise matching the technology fields of citing and cited patents. Inter-Tech equals one if a pair of citing and cited patents is in the same technological field; and zero, otherwise. The knowledge accumulation across geographical boundary (*L*) is measured by comparing the geographical locations of the inventors of each pair of citing and cited patents. *L* equals one if the inventor of a cited patent is located in China; and zero, otherwise. For each pair of citing and cited patents, mature technological knowledge (*M*) is measured by the age of the cited patent when the citing patent was granted. The age is calculated by the difference between the grant years of the citing and cited patents.

We controlled for the grant year of citing patents (*Y*). Moreover, industry dummies (IND) and home country/region dummies (HM) are included to control for the possible industrial and home country/region effects. The food industry and Taiwan are the baseline categories for IND and HM dummies, respectively. We chose Taiwan as the reference group for HM because of the geographical and psychic closeness between Taiwan and Mainland China.

Since *EXT* is a dichotomous variable that takes values of one and zero, a logistic regression technique is employed. The model may be expressed formally as:

Table 5.4   Two-tailed pearson correlation matrix

Variables	N	Mean	Std dev.	1	2	3	4	5
External Knowledge (*EXT*)	3,845	0.7748	0.4178	1				
Inter-Technological Field Knowledge (*Inter-Tech*)	3,845	0.2039	0.403	0.1539	1			
Geographically Local Knowledge (*L*)	3,845	0.0434	0.2039	–0.3616 <0.0001	–0.0698 <0.0001	1		
Mature Knowledge (*M*)	3,845	7.5813	10.0794	0.233 <0.0001	0.0918 <0.0001	–0.119 <0.0001	1	
Year (*Y*)	3,845	2003	1.5287	–0.0152 0.3462	–0.0197 0.2222	0.0534 0.0009	–0.0407 0.0117	1

$$Y = f(X, C) \qquad\qquad (5.1)$$

where

Y is the probability of knowledge coming from external sources, viz. the probability of *EXT* equaling one;

X is a vector of independent variables, and *C* is a vector of control variables.

Table 5.4 reports the two-tailed Pearson correlation matrix of most variables in this study. Given the number of industrial and home country/region dummies, we did not report their correlation coefficients in Table 5.4 (the full correlation matrix is available upon request). No significant correlation is observed among explanatory variables.

The results of Logistic Regression are reported in Table 5.5. All models in the table are statistically significant. Model 1 only includes control variables, and it serves as the baseline model. Models 2 to 4 add independent variables to the baseline model. The coefficients of independent variable '*Inter-Tech*' are positively significant across all models. In other words, CN subsidiaries are more likely to access external knowledge sources for knowledge across technological boundaries, namely, knowledge in technological fields that differ from the technological field in which the patent of CN subsidiaries was generated. Therefore, our Hypothesis 1 is supported. The independent variable measuring CN subsidiaries' access of geographically local knowledge (*L*) is negatively significant. We expected that CN subsidiaries would still utilize external knowledge

Table 5.5 Logistic regression coefficients for variables predicting external knowledge accumulation

Variables	Model 1	Model 2	Model 3	Model 4
Intercept	61.3843	68.2081	-5.3903	134.2**
Inter-Technological Field Knowledge (Inter-Field)		0.7996***	0.7886***	0.7729***
Geographically Local Knowledge (L)			-3.9831***	-3.6053***
Mature Knowledge (M)				0.1873***
Year (Y)	-0.0293	-0.0329	0.0039	-0.0671**
Industry (IND)				
Chemicals	-1.1463*	-1.3462**	-1.4287**	-0.4646
Pharmaceuticals	-1.7471***	-1.6431**	-1.7216**	-0.7913
Metals	0.8904	0.944	0.8988	2.3138****
Mechanical engineering	14.1128	14.2783	14.2166	15.0008
Electrical equipment	-0.631	-0.5119	-0.5170	1.1435*
Office equipment	-0.5351	-0.4081	-0.3713	1.3853**
Motor vehicles	1.6695	1.6476	1.6142	2.7312**
Aircraft	0.3112	0.3405	0.1673	0.6802
Paper products	-0.1936	-0.0602	-0.1980	0.2169
Non-metallic mineral products	-2.6872***	-2.6777***	-2.6294***	-2.2548***
Coal and petroleum products	13.9615	14.0075	14.3639	15.5838
Professional and scientific instruments	13.9595	14.2688	14.1896	15.272
Other manufacturing	-2.3158***	-2.1503***	-2.2602***	-0.7786
Home Country (HM)				
USA	-0.1378	-0.0451	-0.0741	-0.1136
Japan	0.0682	-0.0443	-0.1111	-0.00327
Other countries	-1.2480	-1.1084***	-0.9916***	-0.9459***
Likelihood Ratio – Chi-Square (df)	361.0061 (17)***	399.4918 (18)***	739.9327(19)***	1030.1114 (20)***
Pseudo R-Square	13.66	15.05	26.69	35.83

Note: ***$p < 0.001$; **$p < 0.01$; *$p < 0.05$

from local resources in China given the importance of local embeddedness for the capability development of overseas subsidiaries, even though local knowledge only constitutes a small portion of the overall knowledge accumulation of CN subsidiaries as suggested by Table 5.3 and Figure 5.4. Nevertheless, the negatively significant coefficients of variable 'L' in Models 3 and 4 suggest that our Hypothesis 2 is not supported. Instead of accessing external knowledge from geographically local sources, CN subsidiaries tend to access external knowledge from geographically distant locations and integrate such external knowledge with internally accumulated knowledge within the subsidiary, for example, the knowledge generated through in-house R&D. Finally, the positively significant coefficient of variable 'M' confirms that knowledge from external sources is significantly older than that from internal sources. This result indeed supports our Hypothesis 3.

Control variable 'Y' is negative in all models, and only becomes significant in Model 4. It seems to suggest that CN subsidiaries would increasingly rely on internal knowledge sources over time. On the other hand, while the descriptive statistics in Table 5.1 and Figure 5.2 suggest that the early innovations of CN subsidiaries might be the results of experimental or accidental activities, the coefficients of 'Y' may also implicate the capability upgrade of the subsidiaries by increasingly being able to systematically organize their in-house R&D and thereby accumulating specialized knowledge bases for future innovations. After all, a firm's own problem solving and learning sets the agenda for what is usefully searched for when monitoring the external environment (Cantwell and Barrera, 1998). Industrial controls show that CN subsidiaries in the chemical, pharmaceuticals, non-metallic mineral products and other manufacturing industries are more likely than those in the food industry to rely on internal knowledge sources, and that the dummies of metals, office equipment and motor vehicles industries become positively significant in Model 4. The characteristics of technological innovations in these two sets of industries may partly explain this result; in particular, the technological innovations in the former set of industries are more systematic, whereas those of the latter set of industries are more modular. The latter normally feels more comfortable to access external knowledge even in a location with relatively weak intellectual property protection (Zhao, 2006). Finally, the firms of other countries/regions are less likely than Taiwanese firms to access external knowledge. Given the geographical and psychic closeness between China and Taiwan, it is expected that the subsidiaries of Taiwanese firms would be better embedded in the local environment.

CONCLUSION AND DISCUSSION

Subsidiary evolution has been explained by MNC corporate-level and subsidiary-level characteristics, as well as locational factors. However, little has been said about the capability developed, as well as the overseas subsidiaries in some developing countries that are quickly catching up. This study focuses on the structure and components of technological knowledge accumulated in foreign-owned subsidiaries in China during their early phase of evolution. We employed patents granted by the USPTO to the world's largest firms for inventions attributable to foreign-owned subsidiaries in China between 1996 and 2005. The results support our overall argument that the technological capabilities of foreign-owned subsidiaries in China have been developed over the ten year period. Descriptive statistics illustrate the growth of patenting activities, and thereby technological knowledge generation, among foreign-owned subsidiaries in China. Moreover, the knowledge structure of the patents invented by those subsidiaries has been increasingly comparable with that of some overseas subsidiaries in developed countries. For instance, Table 5.1 and Figure 5.2 show that from 2001 onwards the share of external knowledge in the overall knowledge accumulation of foreign-owned subsidiaries in China was comparable with that of well-established overseas subsidiaries of MNCs in 1990s (Cantwell et al., 2008). We also found in empirical tests that external knowledge sources have been utilized to the larger extent to access technological complex knowledge, namely, knowledge in different technological fields.

This study analyses the knowledge structure and components of USPTO patents invented by foreign-owned subsidiaries in China. This setting is to investigate the technological capabilities of those subsidiaries beyond basic capability development that could be captured by, for instance, their licensing activities. To generate quality technological innovations, foreign-owned subsidiaries may have to increasingly access knowledge from their individual host locations (Birkinshaw et al., 1998; Andersson and Forsgren, 2000; Almeida and Phene, 2004). However, we observed a much less important role of the technological knowledge from external sources located in the host country for the overall knowledge accumulation of foreign-owned subsidiaries in China. Instead, those subsidiaries tend to integrate external knowledge from geographically international locations with internal knowledge accumulated in individual subsidiaries through local in-house R&D. This result seems to contradict the predictions based on previous literature. The characteristics of patents may partly explain this result. In particular, during the studied period patent citations may only be able to capture a small portion of the local knowledge sourcing of foreign-owned subsidiaries in China. As shown in descriptive statistics evidence, those subsidiaries are still in their early stage to develop technological capabilities, and their patenting activities only started to pick up pace from 2000 onwards (Figure 5.1). It is expected that other firms in China, for example, smaller foreign-owned firms and domestic firms, might also have just started their patenting activities around the same time. Consequently, external knowledge in China was not largely available in the format of patents, especially US patents, during the studied period.

Given the emerging status of the host country, China, another possibility would be that foreign-owned subsidiaries in this study were strategically avoiding the knowledge exchange with other firms or organizations in the host country because of their concerns about intellectual property right conditions. As the organization of MNCs could provide an alternative institutional device for intellectual property protection (Zhao, 2006), the subsidiaries may purposely limit the knowledge exchange with other firms/organizations in China, but rely more on internal knowledge exchange. Indeed, this argument might be more relevant for the outflow of technological knowledge, or it at least must be testified by looking at both inflow and outflow of technological knowledge of the subsidiaries. Therefore, an interesting future research would be to look at the antecedents and descendants of technological knowledge developed in different subsidiaries located across weak and strong intellectual property rights regions.

While the findings of this study reveal an interesting phenomenon in the local external knowledge sourcing of overseas subsidiaries in China, we also looked at the age of internal and external knowledge, which has been largely ignored in previous literature. In particular, we found that those subsidiaries are increasingly able to understand newer knowledge (Figure 5.5), and that foreign-owned subsidiaries in China tend to integrate external knowledge, which is well established and requires less further development, with newly generated knowledge through in-house R&D. On the one hand, this finding suggests that firms may access external knowledge for niche applications of the knowledge in their own specialized technological areas. However, given the limited absorptive capacity of foreign-owned subsidiaries in China, they may only be able to understand and integrate older knowledge from external sources. On the other hand, the trend observed indeed illustrates the technological capability development of foreign-owned subsidiaries.

This study is one of the first attempts to understand the accumulation of strategically important knowledge of foreign-owned subsidiaries in their early phase of evolution using patent data. This setting contributes to the better understanding of the technological capability development of overseas subsidiaries located in some developing countries, although the generalization of the results to other developing countries must be undertaken with cautions. This study shows that the knowledge accumulation pattern of foreign-owned subsidiaries in China changed dramatically from 1996 to 2005. Also, the speed of catching up among foreign-owned subsidiaries in China in terms of competence generation has been accelerating since 2000. Consequently, the results of the current study may not be applicable to on those subsidiaries after 2005, given the possibility of more recent changes in their knowledge accumulation pattern. Indeed, future study that can incorporate data after 2005 would contribute to the more accurate understanding of foreign-owned MNCs in China.

REFERENCES

Alcacer, J. and M. Gittelman (2006), 'Patent citations as a measure of knowledge flows: the influence of examiner citations', *Review of Economics and Statistics*, **88**(4), 774–9.

Almeida, P. and A. Phene (2004), 'Subsidiaries and knowledge creation: the influence of the MNC and host country on innovation', *Strategic Management Journal*, **25**, 847–64.

Andersson, U. and M. Forsgren (2000), 'In search of centre of excellence: network embeddedness and subsidiary roles in multinational corporations', *Management International Review*, **40**(4), 329–50.

Andersson, U., I. Bjorkman and M. Forsgren (2005), 'Managing subsidiary knowledge creation: the effect of control mechanisms on subsidiary local embeddedness', *International Business Review*, **14**, 521–38.

Andersson, U., M. Forsgren and U. Holm (2002), 'The strategic impact of external networks: subsidiary performance and competence development in the multinational corporation', *Strategic Management Journal*, Winter, 155–65.

Athreye, S. and J.A. Cantwell (2007), 'Creating competition? Globalization and the emergence of new technology producers', *Research Policy*, **36**, 209–26.

Bartlett, C.A. and S. Ghoshal (1986), 'Tap your subsidiaries for global reach', *Harvard Business Review*, **64**(6), 87–94.

Bartlett, C.A. and S. Ghoshal (1989), *Managing Across Borders: The Transnational Solution*, Boston, MA: Harvard Business School Press.

Birkinshaw, J. and N. Hood (1998), 'Multinational subsidiary evolution: capability evolution and charter change in foreign-owned subsidiary companies', *Academy of Management Review*, **23**(4), 773–95.

Birkinshaw, J., N. Hood and S. Jonsson (1998), 'Building firm specific advantages in multinational corporations: the role of subsidiary initiative', *Strategic Management Journal*, **19**(3), 221–41.

Buckley, P.J. and M.C. Casson (2002), 'A long-run theory of the multinational enterprise', in P.J. Buckley and M.C. Casson (eds), *The Future of the Multinational Enterprise*, 25th anniversary edn, New York: Palgrave Macmillan, pp. 32–65.

Cantwell, J.A. (2006), 'Introduction', *The Economics of Patents*, Cheltenham, UK and Northampton, MA, USA: Edward Elgar publishing.

Cantwell, J.A. and M.P. Barrera (1998), 'The localisation of corporate technological trajectories in the interwar cartels: cooperative learning versus an exchange of knowledge', *Economics of Innovation and New Technology*, **6**(2–3), 257–92.

Cantwell, J.A. and R. Mudambi (2005), 'MNE competence-creating subsidiary mandates', *Strategic Management Journal*, **26**(12), 1109–28.

Cantwell, J.A. and C. Noonan (2007), 'Exploring the Characteristics of technology spillovers using patent citation data', *International Business and Management*, **22**, 95–127.

Cantwell, J.A., C. Noonan and F. Zhang (2008), 'Technological complexity and the restructuring of subsidiary knowledge sourcing in intra-multinational and inter-firm networks', Annual Conference of Academy of International Business, Milan, Italy.

Chesbrough, H.W. (2006), 'Open innovation: a new paradigm for understanding industrial innovation', in H.W. Chesbrough, W. Vanhaverbeke and J. West (eds), *Open Innovation: Researching a New Paradigm*, Oxford: Oxford University Press, pp. 1–140.

China Daily (2005), 'Overseas investment on the up, excerpts from the Chinese Academy of Foreign Trade and Economic Cooperation (CAFTEC)', *China Daily*.

Duguet, E. and M. Macgarvie (2005), 'How well do patent citations measure flows of technology? Evidence from french innovation surveys', *Economic Innovation and New Technology*, **14**(5), 375–93.

Dunning, J.H. (1998), 'Location and the multinational enterprise: a neglected factor?', *Journal of International Business Studies*, **29**(1), 45–66.

Ernst, D. and L. Kim (2002), 'Global production networks, knowledge diffusion and local capability formation', *Research Policy*, **31**(8–9), 1417–29.

Garcia-Pont, C., J.I. Canales, and F. Noboa (2009), 'Subsidiary strategy: the embeddedness component', *Journal of Management Studies*, **46**(2), 182–214.

Ghoshal, S. and C.A. Bartlett (1990), 'The multinational corporation as an inter-organizational network', *Academy of Management Review*, **15**(4), 603–25.

Ghoshal, S. and N. Nohria (1989), 'Internal differentiation within multinational corporations', *Strategic Management Journal*, **10**(4), 323–37.

Granstrand, O., P. Patel and K. Pavitt (1997), 'Multitechnology corporations: why they have distributed rather than distinctive core competencies', *California Management Review*, **39**(4), 8–25.

Griliches, Z. (1990), 'Patent statistics as economic indicators: a survey', *Journal of Economic Literature*, **28**(4), 1661–707.

Howells, J., A. James and K. Malik (2003), 'The sourcing of technological knowledge: distributed innovation processes and dynamic change', *R&D Management*, **33**(4), 395–409.

Jaffe, A.B. and M. Trajtenberg (1999), 'International knowledge flows: evidence from patent citation', *Economics of Innovation and New Technology*, **8**(1/2), 105–36.

Jaffe, A.B., M. Trajtenberg and M.S. Fogarty (2000), 'Knowledge spillovers and patent citations: evidence from a survey of inventors', *American Economic Review*, **90**(2), 215–18.

Kogut, B. and U. Zander (1993), 'Knowledge of the firm and the evolutionary theory of the multinational enterprise', *Journal of International Business Studies*, **24**(4), 625–45.

Kuemmerle, W. (1999), 'The drivers of foreign direct investment into research and development: an empirical investigation', *Journal of International Business Studies*, **30**(1), 1–24.

McEvily, B. and A. Zaheer (1999), 'Bridging ties: a source of firm heterogeneity in competitive capabilities', *Strategic Management Journal*, **20**(12), 1133–56.

Miller, R. (1994), 'Global R&D networks and large-scale innovations: the case of the automobile industry', *Research Policy*, **23**, 27–46.

Nonaka, I. and H. Takeuchi (1998), 'A theory of the firm's knowledge-creation dynamics', in A. D. Chandler, P. Hagstrom and O. Solvell (eds), *The Dynamic Firm: The Role of Technology, Strategy, Organization and Regions*, New York: Oxford University Press, pp. 214–41.

Pavitt, K. (1988), 'International patterns of technological accumulation', in N. Hood and J. E. Vahlne (eds), *Strategies in Global Competition*, New York: Croom Helm, pp. 126–57.

Pearce, R. (1999), 'Decentralised R&D and strategic competitiveness: globalised approaches to generation and use of technology in multinational enterprises', *Research Policy*, **28**(2), 157–79.

Pearce, R. and M. Papanastassiou (1999), 'Overseas R&D and the strategic evolution of MNEs: evidence from laboratories in the UK', *Research Policy*, **28**, 23–41.

Phene, A. and P. Almeida (2003), 'How do firms evolve? The patterns of technological evolution of semiconductor subsidiaries', *International Business Review*, **12**(3), 349–67.

Rosenkopf, L. and P. Almeida (2003), 'Overcoming local search through alliances and mobility', *Management Science*, **49** (6), 751–66.

Schulz, M. (2003), 'Pathways of relevance: exploring inflows of knowledge into subunits of multinational corporations', *Organization Science*, **14**(4), 440–59.

White, R. and T. Poynter (1984), 'Strategies for foreign owned subsidiaries in Canada', *Business Quarterly*, **49**(2), 59–69.

WIR (2005), *World Invesment Report*, Geneva: UNCTAD.

Zhao, M. (2006), 'Conducting R&D in countries with weak intellectual property rights protection', *Management Science*, **52**(8), 1185–99.

6. Corporate hybrids and the co-evolution of institutions and enterprise in China

Simon Collinson and Yanxue Sun

INTRODUCTION

There is a renewed interest, for obvious reasons, in exploring different forms of capitalism. Debates about the role of the state and optimum forms of regulatory intervention in the market follow the aftermath of the systemic problems affecting the neoliberal 'US model' leading to a search for alternatives to these forms of liberal market system (Whitley, 2009a, 2009b). Comparisons between those economies following the US model and emerging economies that are experiencing exceptional growth under the guidance of strong state agencies are part of this debate.

Because of this renewed interest we are also finding clearer evidence of the wide variety of models that already exist in less well-researched parts of the world, where more interventionist states have the combined roles as owner, coordinator, regulator or entrepreneur in the market. The two most prominent models, China and India, illustrate this better than most, with very different parts played by central government (functioning and enabling in China, less so in India) and civil society ('emasculated in China and vibrant in India'; Khanna, 2009).

Differences in the levels and forms of government intervention in the market have resulted in the evolution of a wide variety of forms of enterprise, in terms of governance structures, incentive systems and resource-allocation mechanisms, than we have hitherto fully recognized. Despite the tendency, following Coasian or Williamsonian transactions cost approaches, to adopt a somewhat polarized view of markets and hierarchies, firms in emerging economies are normally a complex combination of market-oriented and state-driven influences.[1] They are hybrids.

This chapter uses the concept of hybrid organizations partly to examine the complex and changing relationship between the state, in its various guises, and enterprise, in China. This includes analysis of the ways in which such organizations are not just passive recipients but actively engage with government agencies to shape both the 'rules-of-the-game' and the institutional context in which they operate. We are also interested in how joint ventures between firms from different home countries represent hybrid organizational forms that result from the merging of characteristics and traits from each. Consequently, two forms of hybrid organization are discussed here, drawing from empirical research by the authors. We primarily focus on international joint ventures (IJVs) in China, involving large multinational enterprises (MNEs) and local state-owned enterprises (SOEs). But in the course of our fieldwork and through close observation of IJVs we came to understand how local Chinese SOEs also operate as hybrid organizations independently of IJVs. They are controlled by state agencies and fulfil public sector contracts but in parallel to this they operate in the private sector, buying and selling in both formal and informal markets. Our analysis draws on evidence from a range of industry sectors, but particularly the aerospace and automotive industries in China.

We start with a brief review of the historical context in China, focusing on how inward foreign direct investment (FDI) has driven the growth of a certain kind of IJV, alongside more general reforms that have changed the nature of SOEs. We then examine the industry context where targeted initiatives by the Chinese government have created different influences on the evolution of both SOEs and IJVs. More detailed illustrations of hybrid structures and behaviours are then presented through individual firm case studies. Finally, we step back to consider the nature of hybrid organizations in China in the broader context of prior research in international business.

THE HISTORICAL CONTEXT IN CHINA FOR THE EMERGENCE OF NEW ORGANIZATIONAL FORM

Much has been written about the significant changes taking place in China as it passes the 30th anniversary of the start of the market liberalization process, such that only a brief review is needed here. We will focus on the factors driving the growth of IJVs and the changing nature of SOEs.

Inward FDI and the Rise of IJVs

In the past 30 years, with gross domestic product (GDP) growth averaging 9 per cent per year, China has evolved from a closed, centrally planned system towards an open, market-oriented economy. Reforms started in the late 1970s with the phasing out of collectivized agriculture, and expanded to include the gradual liberalization of prices, fiscal decentralization, increased autonomy for state enterprises, the foundation of a diversified banking system, the development of stock markets, the rapid growth of the non-state sector, and the opening to foreign trade and investment.

Increased trade and FDI, both inward and outward, have accompanied this economic growth as China has become integrated into the global economy. A central principle of the Chinese government's National Development Plan is to improve domestic scientific and technological capabilities and boost China's competitiveness in high-technology based industries. The state decreed 'Law on Enterprises Operated Exclusively with Foreign Capital' and the 'Provision for Encouraging Foreign Investment' with regard to wholly foreign-owned enterprises (WFOEs) in 1986 was part of this mandate. From 1992 a noticeable inflow of foreign capital surged into China due to the influence of Deng's southern tour. During this period FDI increased dramatically at an annual rate of 7.8 per cent, from US$27.15 billion to US$83 billion between 1993 to 2007, climbing to US$92.4 in 2008 (UNCTAD, 2008).

Most commentators now assert that WFOEs have become the preferred governance form for FDI in China (Child, 2009). But the result has been the largest range of IJVs ever witnessed in an emerging economy and they are still mandatory in some industry sectors. These have also been one of the major drivers of both 'imitation' and learning for Chinese industries (Overholt, 2005; Shenkar, 2005; Collinson et al., 2007), as well as more general enhancement of growth and productivity, stimulation of domestic investment, employment generation and skill upgrading and technology transfer (Banerjee, 2006; Medcof, 2007 Collinson, 2009).

Changing Forms of Local Enterprise

The second major trend during China's economic transition relevant to us here has been the reform of its SOEs. This has taken place gradually in an attempt to increase the pressure of market forces on firms and bring about improvements in efficiency and competitiveness whilst simultaneously providing a degree of ongoing economic stability and employment security for millions of Chinese. From 1978 to 1984, the government strategy was to increase the motivation of SOEs to satisfy production quotas. On the assumption that self-autonomy induces motivation, regulations were introduced allowing SOEs a degree of operational autonomy and some independent economic interests of their own.[2] Later, the new SOE reform goal was established to separate operational rights from ownership rights, to disconnect the function and responsibility of SOEs from that of the state (which continued as the de facto owner) and to establish the SOE as an independent producer and operator.

From 1984 SOEs started to adopt a system of contracting, taking on independent responsibility for finding the means, and increasingly guiding investment of resources, to achieve sustainable operations. Key regulatory milestones in 1987 and 1992 increased their commercial orientation, by reducing guarantees of financial investment from the state and establishing distinctive enterprise property rights. A further step was taken in 1997, when the 15th CCP Congress began the process of strengthening a selected number of large SOEs as champions or 'flagship' firms, to implement the government's industrial policy, improve domestic economic stability and enhance international competitiveness in key sectors. Small and medium-sized SOEs were freed from government ownership under a strengthened monitoring mechanism. Various forms of corporate mechanisms including alliance, merger, leasing, sell-out, bankruptcy and a stock cooperative system were also adopted (Yang Yard Li, 2008).

Ongoing problems with SOEs stem from this historical legacy, including their low (often negative) profitability and high levels of over-employment. For obvious reasons many of them lack managerial, financial and market-related capabilities, relative to their private counterparts. Many also display weak levels of absorptive capacity and are therefore alleged to be 'slower learners' than private sector firms.

As we would expect from what theory tells us about the efficiencies of markets and principal – agent relationships, SOEs are not the best mechanisms for allocating capital. However, in many industries, particularly those that are the target of government drives for efficiency, self-sufficiency, competitiveness and sometimes international expansion, this weakness is often hidden by the very large amounts of finance being invested through SOEs. Moreover, some might argue that these inefficiencies are more than outweighed by the benefits of a state-led, targeted industry policy that leverages the economies of scale and attractiveness of a growing domestic market to give preferential treatment to national firms in the face of global competitors. The debate on whether to further reform SOEs, but maintain state ownership, or privatize them in the more conventional way, continues to be a central issue for China, but has lessons for other economies.

HYBRID ORGANIZATIONS IN CHINA

Evidence of hybrid enterprises and their varied relationships with government agencies and the private sector come from two separate empirical studies by the authors. The first was a large-scale study of British, European and US multinational firms in China, encompassing 30 joint-venture projects in 20 multinational firms in the pharmaceuticals, telecoms, aerospace, automotive, industrial manufacturing, fast-moving computer goods (FMCG) manufacturing and research, and high-tech manufacturing sectors. This involved over 100 semi-structured interviews with Western and Chinese managers, engineers, scientists and plant-level personnel in China. The largest questionnaire-based survey ever on this topic was also conducted, using two different company samples. One sample produced 320 valid responses allowing us to compare the experiences of 51 British firms with those of 181 American firms and 88 from mainland Europe (Collinson et al., 2007).[3]

The second study examined a set of four Sino-foreign IJVs in the auto parts and animal feed sectors. It used quantitative and qualitative measures to compare technology transfer and learning between partners as well as the initial intentions against the realized benefits of JV transfers over time (Sun, 2009).

Variations Across Industry Sectors

Significant variations in the degree to which and mechanisms by which national and local government agencies intervene in the strategies and operations of Chinese enterprises and the rules-of-the-game for IJV partners are very evident at the industry sector level. This is strongly influenced by the overarching development plans of the central government.

The Chinese central government's 11th five-year 'Development Guidelines' (rather than the five-year 'Plan'), from 2006–10, lists integrated circuits and software, internet and digital infrastructure, advanced computing, biomedicine, civil airplane, telecommunications, new materials and environmental and low-carbon technologies as priority targets. This is part of the medium and long-term plan from 2006–20 for science and technology development, where the general aim is to increase overall R&D intensity across the economy, with a strong focus on energy, transport, information technology (IT), public security and national defence, manufacturing technologies, aeronautics and a range of other areas. There are 11 priority fields in total and a wide range of targeted investments in large-scale research and development (R&D) projects (Ministry of Science and Technology, 2006; OECD, 2008). Tax incentives, public procurement policies, support for human resources development and training and targeted R&D programme investments all play a role in guiding enterprise behaviour.

The effects of these interventions were evident in both of the empirical studies we conducted. These showed different levels of and mechanisms for government intervention, both leading to different incentive structures and subsequently different forms of hybrid organization. Both studies included firms in the automotive sector which have been the focus of an explicit strategy to promote technology transfer from foreign firms in IJVs, alongside training and capability development (Duanmu and Fai, 2007; Gou and Li, 2007). This means more financial support for both the big state-owned manufacturers which has helped the 'big 4'; Shanghai Automotive (SAIC), First Auto Works (FAW) of Changchun, Dongfeng of Wuhan and Changan of Chongqing grow to produce over five million units in 2007 compared to less than half a million for the three private firms in the top 15; Geely, Great Wall and BYD.

There are a large number of well-publicized technical centres established as part of the automotive IJVs in China, such as the Pan Asia Technical Automotive Centre (PATAC), a US$50 million, 50-50 joint venture between General Motors China and SAIC. But we also found evidence of smaller firms gaining funds through national technology-promotion programmes such as the 'Torch Plan' approved by the Chinese State Department and the National Science and Technology Ministry and dispersed through the Provincial Science and Technology Offices (totalling 700,000RMB funds to one of the IJVs we studied).

The automotive sector was compared to the animal feeds sector in one of the studies we report on. In the latter, contrasting the former, a longer-term reliance on technologies and innovations from foreign firms is accepted as part of government policy. So, advanced feed products are imported and farmers are introduced to advanced scientific feeding methods, but are not particularly encouraged to develop their own advanced innovation capabilities or explicitly aim to compete with multinational firms.

So the result of the targeted government policy is a highly uneven local playing field as different 'rules-of-the-game' apply both to SOEs and to IJVs depending on central and local government agendas. This has direct effects on the organizational forms that evolve within these industry contexts. The aerospace industry provides another good illustration of this before we move on to examine firm-level differences.

The Chinese government's 10th and 11th five-year plans have explicitly targeted the development of an indigenous aircraft manufacturing industry. A key mechanism to promote this has been to require all foreign aerospace and aviation manufacturers wishing to enter the Chinese market to do so via IJVs with SOEs and to channel commercial and military procurement through these joint enterprises. Growth in the Chinese air transport market has reinforced the bargaining power of national aircraft producers and authorities, allowing them to not only be selective about partnering arrangements but also push for significant technology transfer and training as they give priority to building science and technology capacity in this area (Goldstein, 2005).

The large civil aircraft market has been growing at 9–10 per cent per year and is expected to continue at this rate to become the largest market in the world by 2026. This is why all the big players, including Boeing, Airbus, GE, PW Canada, Honeywell, Collins and Rolls-Royce, have invested in local JVs. The overall Chinese aviation industry is comprised of over 155 large-scale manufacturers and maintenance companies, employing around 300,000 people. These operate within the government umbrella organization known as Aviation Industry China, or 'AVIC1' which has the use of an import-export organization (China International Trust and Investment Corporation, CATIC) and a separate trading company (China Aviation Supplies Corporation, CASC). The AVIC1 institutional structure oversees and coordinates the commercial activities of state-owned and local and foreign private firms in the industry (Dougan, 2002 and survey respondents).

Case studies of two multinational firms, with significant investments in China, were developed as part of the above-mentioned research. Both firms have been required by the government, via AVIC1, to establish a range of technology transfer and training activities with their local JV partners, including the Xian Aircraft Corporation (XAC), the Xian Aero Engine Company and Shenyang Aircraft Corporation (SAC), to facilitate the development of a local aerospace industry. As part of their involvement, however, the multinational firms have also been able to take advantage of opportunities to shape government policy as it relates to their industry. These inputs have led to direct and indirect benefits with regard to their competitive positioning in China's evolving aircraft manufacturing industry. The study observed these effects at both the national and local levels, through different institutional mechanisms, as described in more detail below.

INTERNATIONAL JOINT VENTURES AS HYBRID ORGANIZATIONS

IJVs are the most obvious form of hybrid organization in that they consist of the combined elements (assets, technologies, processes, management procedures, cultural norms and so on) of two independent firms. Table 6.1 shows some common examples of synergies between Western multinational firms investing in China and local Chinese enterprise in alliances

Table 6.1   *Who provides what? Common synergies in international*
partnerships in China

Type of partnership	Foreign multinational firm provides . . .	Local Chinese firm provides . . .
Manufacturing JV or subsidiary-local supplier alliance	Finance. Technology, production systems, management systems (control, coordination best practices, performance measurement, IT etc.). Management expertise, engineering and plant-level training.	Land, labour, facilities, finance. Links to/knowledge of suppliers, buyers, contractors, distributors. Access to local resources, materials. HRM expertise, recruitment capabilities. Local government connections, knowledge about regulations.
Product-development JV	Finance. Technology and product development tools, processes, best practices and expertise. Links to other sources of expertise inside and outside the firm.	Facilities. Finance. Some engineering, technical expertise. Knowledge of regulations, intellectual property rights protection strategies and relevant connections. Links to/knowledge of customer preferences and distribution channels.

Source: Collinson et al. (2007).

and IJVs from the above study. This provides a general checklist of the kinds of contributions each partner makes. However, the study revealed a huge variety of organizational forms existed, depending on the precise kinds of contribution made by each partner, together with a wide range of attributes, from the ownership and agreed governance structure, the range of employees and managers at various levels of the JV hierarchy and the evolving structural forms, practices and procedures adopted by the hybrid organization.

One or other parent can act as the dominant provider or influence over different kinds of organizational characteristics to produce a 'composite' blend of attributes from each side. Whilst assets, technology and other 'tangible' components may be transferred wholesale from the parent firm, intangible characteristics, including knowledge, capabilities and various processes, routines and procedures are integrated and adapted to produce novel forms of organization. This explains why hybrid forms, in detailed ways, are unique. Moreover, respondents reported how changes in the dominance of one or other parent in relation to a particular set of attributes occurs over time, adding to the 'natural' evolution of the organization in response to the usual set of external changes.

A simple approach we adopted, in trying to understand the different roles and influences of each of the parent firms, was to divide these into internal and external organizational differences. The former relate more to the internal contests and compromises between two different organization cultures. The latter, external relationships and responsibilities stem from the industry context in which the IJV is established and develops, as outlined above. In the following sections we will examine the latter after (and more extensively than) the former.

The Internal Hybrid Characteristics of International Joint Ventures

In terms of internal differences, financial reporting structures provide just one example from one of our case studies amongst a variety of practices in operation in different IJVs. In two out of the six IJV case studies examined in one of our studies senior management compiled two sets of financial reports, one for each parent, each following the respective format and protocols demanded by each parent firm. In another case only one system of financial reporting was followed, to meet the requirements of the foreign parent as the dominant shareholder. In another, financial reports were only sent to the local Chinese parent and an experienced local Chinese manager was explicitly hired because of his experience of following such system.

When procedures are relatively clear-cut, as in the case of financial reporting requirements, it is easier to trace which parent firm has the dominant influence over the system or protocol adopted by the IJV. Much of the time, however, the kinds of management practices adopted or 'imitated' at the IJV level represent hybrids in themselves. This is because they are rarely transferred and transplanted wholesale into the new organization, but adopted in an adapted form, according to local capabilities and requirements. Sometimes this may be seen as a 'failure to imitate' (Duanmu and Fai, 2007) but our study suggested that the resulting processes and procedures in place are an evolving outcome of contests and compromises between local and international versions which are a product of the broader 'varieties of capitalism' (Whitely, 1999; 2009b). They will therefore differ from both parent systems and will often represent more appropriate and effective adaptations to the specific organization context in which they exist.

'Boundary spanners' (Carlisle, 2004) form a useful role in identifying, clarifying, 'translating' or mediating between two parent company systems. These are individuals who have experience of both types of organization culture and can build bridges between groups. A specific example of this was found in one of the automotive JVs where the detailed reporting structure characteristic of Chinese firms was found to be clashing with the more devolved structure of the foreign parent firm. One respondent felt stuck between two worlds:

> In the Chinese parent's culture, I have to report almost everything to my leader, otherwise, he will be very unhappy and will possibly consider that I am reluctant to communicate with him. Initially, I did not notice any difference with the foreign culture. So I reported everything to the foreign chairman of the board until I noticed that he was not happy to hear the matters that I had the authority to resolve. Rather, he was of the view that I wanted him to take part of the responsibility for the matter.

This also shows that both systems can operate in parallel, even with individual employees adopting different styles of communication with different senior managers, Chinese and foreign, for sustained periods.

The Interface Between International Joint Ventures and the External Regulatory Environment

Here we examine the ways in which IJVs interact with government agencies which in some cases are also the owners of the Chinese parent firm. This ambiguous boundary between government and owner was a central theme of our studies and is central to the nature of the hybrid organization in China. We focus below on some examples that show how the rules-of-the-game are applied to constrain or benefit IJVs but also how the IJV (and therefore the foreign multinational) influences these rules-of-the-game. These examples illustrate the interactive nature of the relationship between the state and enterprises and the positive and negative effects of the close alliance between public and private.

To begin with, at one level, the 'division of labour' or more specifically the division of strategic responsibilities between the foreign partner and the Chinese partner illustrates how the hybrid is structured. In terms of the external responsibilities, in most cases, but particularly the automotive and aerospace industries (for the reasons outlined above), we found that a common pattern was for the foreign partner to rely heavily on the local partner for managing external networks and partnerships, both with suppliers and customers and with government agencies. Certain types of *guanxi* were important for specific purposes. In automotive IJVs respondents talked of the need for up-to-date information on the 'whole car enterprise's production plan' so that the JV could make their own production modifications in alignment with the flagship manufacturer. These network alliances and bargaining power afforded by strong *guanxi* enabled the local parent firm to secure contracts with the major manufacturers. Similarly relationships with relevant local governmental offices or departments, such as the local tax bureau, land bureau or electricity bureau, were important to gain the necessary preferential treatment including exemption from local service and administration fees.

One multinational firm we studied had invested in a JV with a government-owned aerospace components firm based in a large town which was dominated by this firm and a range of related suppliers, contractors and affiliated companies and public institutions. This kind of industry cluster, although common around the world, has been promoted by the Chinese government policy to develop local industry capabilities in certain key industries and to establish industry concentrations away from the more developed Eastern coastal regions.

Local and regional government agencies were heavily involved in this cluster, to the degree that the Chairman of the Board of the local JV partner was also the town Mayor. This is a relatively common form of hybrid ownership and governance system binding government and industry in China and it gives rise to a number of benefits and constraints for certain multinational firms relative to other firms. Respondents provided evidence of fairly strong preferential treatment through support from the Mayor's office and related government departments. This influenced dealings with local firms as well as providing preferential access to various public services.

There were a number of specific examples, within this context, where the managers in the multinational subsidiary were able to proactively influence local institutions, companies and relevant regulations to benefit their own operations. In the most extreme case this amounted to locking-out a foreign competitor looking to supply components to the Chinese partner through an exclusivity arrangement overseen directly by the Mayor's office.

The institutional alignment between the Mayor's office, related regulatory agencies and the JV partners also provided opportunities for the multinational firm to influence standards legislation pertaining to its operations and those of competitors. Although it is likely that, if given the choice, the multinational firm would have selected a different market-entry mode or set of local partnerships, it clearly took advantage of the circumstances by shaping public policy at the local level to its own advantage.

Another example of this comes from a different multinational firm involved in several local JVs in the aerospace industry. This firm had led six national-level training programmes with the Civil Aviation

Administration of China (CAAC). As part of these programmes the firm had helped develop: (1) the technical safety legislation governing product specifications and (2) health and safety standards for manufacturing plant conditions in aero components firms. In both cases they were based on the firm's own in-house protocols and in both cases the evolving industry rules-of-the-game were configured to benefit this multinational firm and its local (state-owned) JV partners. As regards (1) this meant that the specified tolerances for materials and manufacturing quality of components, linked to the equipment and processes in use in the firm's plants, became the de facto standard under government legislation. As regards (2), the established plant-level routines and practices for maintaining and managing health and safety limitations for the firm, from equipment handling to requirements for protective clothing and working hours, were the benchmark for developing the standard legislation governing the industry. In both respects competitors were compelled to follow the protocols established jointly by this one firm, its local partners and the relevant Chinese government agencies.

At one level we can view this example as an aerospace manufacturer being forced into a set of JVs and a range of technology-sharing and training programmes by a government agenda targeting the development of indigenous industry capabilities. But the case demonstrates how the firm has used this situation to benefit its own position relative to competitors by actively shaping government policy at the detailed level. Note also that both parent and subsidiary were actively involved in discussions with various government agencies. Senior management from the home-base headquarters made the initial JV arrangements and established the training programmes and related initiatives with government agencies, working closely with the regional HQ in Beijing. Relationships between top management from the MNE's global headquarters and senior trade and industry officials provided the context for the deal-making. Subsidiary managers worked at the more detailed level with local technical and legal experts to shape the evolving rules-of-the-game, usually via their local partners.

There were, of course, down sides and disadvantages to these arrangements. The most common problem resulting from the close alignment of IJVs with local government agencies, according to our studies, were disputes over ownership of various kinds. This included intellectual property rights (IPR), brands and blueprints which have been examined and discussed elsewhere in the context of China's evolving legal and institutional infrastructure. But it also included most types of fixed assets such as land, buildings and facilities which were written into JV contracts from the start but were subject to the changing interpretation of local parties regarding which side had claims over which assets. The dual public-private roles of local officials, as in the case of the above-mentioned town Mayor, often underlies this kind of ambiguity, which remains a central, contested legacy of China's recent past.

The very concept of ownership and personal property is ambiguous in China, including but beyond questions of institutional and legal legitimacy. This ambiguity features everywhere, from copy cat automotive designs to fundamental issues of human rights regarding land ownership. It has enabled both the general flourishing of private enterprise and the profiteering by elites that claim ownership rights, often through connections with public sector 'guardians' of the people's land and assets.

Similarly, ambiguity over public versus private ownership rights lies at the heart of the nature of the hybrid organization. As Chinese SOEs evolve away from financial dependence and the guiding hand of the state the boundary between the public and the private is constantly tested and contested.

STATE-OWNED ENTERPRISES AS HYBRID ORGANIZATIONS

As mentioned at the beginning of this chapter, during our empirical studies of IJVs in China it became apparent that SOEs were also evolving hybrid organizations, with some similarities to the IJV type of hybrid described above. Once again the aerospace industry provided some of the clearest examples of these kinds of dual structures.

AVIC1 firms are compelled to follow dual public and private sector agendas. If a factory is using inputs and materials for production that is part of a five-year plan or government project, they do not pay for these inputs. If the supplier is part of the industry '*xitong*' or bureaucratic grouping then AVIC1 simply orders it to supply the parts.[4] Alongside these production activities factories can have a range of 'private' or off-plan projects in operation. Moreover, managers can reinvest the surplus from the private sector businesses into building market-facing assets and capabilities (or rewarding themselves or employees beyond the state levels of remuneration) so long as government projects are serviced. AVIC member firms also swap assets and resources to help each other with off-plan projects. Another 'legacy' from the past is the lifetime employment system characteristic of all SOEs which all aviation manufacturers still adhere to. This can often act as an incentive towards increasing the volume and/or efficiency of off-plan sales.

As Mark Dougan (2002) describes in his excellent book on the political economy of China's civil aviation industry, this process of 'marketization' has involved changes in how decisions are made (planning or market trends and customer demands) and who makes the decisions. Equipment purchases from foreign firms need to go through the AVIC and CATIC structures (and sometimes coordinate with the Ministry of Foreign Trade and Economic Cooperation (MOFTEC)) even when local firms requiring the investment have a relationship or even JV with the foreign firm supplying the new equipment. Foreign component and co-production is also controlled, but less so than in the past. Foreign firms sign contracts with CATIC and investment goes to this organization before being dispersed to local Chinese manufacturers, via AVIC, following a percentage deduction (which can be 20 per cent) for 'central costs'.

Historically, even after liberalization these government bureaucracies would also dictate which local partners the foreign firms would contract or establish JVs with. But in the past ten years there have been moves towards making local firms compete for investment and technology, with foreign multinationals choosing the most appropriate partnerships. In general market-oriented behaviour is less prevalent in the sales of older aircraft models destined for domestic buyers. Larger more powerful firms with '*jituan*' corporate status (state champions or flagship firms backed by the state) get a larger slice of the surplus revenues generated by component manufacturing for multinational firms and for export sales.

In this way the evolution of non-state assets takes place alongside state-owned assets, each with different external market drivers and supplier relationships and internal agency effects. Managers and employees often play split roles serving both government and markets. On the one hand, they have to maintain good *guanxi* relations with the dominant local central government agencies, on the other hand, they are driven to improve their competitiveness in private markets, not least to increase personal remuneration.

At times the mismatch between what the market needs and what the government planning system is driving heightens the differences and internal tensions within these local hybrid firms, particularly when it comes to export markets. One effect of the partial liberalization model highlighted in our study is that firms have diversified to evolve different business portfolios beyond the aerospace industry and beyond the domestic market. This has partly been a response to the fact that better opportunities were seen to exist in other areas of manufacturing (turbines, machinery and even auto components) and services both within and beyond aerospace.

This kind of 'split personality' was evident in a wide range of SOEs we encountered. We particularly noted how this affects the R&D strategies of the Chinese firms in government-dominated industry sectors. In the aerospace and marine technology industries SOEs often had a dual structure for planning, funding and managing government-led and market-driven product or technology development projects. Both involved the development of complementary assets and capabilities with suppliers and external contractors. But the latter would require client or customer-oriented strategies and involved risks related to targeting the right sets of products and technologies and developing cost-effective means of developing them without solid guarantees of market success. In short, these market-facing initiatives required an entrepreneurial style of management. Contrasting this, innovations that were aligned with government-supported science and technology projects were subject to different kinds of risk, particularly those stemming from changes in the government agenda, networks or preferences in terms of favoured SOEs. These kinds of risks were best mitigated through the *guanxi* networks and a different kind of public sector oriented mind-set.

Developing this last point a little further, descriptions of these kinds of networking activities by respondents highlights how the government (or hierarchy) versus market, public versus private dualism over-simplifies the reality of the institutional structures and constituencies involved. As Dougan (2002) notes, the Chinese government system as well as being multilevel is also best characterized as a highly fragmented form of authoritarianism. There are complex inter-group rivalries and continuous contests between constituencies and interest groups, alongside the ability for senior political figures to bulldoze straight through and enforce specific initiatives. Negotiating through this maze to establish and maintain but also shift allegiances to best serve the enterprise (and oneself) presents a greater competitive challenge for senior management in China than most other places.

DISCUSSION: WHAT IS INTERESTING ABOUT HYBRID ORGANIZATIONS IN CHINA

This chapter describes two kinds of hybrid organization in the context of the evolving Chinese industry environment, revealed through two separate empirical studies of IJVs. These show how elements of both markets and hierarchies can co-exist in one enterprise, in terms of incentives and agency, capital allocation mechanisms, organizational culture and strategy. They also provide a reflection of the broader external context, a mixture of government control and market mechanisms, linking internal capital allocation mechanisms, decision-making priorities and incentives to outside combinations of ownership and governance in China.

Buckley et al. (2007, p. 514) conclude from their study of the internationalization of Chinese firms that these firms 'have to straddle environments, institutions and rules that differ probably more than for any other outward-investing country in the world'. This is equally true for multinational firms entering the Chinese market. These firms have one foot back in their home countries and the other in the very different market environment of China. As a consequence IJVs are shaped by the combined influence of both sets of parents and their respective 'selection regimes' and therefore represent a form of organizational 'variety-generation' (Westney, 2009). Moreover, they retain or discard combinations of routines, procedures and capabilities from each parent in response to the changing local environmental pressures.

Chinese SOEs have a different genesis, as national enterprises under the central command-and-control of government agencies. But their hybridization is the result of similar forces as they have developed dual organizational structures to cope with semi-privatization and turned part of their investment efforts and capabilities towards the market. Both types of hybrid examined here demonstrate how firms are not only a product of their environment(s) but shape that environment. To some degree government agencies and firms each represent the selection environment of the other making the evolutionary processes of selection, retention and mutual adaption interdependent.

Many studies of hybrids have built on Oliver Williamson's foundations to understand how 'discrete structural alternatives' emerge. Transactions costs approaches and principal – agent models tend to dominate as does a concern with efficiency effects, as in the recent study by Makadok and Coff (2009). These also tend to adopt a simplified view of incentives structures which we have tried to go beyond in this research.

Other research has, like us, explored alliances and JVs as hybrid forms of organization. Borys and Jemison (1989, p. 234) some time ago proposed that within hybrid organizational arrangements 'breadth of purpose, boundary determination, value creation, and stability mechanisms' form the core of a theory to understand the variety of these forms. We found empirical evidence confirming that these were important dimensions for differentiating between hybrid forms and highlighting variations in the division of responsibilities as well as relative functional dominance in the relationship. But we also found that the division of decision-making responsibilities and to some extent the governance and management systems and procedures adopted were a result not just of agency and incentive structures but also of the relative differences in expertise, capability and network linkages of the two partners. Hence in our cases, for example, the tendency was for the Chinese side to take the lead in external relationships (suppliers, distributors and government) and the foreign multinational managers to lead on technology, production and product development type issues.

It is important to note how these hybrid forms change over time, depending on (to use a simple proxy) the balance between public sector controlled and market-oriented operations and investments they encompass at any one time. Moreover, the drivers of change are not one-way but interactive. Both IJVs, usually through the Chinese partner and SOEs influence the evolving industry rules-of-the-game. This may lead to local advantages (such as tax relief through connections with the local Mayor's office) or a wider influence on the government industry agenda, including the exclusion of competitors.

Stepping back from this observation we can see that this provides a relevant and much-needed example of how multinational firms shape their competitive environment, particularly with regard to the institutional contexts in which they operate. Much needed in that there is a consensus in the field of international business that too little attention has been paid to the degree to which and the ways in which multinational firms shape their competitive environment (Kogut, 2005, Collinson, 2009; Dunning and Lundan, 2009).

This is true of both mainstream international business studies literature and of studies of national business systems. These have explored how national systems differ, institutionally as well as economically, and how such differences present a variety of opportunities and constraints for firms. But in the words of Cantwell et al. (2010) both have 'ignored the active agency of firms and particularly that of MNEs in adjusting to and affecting institutional change'.

China provides an ideal opportunity to research this, because, despite the relatively heavy hand of central and local government agencies, there is an interactive and interdependent co-evolution between policy agendas (and regulations that result from policy implementation) and enterprise-level strategies. Industry policies to promote competitiveness in specific industry sectors including specific technologies and business niches and the regulatory and legal conditions that govern private sector behaviours are not entirely top-down but shaped at the interface between private and public, central and local. Ever-changing alignments between these constituencies drive changes in both the formal and informal rules-of-the-game. Whilst the same may be true of government-enterprise relationships in any national system, the nature of this interface, the effects on the forms of enterprise and the patterns of co-evolution are more apparent in China than elsewhere.

As well as providing insights into how hybrid forms have emerged as a result of the combinations of market and institutional influences, this study provides some details about the mechanisms by which a firm might 'add to, or restructure, its institutional advantages' (Dunning and Lundan, 2009). One strand of international business that has pursued this question and helps provide part of an explanation of the role of hybrids as institution-shapers is broadly referred to as the 'corporate political activities' (CPA) literature. CPA studies examine the ability of multinational firms to adapt to and influence political and institutional environments in host countries. They would tend to describe the behaviour of the firms we observed as public policy shaping (rather than passive reaction; Weidenbaum, 1980), proactive (Hillman et al., 2004), influencing (rather than compliant; Oliver and Holzinger, 2008), bargaining behaviour (Boddewyn and Brewer, 1994). Although much of the CPA research is conducted in domestic market contexts (Wan and Hillman, 2006), studies that have examined CPA capabilities in emerging economies suggest that these account for a considerable part of an MNE's competitive strength in such economies (Peng and Luo, 2000; Luo, 2001) and tend to be located at the subsidiary level (Asmussen et al., 2009).

In some of the firms we analysed there was a strong fit between firm resources and the ongoing government policy with regard to promoting the development of local capabilities in particular target industries and this gave rise to preferential access to the relevant government institutions and opportunities for policy intervention.

Douglass North (1990, 2005) perhaps more than any other scholar laid the foundations for our understanding of institutions at the macro level in relation to the multinational firm. He defines institutions as formal rules (for example constitutions, laws and regulations) and informal constraints (norms of behaviour, conventions and self-imposed codes of conduct). Institutions (and their enforcement mechanisms) set the rules-of-the-game, which organizations, in pursuit of their own goals regarding resource allocation, innovation and performance, must follow. An institutional system can only be fully understood when both formal and informal institutional structures are taken into account.

China probably does not fit precisely with North's views, as an economically underdeveloped country with arguably sophisticated governance institutions. But his work has led us to better understand the ambiguous interplay between the visible hand of government and invisible hand of the market. This perspective connects with the broader field of heterodox institutional economics in viewing markets as a result of the complex interaction of various institutions including firms and government agencies at a variety of levels. Our studies find some echoes of Galbraith's

(1972) 'new industrial state' but the 'technostructure' that he describes is comprised in China of a complex and ever-changing balance of public and private. Moreover, individuals within this system are incentivized by both government and market simultaneously. Nee (1992, p. 1) also takes this view describing China as a mixed economy 'characterized by a diversity of organizational forms and a plurality of property rights' as it transitions from state socialism towards a capitalist market economy.

A persistent feature of all of these perspectives, however, is the tendency to think of hybrid organizations as a temporary form of enterprise, as China moves along a linear path to full market liberalization. This might be a false assumption based on a Western view that the Anglo-American neoliberal form of market capitalism is the 'most advanced' state for a national economy to aspire to. At the very least they may be around for longer than many seem to expect.

NOTES

1. It is important to note, however, that Williamson himself recognized hybrids as a third form of structural alternative (Williamson, 1991). Common interpretations of his work, however, usually focus on only two of these; markets and hierarchies
2. During the Third Plenary Session of the 14th National Party Congress, Deng Xiao Ping called for the quickening of the pace of reform and no further arguing as to whether the reform policy had the name of socialist or capitalist, using the famous phrase: 'As long as a cat can catch a mouse, it is a good cat regardless of whether it is white or black' (Moore and Wen, 2006).
3. Funding for this research came from the UK's Economic and Social Research Council (ESRC) and Engineering and Physical Sciences Research Council (EPSRC) via the Advanced Institute for Management (AIM) in the UK, and is gratefully acknowledged.
4. *Xitong's* are part of the Chinese '*Taio-kuai*' quasi-federal arrangement of administration. Functional vertical structures (the Tiao structures, such as Ministries) have evolved as a top-down hierarchy emanating from central government. But horizontal territorial structures, (the *kuai* structures, like provincial governments or mayoral offices in cities) have a large degree of autonomy and the boundaries of control are constantly contested (Dougan, 2002).

REFERENCES

Asmussen, C.G., T. Pedersen and C. Dhanaraj (2009), 'Host-country environment and subsidiary competence: extending the diamond network model', *Journal of International Business Studies*, **40**(1), 42–58.

Banerjee, A. (2006), 'FDI in China and its economic impact', *World Review of Entrepreneurship, Management and Sustainable Development*, **2**, 36–56.

Boddewyn, J. and T. Brewer (1994), 'International business political behaviour: new theoretical directions', *Academy of Management Review*, **19**(1), 119–43.

Borys, B. and D.B. Jemison (1989), 'Hybrid arrangements as strategic alliances:

theoretical issues in organizational combinations', *Academy of Management Review*, **14**(2), 234–49.

Broadman, H.G. (2001), 'The business(es) of the Chinese State', *The World Economy*, **24**(7), 849–75.

Buckley, P.J., J. Clegg, A.R. Cross, X. Liu, H. Voss and P. Zheng (2007), 'The determinants of Chinese outward foreign direct investment', *Journal of International Business Studies*, **38**, 499–518.

Cantwell, J.A., J.H. Dunning and S.M. Lundan (2010), 'An evolutionary approach to understanding international business activity: the co-evolution of MNEs and the institutional environment', *Journal of International Business Studies*, **41**(4), 567–86.

Carlisle, P.R. (2004), 'Transferring, translating, and transforming: an integrative framework for managing knowledge across boundaries', *Organizational Science,* **15**(5), 555–68.

Child, J. (2009), 'China and international business', in A.M. Rugman (ed.), *The Oxford Handbook of International Business*, 2nd edn, Oxford: Oxford University Press.

Child, J. and S.B. Rodriques (2005), 'The internationalisation of Chinese firms: a case for theoretical extension?', *Management and Organisation Review*, **1** (November), 381–410.

Collinson, S.C. (2009), 'The multinational firm as the major global promoter of economic development', in S.C. Collinson and G. Morgan (eds), *Images of the Multinational Firm*, Chichester: Wiley, pp. 69–93.

Collinson, S.C., B. Sullivan-Taylor and J.L. Wang (2007), 'Adapting to the China challenge: lessons from experienced multinationals', Advanced Institute of Management (AIM) Research Executive Briefing, London, available at http://www.aimresearch.org/publications/adaptingtochina.pdf.

Deng, P. (2004), 'Outward investment by Chinese MNCs: motivations and implications', *Business Horizons*, **47**(1), 8–16.

Dougan, M. (2002), *A Political Economy Analysis of China's Civil Aviation Industry*, London: Routledge.

Duanmu, J.L. and F.M. Fai (2007), 'A processual analysis of knowledge transfer: from foreign MNEs to Chinese suppliers', *International Business Review*, **16**, 449–73.

Dunning, J.H. and S.M. Lundan (2009), 'The multinational as a creator, fashioner and respondent to institutional change', in S.C. Collinson and G. Morgan (eds), *Images of the Multinational Firm*, Chichester: Wiley, pp. 93–117.

Galbraith, J.K. (1972), *The New Industrial State*, 2nd edn, Princeton, NJ: Princeton University Press.

Goldstein, A. (2005), 'The political economy of industrial policy in China: the case of aircraft manufacturing', William Davidson Institute Working Paper No. 779, Organisation for Economic Co-operation and Development (OECD).

Gou, H.P. and Z.F. Li (2007), 'Competition situation and strategy selection in China auto part industry', *Automotive Engineering*, **11** 1018–24.

Hillman, A., G. Keim and D. Schuler (2004), 'Corporate political activity: a review and research agenda', *Journal of Management*, **30**(6), 837–57.

Khanna, T. (2009), 'Learning from economic experiments in China and India', *Academy of Management Perspectives*, **23**(2), 36–44.

Kogut, B. (2005), 'Of beauty finding the beast: the field of international business and the dialogue of fact and theory', in P.J. Buckley (ed.), *What is International Business?*, New York: Palgrave Macmillan, pp. 57–67.

Lardy, N.R. (1998), *China's Unfinished Economic Revolution*, Washington, DC: Brookings Institution.

Liu, X. and S. White (2001), 'Company innovation systems: a framework and application to China's transition context', *Research Policy*, **30**(7), 1091–114.

Luo, Y. (2001), 'Towards a cooperative view of MNC-host government relations: building blocks and performance implications', *Journal of International Business Studies*, **32**(3), 401–19.

Makadok, R. and R. Coff (2009), 'Both market and hierarchy: an incentive-system theory of hybrid governance forms', *Academy of Management Review*, **34**(2), 297–319.

Mallumpally, P. and K.P. Sauvant (1999), 'Foreign direct investment in developing countries', *Finance and Development*, **36** (March).

Medcof, J.W. (2007), 'Subsidiary technology upgrading and international technology transfer with reference to China', *Asia Pacific Business Review*, **13**, 451–69.

Ministry of Science and Technology (2006), 'Medium-to-long-term plan outline for the development of national science and technology (2006–2020) (MLP)', *China Science and Technology Newsletter*, **456**, Ministry of Science and Technology of the People's Republic of China.

Moore, S. and J.J. Wen (2006), 'Reform of state owned enterprises and challenges in China', *Journal of Technology Management in China*, **1**(3), 279–91.

Nee, V. (1992), 'Organizational dynamics of market transition: hybrid forms, property rights, and mixed economy in China', *Administrative Science Quarterly*, **37**, 1–27.

North, D.C. (1990), *Institutions, Institutional Change and Economic Performance*, Cambridge: Cambridge University Press.

North, D.C. (2005), *Understanding the Process of Economic Change*, Princeton, NJ: Princeton University Press.

OECD (2008), *Science, Technology and Industry Outlook*, Paris: OECD publications.

Oliver, C. and I. Holzinger (2008), 'The effectiveness of strategic political management: a dynamic capabilities framework', *Academy of Management Review*, **33**(2), 496–520.

Overholt, W.H. (2005) 'Selling foreign investment short', *Management and Organization Review*, **1**(3), 19–27.

Peng, M.W. and Y. Luo (2000), 'Managerial ties and firm performance in a transition economy: the nature of macro-micro link', *Academy of Management Journal*, **43** (3), 486–501.

Shenkar, O. (2005), 'China, economics, and FDI: reflections on selling China', *Management and Organization Review*, **1**(3), 15–18.

Sino Cast Business News Daily (2005), 'TCL to expand overseas market with CNY 8 bn loans from CDB', 9 August, p. 1.

Sun, Y.X. (2009), 'How recipient firms benefit from international joint ventures: resource and knowledge transfer, learning mechanisms and R&D spillovers in the China context', Unpublished PhD Thesis, Warwick Business School, University of Warwick.

UNCTAD (2008), *World Investment Report 2008: Transnational Corporations, and the Infrastructure Challenge*, Geneva: UN Conference on Trade and Development.

Wan, W. and A. Hillman (2006), 'One of these things is not like the others: what contributes to dissimilarity among MNE subsidiaries' political strategy', *Management International Review*, **46**(1), 85–107.

Wang, J. and S. Chan (2003), 'China's outward direct investment: expanding worldwide', *China: An International Journal*, **1**(2), 273–301.

Weidenbaum, M. (1980), 'Public policy: no longer a spectator sport for business', *Journal of Business Strategy*, **3**, 48–53.

Westney, D.E. (2009), 'The multinational firm as an evolutionary system', in S. Collinson and G. Morgan (eds), *Images of the Multinational Firm*, Chichester: Wiley, pp. 117–44.

Whitley, R. (1999), *Divergent Capitalisms: The Social Structuring and Change of Business Systems*, Oxford and New York: Oxford University Press.

Whitley, R. (2009a), 'U.S. capitalism: a tarnished model?', *Academy of Management Perspectives*, **23**(2), 11–23.

Whitley, R. (2009b), 'The multinational firm as a distinct organisational form', in S. Collinson and G. Morgan (eds), *Images of the Multinational Firm*, Chichester: Wiley, pp. 145–67.

Williamson, O.E. (1991), 'Comparative economic organization: the analysis of discrete structural alternatives', *Administrative Science Quarterly*, **36**, 269–96.

Yang, J.Y and J.T. Li (2008), 'The development of entrepreneurship in China', *Asia Pacific Journal of Management*, **25**, 335–59.

Zhu, R. (2001), Report on the Outline of the Fifth Five-Year Plan for National and Social Development (Excerpts) in Almanac of China's Foreign Economic Relations and Trends 2001, Beijing: MOFCOM.

7. The emergence of Chinese firms as multinationals: the influence of the home institutional environment

Peter J. Buckley, Hinrich Voss, Adam R. Cross and L. Jeremy Clegg[1]

INTRODUCTION

Much of the research to date on the evolution of mainland China's outward foreign direct investment (OFDI) is based on analyses of official secondary data and in-depth case studies of a small number of high-profile Chinese multinational enterprise (MNEs) (for example, Bonaglia et al., 2007; Buckley et al., 2007; Rugman and Li, 2007; Rui and Yip, 2008; Teagarden and Cai, 2009). While this research sheds some important light on the motives underpinning the internationalisation of Chinese firms, much of it is limited by the application of established international business theories to understanding the phenomenon (for example, Liu and Li, 2002; Wang and Chan, 2003; Deng, 2004). Consequently, and as we argue in this chapter, important dimensions which derive from the specific context of emerging countries are often overlooked or underdeveloped in extant theorising. In particular, we assert that the institutional environment of the home country is an important explanatory factor. In this chapter, we propose a conceptual framework for analysing the effect of this dimension on the overseas investment behaviour of Chinese MNEs. This, we argue, also has relevance for investigating the internationalisation of firms from other developing and transition economies, as we illustrate in the conclusion. A number of propositions are advanced to inform future research on Chinese OFDI, and these can be extrapolated to the investigation of developing country OFDI in general.

The framework we develop in this chapter is derived from established international business theory which is extended by the inclusion of aspects of institutional theory and social network theory. In doing so, our framework incorporates the role of home country institutions. Such institutions coordinate aspects of the domestic economy, are partially codified and contain an element of enforcement and sanction. They comprise a country's legislature, judiciary and bureaucracy, government structures and market mechanisms (that is, formal institutional elements) as well as social networks (that is, informal elements) (North, 1990). These institutions have been identified in previous studies (especially Oliver, 1997; Peng, 2003; Meyer and Nguyen, 2005) as crucial factors in shaping the economies of developing countries and, it follows, the business behaviour of inward investing firms. However, to date these elements have not been fully integrated into a formal analysis of the outward investment behaviour of developing country firms.

The chapter is organised as follows. In the next section, we begin our analysis by considering the relationship between inbound FDI and host country institutions. We then take a number of themes developed in this discussion and apply them to an analysis of the literature on how domestic institutions have the potential to influence, through the implementation of home country measures (HCMs), the international investment behaviour of domestic firms (UNCTAD, 2001; Buckley et al., 2009). Four dimensions to this analysis are considered, namely, (i) domestic institutions and government administration, (ii) domestic government-business linkages, (iii) international business and social networks, (iv) international government linkages.. We assess how each of these dimensions has the potential to interact or impinge upon market imperfections, transaction costs and the internationalisation processes of developing country firms. From this we develop a series of propositions for each of the dimensions to guide future research. The concluding section summarises our work, considers possible extensions to other emerging market contexts and proposes areas where future research is needed to generate further insights into the phenomenon of developing country OFDI.

INSTITUTIONS AND INTERNATIONAL BUSINESS

Institutions coordinate aspects of an economy by determining the 'rules of the game' and influencing 'how the game is played' (North, 1990; Brewer, 1993). To do so, institutions contain an element of enforcement and sanction. Institutions that are characterised by codified and rule-based enforcement and sanction procedures (that is, formal institutions) comprise government structures such as legislature, judiciary and bureaucracy, as well as market mechanisms. Informal institutions lack such rigid structures and are based on conventions and norms of behaviour as exemplified by social networks (North, 1990). Such formal and informal institutions can create two types of market imperfection: (i) structural market imperfections (for example, government intervention, market concentration and collusion) and (ii) endemic market imperfections (for example, information problems and high uncertainty). Both types of market imperfection have the potential to influence the level of transactions costs in an economy – in other words, they give rise to costs that prevent perfect competition. Such imperfections can be created by home country governments and their agencies with intent and do not necessarily evolve by accident (North, 1990; Dunning, 1992; Hämäläinen, 2003). This is done to achieve certain political, economic or social goals and is reflected in different ways with respect to inward and outward FDI activities. Likewise, some institutional arrangements can be created to circumvent the transactions costs caused by a misalignment of an existing configuration of other parts of the institutional environment, but without removing them. In order to establish a framework for an understanding of how the reach and actions of institutions influence the internationalisation behaviour of indigenous firms, we first consider a number of contributions to the literature on the relationship between inward FDI and emerging country institutions (a subject that has been much more comprehensively researched) since this has yielded several important and relevant insights. Our discussion of extant work on inward FDI and institutions identifies four dimensions which we take forward to structure our assessment of the institutional regime within which Chinese OFDI takes place.

INSTITUTIONS AND INWARD FDI

The influence of host country institutions on inward FDI and the business strategies of foreign MNEs is well documented, especially in the case of investments to emerging markets (see, for example, Dunning, 1992; Lipsey, 2002; Makino et al., 2004; Meyer, 2004). Generally, host country institutions support its national locational advantages for the attraction of inward FDI by putting emphasis on policies that target, inter alia, foreign exchange liberalisation, international trade and domestic market liberalisation, and that support private ownership (for example, Gastanaga et al., 1998; Globerman and Shapiro, 1999; Taylor, 2000; Sethi et al., 2002; Bevan et al., 2004). Especially in the case of emerging markets, transparent and accountable institutions are seen by investors as an insurance against those political and commercial risks that MNEs generally do not encounter when investing in more advanced economies (for example, Loree and Guisinger, 1995; Drabek and Payne, 2002). Such institutions are intended to remove those market imperfections which were put in place by an emerging country government for political and industrial policy reasons and which have the effect of increasing the costs of establishing and operating a business in that market for foreign firms. Likewise, domestic institutions can cause strategic and operational problems to MNEs due to unexpected nuances and unforeseen changes (Henisz and Swaminathan, 2008) which raise transaction costs for MNEs and have the potential to jeopardise their profit-maximising strategy. Mainland China is a good example. China has become one of the most attractive locations for inward FDI, not least because, since 1978, it has undergone an institutional transformation that has helped to release its potential as a production base for exports and for the servicing of a growing domestic market by foreign firms (for example, Henley et al., 1999; Ng and Tuan, 2001, 2002; Zhang, 2001; Buckley et al., 2005). Meyer and Nguyen (2005) extend the scope of analysis by demonstrating that host country institutions at both the national and subnational levels influence the strategy of MNEs, and that both levels should be considered when seeking theoretical explanations for the inward investment behaviour of foreign firms. We label this aspect the 'domestic institutions and government administration' dimension of FDI.

Host country governments sometimes seek to actively exploit the potential benefits from inward FDI. These benefits include an increase in the competitiveness of domestic firms through spillover and demonstration effects, as well as through the establishment of domestic value chains which may attract further foreign investors and thus lead to positive agglomeration effects. At the same time, the government may work to minimise the possibility of crowding-out effects arising from inward FDI that might be caused by the higher productivity of MNEs vis-à-vis domestic firms. In the case of China, several measures have been taken since 1978 to achieve both goals. Despite the formal openness to inward investments, only selected sectors were opened in the early 1980s to foreign participation. The breadth of sectors has been subsequentially increased and regularly updated using the instrument of inward FDI catalogues issued by the Ministry of Commerce and the National Development and Reform Commission. These catalogues set out in which sectors FDI is 'encouraged', 'welcomed', 'restricted' or 'prohibited' (the most recent version dating from 2007; MOFCOM and NDRC, 2007). Moreover, the establishment of a joint venture with a domestic firm and tight local content requirements were prerequisites for the approval of particular FDI projects as recently as the late 1990s. This alignment of objectives between the government and the business sector for mutual benefit falls into what we describe as the 'domestic government-business network' dimension.

In instances when domestic formal institutions are weak, at either the national or subnational level, informal institutions – such as personal networks and relationships – can be used by MNEs as a substitute in order to provide channels for obtaining business intelligence, securing greater investment certainty and other benefits. When the formal institutions are perceived to work well, informal institutions may supplement rather than replace them (Wang, 2000; Gao, 2003; Li et al., 2004). In the context of China, informal institutions play an important role. To illustrate, businesses owned by the overseas Chinese community in Southeast Asia were among the first to take the opportunity to invest in mainland China after it opened its economy to foreign investors, and familial and cultural linkages (which are often connected to ancestral homelands) helped them to advance their business operations in particular regions of China (Yeung and Olds, 2000). The importance of personal networks and relationships – called '*guanxi*' in the Chinese context – is reported in a number of studies on establishing, running and expanding businesses in China (for example, Hwang, 1987; Björkman and Kock, 1995; Park and Luo, 2001; Fan, 2002; Standifird, 2006). Such considerations are encapsulated in our 'international business and social networks' dimension.

Following a similar line of argument, international investment agreements (IIAs) based on bilateral or multilateral contacts and negotiations between governments and between governments and international organisations can support FDI flows by lowering institution-derived transaction costs (Bandelj, 2002; Buckley et al., 2008a; UNCTAD, 2004). China started early to sign IIAs with other countries to protect foreign investors and increase inward FDI. Another step in this direction was the accession of China to the World Trade Organization (WTO) in 2001. One concession made by China during accession negotiations was the phased opening of previously closed sectors to foreign investors. Moreover, due to the principles underlying WTO membership, foreign and domestic firms have to be treated equally by Chinese institutions, and Chinese companies have to comply with international standards on, for example, anti-dumping and other fair business practice measures. WTO membership therefore provides foreign firms with a tool for dispute settlement through an independent entity. Such interactions are embraced by our 'international government linkages' dimension.

This review of how institutions affect inbound FDI provides us with a foundation for understanding how institutions have the potential to influence the scale of OFDI from developing and emerging economies and the investment behaviour of firms. In the following section, we discuss this framework under each of the four dimensions identified above. Figure 7.1 depicts the institutional framework within which OFDI from a developing economy occurs.

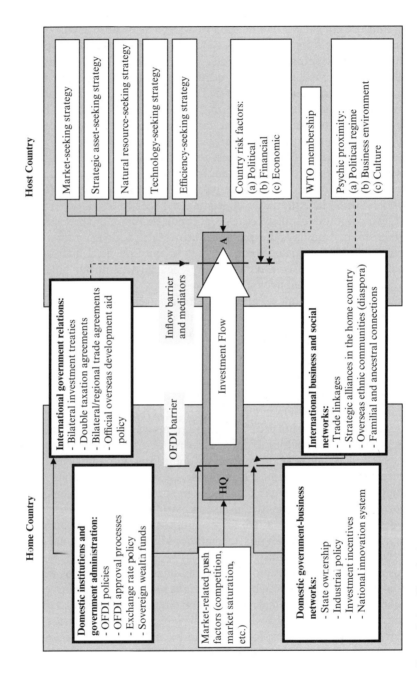

Home Country

Host Country

Domestic institutions and
government administration:
- OFDI policies
- OFDI approval processes
- Exchange rate policy
- Sovereign wealth funds

International government relations:
- Bilateral investment treaties
- Double taxation agreements
- Bilateral/regional trade agreements
- Official overseas development aid
  policy

Market-related push
factors (competition,
market saturation,
etc.)

Domestic government-business
networks:
- State ownership
- Industrial policy
- Investment incentives
- National innovation system

International business and social
networks:
- Trade linkages
- Strategic alliances in the home country
- Overseas ethnic communities (diaspora)
- Familial and ancestral connections

OFDI barrier

HQ

Investment Flow

Inflow barrier
and mediators

A

Market-seeking strategy

Strategic asset-seeking strategy

Natural resource-seeking strategy

Technology-seeking strategy

Efficiency-seeking strategy

Country risk factors:
(a) Political
(b) Financial
(c) Economic

WTO membership

Psychic proximity:
(a) Political regime
(b) Business environment
(c) Culture

Figure 7.1   Chira's OFDI regime

130

INSTITUTIONS AND OUTWARD FDI – THE CASE OF CHINA

Extant international business literature on inward FDI generally takes the standpoint of a developed country MNE and how such firms can best defend and exploit their ownership advantages in a new country (for example, Luo, 2000; Enderwick, 2007). Such a perspective generally perceives the 'visible hand' of emerging country institutions as serving as an impediment to international expansion and questions how a firm can cope with and overcome its liabilities of foreignness. It can be argued that these standpoints are misplaced when it comes to the analysis of OFDI from developing countries. The same institutions that may be considered as serving as a constraint for foreign investors can serve as an important source of competitive advantage for domestic firms. In this respect, the policies and institutions of home countries may actually contribute to the international competitiveness of indigenous firms.

When countries are considered as sources of outward investment, an 'invisible hand' approach towards the internationalisation of domestic enterprises and the domestic economy is often assumed. Consequently, past research has tended to disregard or underestimate how the domestic institutional environment affects the international development and strategies of local firms (for example, Liu and Li, 2002; Cui and Jiang, 2009; Teagarden and Cai, 2009). We propose that future analysis of OFDI from a developing country such as mainland China needs to adopt a more holistic approach and take better account of those institutions that operate on the subnational level, the national level and, as we introduce here, the international level that can play a key role in shaping the international investment decision-making of Chinese MNEs through the creation of market imperfections and other effects. Our framework builds upon, extends and systemises the work of Buckley et al., (2007) and Buckley et al., (2008a) in order to assess the influences of each of the four dimensions identified above on the institutional environment within which developing country OFDI takes place. In doing so, we relate the four dimensions to policies and economic development in China. Our analysis is restricted to the post-1978 period and covers the period of transition of China from an autarkic planned economy towards a more market-influenced economy. In the following sections, we discuss in turn the likely effect of each of the four institutional dimensions on OFDI in general, and then extend our analysis to the specific case of China.

Domestic Institutions and Government Administration

Countries introduce economic policies and regulatory frameworks with a clear goal in mind, namely, to advance national economic development. Intentionally or not, this can have negative effects on OFDI (or, in other words, they constitute negative HCMs). Amongst the measures that may have negative side effects on OFDI are those actions that target the international economic interaction of domestic businesses (for example, balance of payments controls, international investments approval processes and foreign exchange controls), while other measures have a domestic policy focus such as domestic investment promotion and control, and the identification and support of industry sectors considered to be important for the economic future of the country. The intention behind all of these types of policies is to ensure that there is sufficient long-term capital for domestic investment that will create employment and economic growth. However, by curbing the international investment possibilities of domestic firms, their competitiveness potential may be diminished because they cannot develop and exploit their resources and capabilities to the fullest extent possible.

On the other hand, the domestic institutional framework may have positive effects on some indigenous firms and can augment their ownership advantages (that is, it gives rise to positive HCMs). Companies that originate from a restrictive institutional framework will gain substantial experience of how to cope with such an environment and, indeed, how to exploit those imperfections associated with the local market which may assist them in being successful in countries with similar institutional conditions. Of itself, this can constitute a firm-specific advantage, and one that may enable firms to internalise even the smallest changes and opportunities provided by the governance system – regardless of whether it is a 'rules-based' or 'relations-based' system. By extension, such firms are likely to exploit these advantages in a similarly structured host country – a notion that accords with the spirit of the 'Uppsala' model of incremental firm internationalisation (Johanson and Vahlne, 1977). These are the advantages of home country embeddedness, and they can include the ability of firms to cope effectively with (rapidly) changing institutional settings and discretionary policies, to economise on the use of scarce capital and other factor inputs, to exploit domestic and international network capacities to circumvent market imperfections, and to scale products and production systems to suit foreign market needs and conditions. In fact, companies might feel more comfortable investing in a country with a similar institutional setting and governance system to their home country as they can better appreciate it, utilise existing operational leeway and better foresee any political developments and administrative decisions that might ensue (Johanson and Vahlne, 1977; Lecraw, 1977; Lall, 1982; Wells, 1983). In contrast, the institutional environment may be designed in such a way that any international investment by domestic firms is prohibited: that is, when structural market imperfections are put in place (Hämäläinen, 2003). Companies operating in such an environment may find it costly and cumbersome to (illegally) circumvent investment barriers to take advantage of their international competitiveness. But firms with only a few short-term ownership advantages have to proceed with their internationalisation at a point in time when they are in possession of the advantage. If the foreign investment is delayed, their ownership advantage may become eroded before they are able to invest, and this may render the investment unfeasible (Rivoli and Salorio, 1996).

It should be noted that this discussion about the role of domestic institutions is in contrast with the view of Dunning (1996) who argues that domestic institutions have either a neutral effect or an adverse effect on the ownership advantages of industrialised country MNEs. It is also at odds with Tsang and Yip's (2007) empirical evidence that firms are more successful when they invest in countries that have greater institutional distance from their home country.

The Chinese government is renowned for having a 'hands-on' approach towards domestic economic issues, and this can give rise to market imperfections. One recent example can be found in the telecommunications industry, whereby the Chinese government has formed three companies which it perceives as being sufficiently strong and large enough to compete with each other and, potentially, with foreign firms in the future. To achieve this, China Unicom sold in the spring of 2008 its Code Division Multiple Access (CDMA) mobile phone business to China Telecom and incorporated the businesses of China Netcom. The three companies are each listed on at least two stock exchanges (China Netcom: Hong Kong and New York; China Union: Hong Kong, New York and Shanghai; and China Telecom: Hong Kong and New York) but each one is majority state-owned (Lau and Dickie, 2008). Similar government involvement can be observed for most of the period since 1978 in other industry sectors (for example, Child and Yuan, 1996; Lu, 2000; Nolan and Zhang, 2002).[2] But government intervention in China is not restricted to the domestic realm: it is also directed towards the international business activities of Chinese firms. China prohibited OFDI prior to 1978 and, as with many other developing countries, it was controlled and restricted for a significant period of time after 1978. This was done in the conviction that scarce capital should be invested domestically because this would be most beneficial to the economy. The Chinese government also sought to increase foreign exchange reserves to achieve security from international financial volatility (Sauvant 2005). It is therefore not surprising that the Chinese government has employed a number of legal, regulatory and financial instruments and measures that either directly (through administrative fiat) or indirectly (using economic policy implementation and other measures) affect Chinese OFDI (Buckley et al., 2008b). These initiatives have resulted in both positive and negative outcomes in respect to Chinese OFDI. Examples of the latter include the outward investment approval process (which involves several ministries and government agencies), restrictions that permitted only state-owned enterprises (SOEs) to invest abroad and foreign exchange controls (all of which are negative HCMs). These are counterbalanced somewhat by a number of positive HCMs which are embodied within the 'Go Global' policy initiated in 1999 which has led to the introduction of various OFDI liberalisation measures. These positive HCMs have been undertaken with the support of international organisations such as the United Nations Conference on Trade and Development (UNCTAD) and professional organisations such as foreign regional development agencies (RDAs) and consultancies. In the long run, the policy of creating favourable conditions for domestic enterprises should see increasing numbers of Chinese firms locate productive activities abroad. All the HCMs discussed above are clearly time bound and imply changes over time to the regulatory framework within which Chinese OFDI occurs and to the emergence of Chinese MNEs.

To illustrate the impact of a positive HCM, the most recent and far-reaching national measure directly linked to Chinese OFDI, the 'Go Global' policy, is now discussed. This policy was supported by the former Chinese President Jiang Zemin and the former Chinese Premier Zhu Rongji (Zhu, 2001) and became formal policy by its incorporation into the tenth Five-Year Plan in 2001 (Child and Rodrigues, 2005). The 'Go Global' policy represented a strong public commitment to the adoption of an institutional environment that encourages and fosters (both financially and administratively) the outbound investments of Chinese firms. The policy has been translated into national and subnational regulations and various investment support measures. The Chinese authorities have substituted OFDI-restricting measures and indirect, 'hands-off' economic policies for direct, 'hands-on' administrative methods of management (Sauvant, 2005; Buckley et al., 2008b). In particular, the response of relevant Chinese government agencies has been to provide greater support and promotion of OFDI by offering favourable policies and various 'hard' and 'soft' HCMs to investors in many areas. These include 'hard' measures such as improvements to the availability of commercial loans and funding from the Export-Import Bank of China and the China Investment

Corporation for earmarked projects (using China's substantial foreign exchange reserves),[3] and preferential arrangements concerning foreign exchange usage. They also include corporate income tax exemptions to qualified firms and projects, overseas investment insurance, provision of human resources and liberalisation of the legal and regulatory environment. 'Soft' measures include, for example, the provision of information services and training courses on international business and foreign languages, and the establishment of an Overseas Business Service Centre in Beijing and Chinese Chambers of Commerce in foreign countries. One example of a 'hands-off' measure is the intention of the Chinese government to improve the quality of OFDI-related services by further devolving decision-taking on outward investment approvals to local government (that is, to the provincial level). Also in this category is the policy to mini-mise competition among Chinese companies abroad by introducing meas-ures to coordinate the international dispersion of Chinese firms in a way that prevents OFDI in the same industries in the same countries (Wang, 2001). International 'market cannibalism' amongst Chinese firms is seen by the Chinese authorities as being detrimental to the competitiveness of Chinese firms.

Irrespective of the level of government support, domestic Chinese firms will also have gained considerable experience of how to operate under an opaque or idiosyncratic institutional arrangement, as we alluded to in our earlier discussion. With certain ownership advantages gained from their context-specific institutional framework, Chinese MNEs (like other devel-oping country MNEs) are likely to have a distinctive foreign investment strategy in terms of location, as exemplified by an idiosyncratic reaction to risk not observed by studies on the FDI behaviour of industrialised country firms (Buckley et al., 2007). We return to this point below. This discussion helps us to derive our first set of propositions, as follows:

Proposition 1a: *Chinese companies that invest abroad benefit from positive home country measures (HCMs) that augment their stock of firm-specific advantages.*

Proposition 1b: *Chinese companies that invest abroad benefit from negative home country measures which increase their institutional sensitivity.*

Domestic Government-Business Networks

The character of the government-business networks of a country can exert considerable influence on the domestic and international development of companies. Economic systems which are built upon 'relation-based' governance systems may reward personal linkages between businesses and governments. This can be reflected in the protection of companies against internal and external competition through government-imposed market entry barriers and the preferential treatment of selected companies (Li et al., 2004). Such behaviour is more difficult to sustain in a 'rules-based' system, which tends to be more transparent and independent.

Close relationships and collusion between the government and domestic businesses can lead to structural and endemic market imperfections which are exploitable by companies that enjoy good relationships with the administration. 'National champion' policies, for example, favour a small number of companies in selected industries with the aim of raising these firms to national and, eventually, international excellence. Industrial policy which focuses on the development of certain business sectors can also be regarded as a structural market imperfection when government involvement leads to the artificial adjustment of factor prices in favour of companies that have preferential access to critical inputs (Dunning, 1992). Though such policies have been in place for a number of years in numerous European and Asian economies (see, for example, Hayward, 1995) they tend to be more commonplace in economies where state ownership of firms dominates (and where these firms are an important pillar of the domestic social and economic security system) or in economies which are built on 'relation-based' governance systems. There are two reasons for this. First, within 'relation-based' governance systems, it becomes difficult to distinguish between formal and informal institutions because they intermingle. Laws, regulations and procedures are interpreted and applied in a discretionary way by certain actors in society to the advantage of a selected few. The informal, personal linkages between firms and government officials can lead to economically unjustified protectionism and favouritism (that is, regulatory capture and adverse selection problems) (Li et al., 2004). As a consequence, one important market imperfection that may manifest itself at the interface between government and businesses concerns the capital market. Capital markets evolve alongside the general economic development of a country and are therefore often underdeveloped in developing countries (cf. Levine, 1999; Freire and Petersen, 2004). This leads to an inefficient allocation of capital. Soft budget constraints are a form of domestic capital market imperfection (Buckley et al., 2007). Soft budget constraints arise, for example, when an organisation's spending is not restricted to the boundaries of an annual budget but can be extended with extra-budgetary funding from the supervising (government) authority (Kornai, 1986). This creates a semi-permanent disequilibrium in the capital market. Outward investors can potentially exploit this and obtain the necessary marginal funding to pursue an internationalising strategy. In particular, companies with excess capital may use it to: (i) invest internationally on a trial-and-error basis without putting the domestic business at risk, (ii) outbid competitors in a fight for resources (especially energy and raw materials, brands and technology), or (iii) fund overseas investment in the first place. For this reason, capital market imperfections can become an ownership advantage for companies (Buckley et al., 2007).

In the case of China, both structural and endemic market imperfections are observable. Both types of imperfections affect the way firms can access external capital and technology, as we now discuss.

Access to Capital

The national government of China is the ultimate owner of its SOEs, and these dominate the list of the top 30 outward investors in terms of OFDI stock in 2006 (MOFCOM, 2006). In this role, the government effectively has a key operational decision-taking role in many investment projects (Buckley et al., 2008b). It frequently is also consulted by companies to ensure that business strategies receive the endorsement of government supervisors (Zhang, 2007). State-owned firms may enjoy different but co-existing forms of soft budget constraint. They have capital made available to them at below market rates or receive capital at market rates without the requirement to pay it back (Xiao and Sun, 2005). For example, Zhao and Shen (2008) report that the State Council requests the Ministry of Finance and state-owned banks to support Chinese construction companies in their international endeavours on preferential terms. Government support of internationalisation is not restricted to the construction industry. For example, the China National Offshore Oil Corporation (CNOOC) received a US$7 billion loan from the Chinese government in 2005 to support its take-over bid for Unocal, a California-based oil company, US$2.5 billion of which was interest-free and the remainder was to be repaid at an interest rate of 3.5 per cent over 30 years (Xiao and Sun, 2005). The aspiration to support the internationalisation of Chinese companies is also reflected in the loan (of US$10 billion over five years) granted in late 2004 by the China Development Bank to Huawei, the telecommunication equipment producer, which reported international sales of US$2.3 billion in 2004 (Huawei, 2004; Forney, 2005). This loan was almost equivalent to the total amount of OFDI flows from China in the preceding three years. TCL, the brown goods manufacturer (and acquirer of a number of ailing European firms), received a combined credit and overseas business insurance package of about US$3.5 billion in 2004 from the Import and Export Bank of China, the China Export Credit Insurance Company and the China Development Bank to support its international expansion (SinoCast China

Business Daily News, 2005). Another scheme which arguably constitutes a cheap source of external capital is illustrated by Central Hujin Investment Company, a government-controlled investment company. Hujin has used China's foreign exchange reserves to become a leading shareholder in a number of major Chinese banks (Heep, 2008). This type of phenomenon may be more prevalent in an economy with poor corporate governance on the part of the lender or borrower (or both) (Lardy, 1998), or where SOEs play a significant socio-economic role (Broadman, 2001), or where 'relations-based' governance systems prevail (Li et al., 2004). Indeed, Zhang (2007) finds that, despite the relatively advanced process of corpo-ratisation of China's SOEs, corporate governance mechanisms in China remain underdeveloped and this is likely to have contributed to the soft budget constraints enjoyed by many Chinese MNEs.

Arguably, these examples and many of the administrative developments discussed above reflect access to cheap capital: that is, they constitute a soft budget constraint. Besides these soft budget constraints, two further capital market imperfections have been identified in China which can be exploited by some (state-owned) Chinese MNEs (Antkiewicz and Whalley, 2006; Buckley et al., 2007). First, because of inefficiencies in the banking systems loans are granted to companies which are not able to be repaid in time or completely. Such debtors may include (potential) outward investors which are supported either as policy to spur their domestic and international growth or through inefficiency. This may be the result of negligence of, or nescience concerning, risk assessment, or both. It may occur because, as Lardy (1998) argues, the capital made available by state-owned banks to SOEs may be perceived as 'remaining within' the state system. Consequently, the close and rigorous scrutiny of the transaction that is required may become compromised because of the view of the Chinese authorities that capital cannot be 'lost'. China's banking system is dominated by four state-owned banks which, though corporatised and listed, also follow state directives and are burdened by a large amount of non-performing loans, and this indicates inefficien-cies in the system. However, a survey conducted in 2003 by Ayyagari et al. (2008) found that Chinese firms grew faster and have higher returns when they are able to access bank financing relative to firms that relied on informal sources of investment funding. This finding holds regardless of firm size. Second, firms and business groups that operate an internal capital market when the external market is underdeveloped can allocate funds to new and ongoing operations as this provides them with access to cheap funding. This internal capital market can be used to cross-subsidise international business activities when the firm is not capable of competing on technological grounds. The necessary funds for such an internal market are generated in (an often protected) domestic market and by the exploitation of business opportunities in related and unrelated business sectors (Keister, 1998; Ma and Lu, 2005; Yiu et al., 2005). It is interesting to note here that the majority of the top 30 Chinese outward investors (as of 2005) are state-owned and are organised as business groups. Two research propositions therefore arise:

Proposition 2a: Chinese MNEs utilise domestic capital market imperfections to support them in funding their international investments.

Proposition 2b: The ability of Chinese firms to exploit domestic capital market imperfections is not equally distributed across firms. SOEs and large private firms are better positioned to do so than others.

Access to Technology

The Chinese government is attempting to establish a comprehensive national innovation system through the adoption and implementation of internal and external measures. As part of the internal measures, the government has implemented a range of national technology- and innovation-funding schemes since the 1990s and in 1994 it identified five pillar industries to support (Liu and White, 2001; Zhang and Taylor, 2001; Sigurdson, 2005).[4] Another strategy is concerned with the acquisition of foreign knowledge, that is, through the use of external measures. The Chinese government has supported the catching-up process of domestic firms by requesting foreign firms to establish joint ventures with domestic firms in certain industries, to transfer advanced technology to the joint ventures and to source locally. The success of the policy has been proven by various empirical studies that have found positive spillover effects arising from inward FDI on Chinese firms (for example, Buckley et al., 2002; Liu and Wang, 2003). The influx of foreign investment and the technology and knowledge transfers which this brings may have helped Chinese firms to develop capabilities that enable them to internationalise today (Liu et al., 2005). A good example can be found in the Chinese automobile industry, one of the five pillar industries. Foreign car assemblers are not permitted to operate wholly owned enterprises in China. As a consequence, Shanghai Automotive Industry Corporation (SAIC) has joint ventures with Volkswagen and General Motors, as do Nanjing Automobile Corporation (NAC) with Iveco, and First Automobile Works with Volkswagen/Audi (Zhang and Taylor, 2001). SAIC acquired the South Korean car manufacturer Ssangyong in 2004 and SAIC and NAC acquired the assets of the ailing British car manufacturer MG Rover in

2004 and 2005, respectively, before combining their car production activities in late 2007. The exposure to foreign technology, and managerial and organisational expertise in their respective joint ventures, in combination with domestic government support and the newly obtained foreign production facilities and technologies, has provided SAIC and NAC with some leverage to pursue an internationalisation strategy.

Proposition 3a: *Chinese firms that participate in nationally funded technology and innovation schemes are likely to have the resources and capabilities to internationalise through direct investments.*

Proposition 3b: *Chinese firms that enjoy an international technology and knowledge exchange agreement are likely to have the resources, capabilities and mindset to internationalise through direct investments.*

International Government Relations

Companies in countries in which the government plays an important role in the domestic economy may benefit from the government taking an active role in establishing international ties with other countries (Bandelj, 2002). Such activities can be directed towards the conclusion of bilateral and multilateral agreements, the accession to supranational institutional arrangements which shape international business activities and other less codified measures. The intention is generally to reduce both structural and endemic market imperfections in and about the host country in order to lower transaction costs for domestic companies in the foreign market. The Chinese government is in the process of negotiating a number of bilateral and multilateral trade and investment agreements in order to support and strengthen the outward orientation of Chinese companies, amongst other things. It has concluded a growing number of bilateral investment agreements and double taxation treaties over the past two decades to protect Chinese investors and their interests (Wang, 2001), and to coordinate China's foreign affairs and official development aid policy for 'mutual' benefit (Chen, 2006). The impact of these activities on the international investment decision-making of Chinese firms depends largely on the perceived credibility of these government-led initiatives (Murtha and Lenway, 1994). Given the current high levels of government support, Chinese firms have to be certain that it is either sufficiently long term or provides sufficient (monetary) short-term benefits to merit the internalisation of market imperfections and that the long-term growth of the firm is not impeded. Below we discuss in turn these types of bilateral, multilateral and other government-led initiatives.

Bilateral Agreements

IIAs, especially bilateral investment treaties (BITs), double taxation treaties (DTTs) and trade agreements are often seen as policy instruments which countries introduce to improve their locational attractiveness to MNEs (Mallampally and Sauvant, 1999). A BIT provides a legally binding situation in which investors from the signatory countries enjoy greater investment protection for their tangible and intangible assets than domestic laws would otherwise provide. A BIT is therefore generally argued to reflect a progressive and positive attitude towards economic liberalism on the part of contracting parties (Vandevelde, 1998). The conclusion of a BIT should ensure a relatively high level of investment protection which helps the internationalising firm to attenuate risk considerations in the investment decision and to focus more attention on commercial considerations. In other words, a BIT regulates a distorted market and dilutes those market imperfections created by inefficient and (potentially) hostile host country governments. A BIT can also help to mitigate the risk of them behaving opportunistically. Consequently, a BIT may trigger FDI since overall investment costs and risks are decreased and business opportunities are widened (Ramamurti, 2001; Egger and Pfaffermayer, 2004). Although BITs are generally aimed at protecting developed country businesses in emerging markets, they should also be of advantage for Chinese firms. China signed its first BIT with Sweden in 1982 to protect domestic firms (Cai, 1999) and it is now second only to Germany as a signatory nation in terms of the numbers of BITs concluded. China concluded 116 BITs by February 2006, of which 63 have been agreed with other developing countries (UNCTAD, 2005, 2006).

Similar to a BIT, a DTT is concluded between two countries to avoid the duplicated taxation of companies operating in both countries for the same activity. Host country attractiveness is increased because future tax rates on (profitable) foreign affiliates are made more predictable for the investing parent company (Davies, 2004). Regional and bilateral trade agreements, on the other hand, have the potential to help domestic firms establish themselves in a foreign market first through exports and subsequentially through FDI, especially as such agreements often include provisions concerning the liberalisation of the host country's inward investment regime and can therefore stimulate intra-regional FDI (Globerman and Shapiro, 1999; Jaumotte, 2004; UNCTAD, 2005). Under the sphere of bilateral agreements also fall aspects of foreign policy such as official development aid and state visits by leading politicians to and from the host countries concerned. State visits are generally intended to appease and befriend the visited country but bear no codifiable and enforcement mechanisms like home country government action. Such visits may, however, be followed by the negotiation and conclusion of bilateral arrangements between the governments and, as we have seen above, this can affect the foreign investment behaviour of domestic firms positively as transactions costs are reduced. Thus:

Proposition 4: The international investment behaviour of Chinese MNEs is positively influenced by the bilateral agreements that the Chinese government concludes and conducts with (potential) host nations.

Multilateral Agreements

The most important supranational organisation that shapes international business on a global scale is the WTO. The WTO is responsible for administering around 30 international treaties and agreements, and these include the General Agreement on Tariffs and Trade (GATT), the agreement on Trade-Related Intellectual Property Rights (TRIPs) and the agreement on Trade-Related Investment Measures (TRIMs). These agreements govern much of the framework for international trade and investment (such as most favoured nation terms and equal treatment of domestic and foreign firms, trade dispute resolution, market access, reductions in preferential trading arrangements and so forth) (Sornarajah, 2004). Membership of the WTO signals to foreign firms that a country is likely to conform to its strictures and obligations with respect to international trade and investment, and signals to domestic firms that the home government is capable of supporting them legally in cases of, for example, dumping accusations and other unfair practices. The WTO thus constitutes an important supranational component of the institutional framework within which MNEs operate. National membership of other region-specific organisations such as the ASEAN, EU, MERCUSOR, and NAFTA can offer similar benefits to investing firms.[5] China is increasingly participating in various supranational agreements and treaties administered by multilateral bodies such as the WTO. Through its active membership, the Chinese government can influence standards and procedures in a way that supports the internationalisation of domestic firms. With regards to the WTO this relates, for example, to the current Doha Round of trade negotiations and possible amendments to the GATT, TRIPS and TRIMS agreements. However, China only joined the WTO in 2001 and the influence of its government in this respect will have begun in 2002.

This period marks a sharp increase in annual FDI outflows from China. Though this may be coincidental, it is worth noting that WTO membership generally signals to host countries that a signatory country will comply with its strictures and obligations with respect to international trade and investment and this may have contributed to at least a proportion of the sharp rise in Chinese OFDI seen since 2002.

Since acceding to the WTO, China has negotiated trade agreements with a number of countries and regional organisations. These agreements contain provision for greater trade and investment liberalisation than is provided for by China's commitments under its WTO membership (Wang, 2004). To date, China has been able to conclude or agree upon frameworks with ten countries and regions (Antkiewicz and Whalley, 2005; Chen, 2006).[6]

Proposition 5: Chinese MNEs benefit from the engagement of the Chinese government in multilateral trade and investment agreements because regulations and standards take better account of the needs and objectives of Chinese firms.

Other Measures: Investment and Trade Hubs

Besides concluding bilateral and multilateral trade and investment agreements, the Chinese government is actively trying to facilitate the export of small and medium-sized domestic enterprises through the establishment of Special Economic Zones (SEZs) and trade hubs in places such as Africa, Europe and the Middle East. The British city of Wigan, for example, has been identified by Chinamex (a SDE under the supervision of the Chinese Ministry of Commerce) and the China Chamber of Commerce for Import and Export of Textiles as a future hub for Chinese clothing and textiles firms with intentions of trading within Europe (Guardian, 2007; NWDA, 2008). In Dubai, Chinamex has opened the so-called 'Chinese Dragon Mart' which offers trading space for up to 4,000 Chinese companies. Chinamex has undertaken similar activities in Amsterdam (the Chinamex Europe Trade and Exhibition Centre (CETEC)) (Netherlands) and it is considering opening a centre in Atlanta (USA). Likewise, the Foreign Trade and Economic Department of the city of Shanghai is to open a trading hub in St Petersburg (Russia) (Chinamex, 2009). Government-led SEZs have been, or will be, established in Egypt, Mauritius, Nigeria, Tanzania and Zambia (Chambishi) (Russell, 2008), and are under discussion and evaluation in Cape Verde, Pakistan (supported by the bilateral Free Trade Agreement concluded in 2006), Rwanda and Uganda. These zones are designed to attract Chinese companies into the regions and to set up manufacturing operations. The facility in Mauritius is being financed by the China Development Bank and run by a private Chinese entrepreneur.

Proposition 6: Government and SOE-led investment parks, SEZs and trading hubs abroad provide a familiar or facilitating institutional environment that encourages first-time investors and small and medium-sized enterprises from China to expand there.

International Business and Social Networks

Access to an international social or business network has the potential to increase investment flows between countries by lowering transaction costs and by pointing a company to existing business opportunities. Such a network exists between a potential outward investor and (i) an ethnically close overseas community, (ii) established foreign trade and contract partners, (iii) international business facilitators (such as investment promotion agencies, consultancies and trade promotion organisations), and (iv) a foreign business partner with whom the potential investor already collaborates in its home country (for example, in the form of a joint venture). All four of these potential linkages exist in the Chinese economy to varying degrees and are described below.

Overseas communities can take different configurations which range from recently emigrated nationals that study or work in the host country or region to communities that have lived in the host country for several generations and retain strong links to their ancestral homelands. Chinese emigrants that moved to Southeast Asia some generations ago have established themselves as strong forces in the local economies of countries such as Indonesia, Malaysia and Singapore (Yeung, 2006) while Australia, Europe and the USA have attracted large numbers of migrants and Chinese students that can help build valuable social and businesses links between the countries (cf. Saxenian, 2002).

Moreover, 'inward internationalisation' (Welch and Luostarinen, 1993) in the form of strong buyer-supplier relationships and contract work for foreign MNEs (for example, original equipment manufacturing (OEM) and original design manufacturing (ODM) arrangements) are all channels of knowledge transfer to emerging market firms. These types of collaboration bring information about product and process standards, as well as technology and quality control mechanisms which help to upgrade the intellectual capital of domestic firms. Galanz, for example, started production of microwaves in 1992 and developed quickly into a major OEM producer for leading foreign brands. It also started selling its own branded microwaves in Europe and South America (Gao et al., 2003; Zeng and Williamson, 2003). In Europe, Galanz gained a 40 per cent market share in 2002. Moreover, its technical expertise has made it an invaluable partner for foreign firms (Zeng and Williamson, 2003). The importance and power of these activities is further reflected in China's position in world trade. From 1980 to 2008, China's share of world exports of merchandise products rose from 0.89 to 8.86 per cent and its share of world imports from 0.96 per cent to 6.90 per cent (WTO, 2009). These figures reflect the increasing integration of China into the global economy, and allude to the growth in opportunity for Chinese firms to augment their capabilities through greater engagement with foreign firms.

National and subnational investment promotion agencies from a wide range of countries have internationalised over the past decade in order to identify and attract potential foreign investors (Table 7.1). These agencies offer crucial first-hand business information and contacts, and provide professional services to businesses that are considering internationalising and, in so doing, they support the investment decision process. Interested firms can also take advantage of professional services firms operating internationally that disseminate 'best practices'. A good example of a national investment promotion agency is the UK Trade and Investment (UKTI) and its 12 RDAs in Britain. The UKTI's mandate is to strengthen the international competitiveness of British firms and the British economy. To fulfil this mandate, the UKTI has investment promotion offices in Beijing, Chongqing, Guangzhou and Shanghai that target Chinese businesses in their respective regions. In addition, eight of the British RDAs have at least one office of their own in China to approach and attract Chinese firms that fit the particular business and development agenda of their respective region in the UK.[7] These offices provide Chinese firms with an opportunity to learn about the potential of the British economy and help them to establish important business contacts.

Local firms can also absorb knowledge through direct and indirect business linkages. Direct linkages involve both backward (supplier) and forward (customer) linkages, as well as any kind of business collaboration, such as license arrangements, outsourcing agreements and the purchase of factor inputs (Pack and Saggi, 1997). Indirect linkages, on the other hand, derive from 'watching' the business operations, functions and products of other firms and imitating them (Inkpen, 2000). Both kinds of linkages are present in China: Sino-foreign joint ventures, the dominant entry mode employed by investors during the 1990s (Teng, 2004), have given Chinese partners multiple opportunities to learn directly from their foreign partners while the growing presence of (wholly owned) foreign firms per se provides them with ample examples to follow and copy (Khanna et al., 1998; Inkpen, 2000; Buckley et al., 2002). For example, Haier has benefited from the transfer of technology in its Sino-foreign joint venture with Liebherr, the German refrigerator company. Haier has also relied on international consultancy firms to help it implement an internationalisation and growth

Table 7.1   The impact of home country institutions on international business strategy

Dimension	Characteristics	Theoretical impact	Evidence from Chinese MNEs
Domestic institutions and government administration	– Strong governmental/ administrative involvement	– Increase of transaction costs – Creation of structural market imperfections	– OFDI approval system involves State Council, NDRC, MOFCOM (national and province) and SAFE (national and province) – Monitoring and adjusting OFDI flows
Domestic government- business networks	– State ownership – Industry policy	– Creation of structural and endemic market imperfections	– Establishment of the China International Trade and Investment Corporation (CITIC) in 1978 – Domestic capital market imperfections
International government relations	– Alignment of foreign policy and aid policy	– Creation of structural market imperfections – Reduction of endemic market imperfections, especially transaction costs, information problems and uncertainty	– China-Africa Fund of up to US$5 billion to support Chinese firms in Africa – Preferential government to government loans which are linked to commissioning contract work to Chinese firms
International business and social networks	– International strategic alliances – OEM, ODM and others – Ethnic overseas Chinese communities	– Decrease of transaction costs – Channels of knowledge transfer	– Top inward FDI destination since the mid-1990s – Domestic policy focusing on local sourcing and establishment of joint ventures – Extensive overseas Chinese network – Extensive overseas student network

strategy (Liu and Li, 2002). As a consequence, Chinese firms enjoy considerable spillover and demonstration effects from the engagement of foreign firms in their economy.

Proposition 7: Chinese firms that are involved in one or more social and business networks enjoy lower transactions costs in identifying business opportunities abroad and are therefore more likely to internationalise than those that are not.

IMPLICATIONS AND CONCLUSIONS

Central to this chapter is the notion that the internationalisation of mainland Chinese companies has been influenced greatly by the domestic institutional framework in which they are embedded. Clearly, these facilitating elements alone are unlikely to fully explain OFDI from China. The role of institutional factors needs to be disentangled from other influences such as demand conditions and competition levels in the host country and the nature and extent of the firm-specific advantages of the profit-maximising firm. Likewise, abstracting from the institutional side and applying standard international business theories risks missing crucial explanatory factors. Hence, we assert that a combined model that takes account of institutional factors as well as the traditional explanations of FDI is likely to have greater explanatory power than a less holistic model can accomplish alone. Our framework therefore integrates the internalisation theory of the MNE and institutional theory. It does so in a novel way by reflecting on the institutional factors that shape the character of inward FDI into an emerging economy. A significant body of literature has grown on this subject which contains invaluable insights on how emerging markets work and what the role is of institutions in those markets. From a review of this literature we identified four institution-related dimensions that, we argue, have the potential to impinge on inward FDI. We use this to develop ten propositions that capture the potential effect of these institution-related dimensions on outward FDI from mainland China. The four dimensions are: (i) 'domestic institutions and government administration', (ii) 'domestic government-business networks', (iii) 'international government relations' and (iv) 'international business and social networks'. Underpinning this chapter is our assertion that future research that seeks to explain the emergence and expansion of Chinese MNEs needs to take better account of the institutional environment in which it takes place along each of these four dimensions. Although investigation of the role of a single dimension is likely to reveal valuable insights, because the dimensions are interrelated and interact with each other, a research framework which incorporates most if not all of them is likely to generate greater understanding.

Moreover, our framework and the ten propositions we advance have the potential to open new avenues of research, not only on Chinese MNEs specifically but also on the international expansion of emerging market MNEs in general. First, the dynamic interplay between firm- and institution-based ownership advantages requires further exploration. Competitive advantages that are derived from the institutional idiosyncrasies of the home country may complement firm-created ownership advantages at particular points in time. However, institutions do not change and develop as quickly as do businesses and, therefore, the benefits of institution-based ownership advantages may lessen over time. Companies that internationalise on the back of such a combination of ownership advantages would thus need to identify their shortcomings and place particular emphasis on competence-enhancing activities to enable them to sustain their international expansion when the gains from domestic institutional support reduce. To illustrate, the global economic crisis that began in 2008 has tested the international competitiveness and resilience of Chinese MNEs. If their international competitiveness has been derived mainly from their domestic institutional environment and the soft budget constraints that they have enjoyed, then their future international expansion may be hampered. China experienced a steep increase in inflation and struggled to sustain subsidies for commodities such as gasoline in 2008 (BBC, 2008; World Bank, 2008). Thus, it is possible to assume that certain financial resources and administrative efforts which were once directed to supporting Chinese MNEs are increasingly likely to be redirected towards easing domestic economic (and social) pressures. At the same time, the reform and modernisation of the Chinese banking sector that is currently underway may see soft budget constraints harden. For these reasons, Chinese MNEs may have to rely more heavily in future on their firm-specific competitive advantages and show that they can compete and survive internationally without benefiting from the same level of institutional support at home that they have enjoyed over the past decade or so. It remains to be seen to what extent the Chinese government and other institutional actors will reduce their current and future support of OFDI and the effect that this will have on the international expansion of Chinese firms.

Second, research on precisely how international social and business networks facilitate the internationalisation of emerging market firms is likely to be informative. Research is needed to explain how such firms (especially smaller and privately owned firms) pursue their international investment strategy and overcome their resources and capability constraints. China is not unique in having a large overseas ethnic community. For example, significant numbers of ethnic Mexicans and Indians live in the USA and the UK is host to a wide range of ethnic communities originating from the Commonwealth countries. Research on the establishment and exploitation of social and business networks by emerging market firms should link into the wider body of research on trust and strategic alliances.

Third, the framework we propose here to analyse Chinese OFDI can also be applied to other emerging countries with appropriate contextualisation. The examples of Russia and India illustrate this point. Although the two countries share some characteristics of an emerging country with China, they also show differences which have to be taken into account. The Russian economy, for example, is dominated by a tightly knit oligarchy-polity network with strong government influence in strategic industries such as oil and gas, minerals, banking, telecommunications and aviation. The existence of purely private and independent domestic companies in these sectors is therefore often questioned. The internationalisation of companies from these industries is therefore likely to be influenced by the objectives of, and negotiations within, the oligarchy-polity network (for example, Barnes, 2001; Guriev and Rachinsky, 2005; Kryshtanovskaya and White, 2005). By contrast, the Indian economic system is embedded in a democratic institutional environment and it has a society that is characterised by a caste system (Deshpande, 2000; Banjerjee and Somanathan, 2007). Large and diversified business groups such as Ranbaxy, Reliance, Tata and Wipro play a very important role in the Indian economy (for example, Ghemawat and Khanna, 1998; Khanna and Palepu, 1999; Kedia et al., 2006; Khanna and Yafeh, 2007). Greater understanding is needed of how such corporate governance structures influence the internationalisation of Indian firms. Social networks also prevail in both Russia and India, but as Michailova and Worm (2003) show, the personal relationship models in the cases of China and Russia exhibit significant differences and this needs to be accounted for when integrating the role of social and business networks into models of emerging country FDI.

Finally, and it follows from the above discussion, more research is needed to understand the nature of the interface between outward investing firms and home country institutions, how one influences and shapes the behaviour of the other, and whether or not variation in such interactions can be observed over, for example, time or geographic space or, in the case of state-owned Chinese MNEs, by controlling authority. In much of the account above, the assumption is made that interactions are mostly unidirectional (that is, from institution to firm). Yet it is likely that those emerging country firms with considerable political or economic influence (or both) may well be in a position to shape the nature of the institutional environment within which they operate (cf. regulatory capture) in ways which, arguably, the current application of institutional theory to the understanding of developing country OFDI takes insufficient account.

To conclude, this chapter shows that home country institutions can play an important role, and in some instances a critical role, in shaping and directing OFDI flows from an economy. This finding has consequences not only for firm- and country-level research on the phenomenon, as we have seen, but also for policy-making. Home country policy-makers have to assess the wider effects of their current and future policies on the international competitiveness of domestic firms. Besides liberalising the OFDI regime, policies and initiatives concerning, for example, education, science and technology programmes can advance the national innovation system of a country and, as such, they can indirectly contribute to the internationalisation of local firms by strengthening their firm-specific advantages, perhaps in a way that brings greater returns to the domestic economy than direct OFDI promotion schemes. Home country governments therefore need to carefully balance the benefits of OFDI liberalisation and the adoption of positive HCMs against the direct costs of implementing such measures and the opportunity cost of not investing in other aspects of national economic development (Buckley et al., 2009). Similarly, host country policy-makers need to have greater understanding of the institutional environment from which investing firms come. The level of institutional support and the constraints these firms experience can influence their long-term commitment to a host economy and their potential for contributing to the host economy in terms of, for example, the financial resources, linkages and spillover effects which they bring. It follows that not only the academic community but also the policy realm would benefit from a more holistic framework for understanding the institutional environment within which OFDI from emerging countries takes place.

NOTES

1. We are grateful for funding received from the Economics and Social Research Council (PTA-030-2005-00553) and the National Institute for Chinese Studies (NICS) in the White Rose East Asia Centre (WREAC) of the University of Leeds (UK) to conduct this research.
2. For industry studies see Huang (2002), Thun (2004) and Tian (2007) for the automobile sector and Sun (2005, 2007) for the steel sector.
3. China's foreign exchange reserves were valued at more than US$1,954 billion in March 2009 which, at the time of writing, was the largest in the world (Chinaview, 2009).
4. Five pillar industries were identified by the then State Planning Commission in 1994 as

follows: machine-building, electronics, automotive, petroleum and construction (Zhang and Taylor, 2001).
5. The acronyms stand for: ASEAN: Association of Southeast Asian Nations, EU: European Union, MERCUSOR: Southern Common Market (from the Spanish Mercado Común del Sur) and NAFTA: North American Free Trade Agreement.
6. As of January 2009, China has concluded free trade agreements with ASEAN (2007), Chile (2005), Hong Kong (2004), Macao (2004), Pakistan (2007), Peru (2008), New Zealand (2008), Singapore (2008), Senegal (2008) and Thailand (2003). China is also negotiating trade agreements with Australia, Costa Rica, the Gulf Cooperation Council, Iceland, India, Japan, the Southern African Customs Union, South Korea and Switzerland (http://www.bilaterals.org).
7. As of April 2009, the following RDAs in Britain have at least one office in China: International Business Wales (Beijing and Shanghai), Locate in Northern Ireland (Shanghai), One North East (Shanghai), Think London (Beijing), Scottish Development International (Beijing and Shanghai), Southeast England Development Agency (Shanghai), Southwest England (Shenzhen) and Yorkshire Forward (Hangzhou) (RDAs' home pages).

REFERENCES

Antkiewicz, A. and J. Whalley (2005), 'China's new regional trade agreements', *World Economy*, **28**(10), 1539–57.
Antkiewicz, A. and J. Whalley (2006), 'Recent Chinese buyout activity and the implications for global architecture', National Bureau of Economic Research (NBER) Working Paper 12072, NBER, Cambridge, MA.
Ayyagari, M., A. Demirgüç-Kunt and V. Maksimovic (2008), 'Formal versus informal finance: evidence from China', World Bank Policy Research Working Paper 4465, World Bank, Washington, DC.
Bandelj, N. (2002), 'Embedded economics: social relations as determinants of foreign direct investment in Central and Eastern Europe', *Social Forces*, **81**(2), 409–44.
Banjerjee, A. and R. Somanathan (2007), 'The political economy of public goods: some evidence from India', *Journal of Development Economics*, **82**, 287–314.
Barnes, A. (2001), 'Property, power, and the presidency: ownership policy reform and Russian executive–legislative relations, 1990–1999', *Communist and Post-Communist Studies*, **34**, 39–61.
BBC (2008), 'China to raise the price of fuel', 19 June, available at http://news.bbc.co.uk/2/hi/business/7464040.stm (accessed 14 April 2009).
Bevan, A., S. Estrin and K. Meyer (2004), 'Foreign investment location and institutional development in transition economies', *International Business Review*, **13**(1), 43–64.
Björkman, I. and S. Kock (1995), 'Social relationships and business networks: the case of Western companies in China', *International Business Review*, **4**(4), 519–35.
Bonaglia, F., A. Goldstein and J.A. Mathews (2007), 'Accelerated internationalization by emerging markets' multinationals: the case of the white goods sector', *Journal of World Business*, **42**(4), 369–83.
Brewer, T.L. (1993), 'Government policies, market imperfections, and foreign direct investment', *Journal of International Business Studies*, **24**(1), 101–20.

Buckley, P.J., L.J. Clegg and C. Wang (2002), 'The impacts of FDI on the performance of Chinese manufacturing firms', *Journal of International Business Studies*, **33**(4), 637–55.

Buckley, P.J., L.J. Clegg, A.R. Cross and H. Tan (2005), 'China's inward foreign direct investment success: Southeast Asia in the shadow of the dragon', *Multinational Business Review*, **13**(1), 3–31.

Buckley, P.J., L.J. Clegg, A.R. Cross, X. Liu, H. Voss and P. Zheng (2007), 'The determinants of Chinese outward foreign direct investment', *Journal of International Business Studies*, **38**(4), 499–518.

Buckley, P.J., L. Jeremy Clegg, Adam R. Cross, H. Voss, M. Rhodes and P. Zheng (2008a), 'Explaining China's outward FDI: an institutional perspective', in K. Sauvant (ed.), *The Rise of Transnational Corporations from Emerging Markets: Threat or Opportunity?*, Cheltenham, UK and Northampton, MA, USA: Edward Elgar Publishing, pp. 151–224.

Buckley, P.J., A.R. Cross, H. Tan, X. Liu and H. Voss (2008b), 'Historic and emergent trends in Chinese outward direct investment', *Management International Review*, **48**(6), 715–48.

Buckley, P.J., L. Jeremy Clegg, Adam R. Cross and H. Voss (2009), 'What can emerging countries learn from the outward direct investment policies of advanced countries?', in K. Sauvant, W.A. Maschek and G. McAllister (eds.), *Foreign Direct Investment from Emerging Markets: Its Challenges Ahead*, Cheltenham, UK and Northampton, MA, USA: Edward Elgar Publishing.

Cai, K.G. (1999), 'Outward foreign direct investment: a novel dimension of China's integration into the regional and global economy', *China Quarterly*, **160** (December), 856–80.

Chen, J. (2006), 'Implementing the strategy of Going Global to speed up the pace of foreign economic cooperation', in *China Commerce Yearbook*, Beijing: MOFCOM, pp. 406–8.

Child, J. and L. Yuan (1996), 'Institutional constraints on economic reform: the case of investment decisions in China', *Organization Science*, **7**(1), 60–77.

Chinamex (2009), http://www.chinamex.com.cn/english/news/01lm.jsp/p_id=3. html, Press Release (accessed 2 January 2009).

Chinaview (2009), China's foreign reserves hit $1.95 trillion at end of March, 11 April, available at http://news.xinhuanet.com/english/2009-04/11/content_11167852.htm (accessed 14 April 2009).

Cross, A.R., P.J. Buckley, L. Jeremy Clegg et al. (2007), 'An econometric investigation of Chinese outward direct investment', in J.H. Dunning and T.-M. Lin (eds), *Multinational Enterprises and Emerging Challenge of the 21st Century*, Cheltenham, UK and Northampton, MA, USA: Edward Elgar Publishing, pp. 55–85.

Cui, L. and F. Jiang (2009), 'FDI entry mode choice of Chinese firms: a strategic behavior perspective', *Journal of World Business*, **44**(4), 434–44.

Davies, R.B. (2004), 'Tax treaties and foreign direct investment: potential versus performance', *International Tax and Public Finance*, **11**(6), 775–802.

Deshpande, A. (2000), 'Does caste still define disparity? A look at inequality in Kerala, India', *AEA Papers and Proceedings*, **90**(2), 322–5.

Drabek, Z. and W. Payne (2002), 'The impact of transparency on foreign direct investment', *Journal of Economic Integration*, **17**(4), 777–810.

Dunning, J.H. (1992), 'The global economy, domestic governance, strategies and transnational corporations: interactions and policy implications', *Transnational Corporations*, **1**(3), 7–45.

Dunning, J.H. (1996), 'The geographical sources of competitiveness of firms: some results of a new survey', *Transnational Corporations*, **5**(3), 1–30.

Egger, P. and M. Pfaffermayer (2004), 'The impact of bilateral investment treaties on foreign direct investment', *Journal of Comparative Economics*, **32**(4), 788–804.

Enderwick, P. (2007), *Understanding Emerging Markets: China and India*, London: Routledge.

Fan, Y. (2002), 'Questioning guanxi: definition, classification and implications', *International Business Review*, **11**(5), 543–61.

Forney, M. (2005), 'China's going-out party', *Time*, available at http://www.time.com/time/magazine/article/0,9171,1018167,00.html (accessed 6 August 2008).

Freire, M. and J. Petersen (eds) (2004), *Subnational Capital Markets in Developing Countries: From Theory to Practice*, Washington, DC: World Bank.

Gao, P., J.R. Woetzel and Y. Wu (2003), 'Can Chinese brands make it abroad?', *McKinsey Quarterly*, Special edn, December, 3–13.

Gao, T. (2003), 'Ethnic Chinese networks and international investment: evidence from inward FDI in China', *Journal of Asian Economics*, **14**(4), 611–29.

Gastanaga, V.M., J.B. Nugent and B. Pashamova (1998), 'Host country reforms and FDI inflows: how much difference do they make?', *World Development*, **26**(7), 1299–314.

Ghemawat, P. and T. Khanna (1998), 'The nature of diversified business groups: a research design and two case studies', *Journal of Industrial Economics*, **46**(1), 35–61.

Globerman, S. and D.M. Shapiro (1999), 'The impact of government policies on foreign direct investment: the Canadian experience', *Journal of International Business Studies*, **30**(3), 513–32.

Guardian (2007), 'Chinese project may revive Wigan's cotton industry', Monday 28 May, available at http://www.guardian.co.uk/uk/2007/may/28/china.world (accessed 2 January 2009).

Guriev, S. and A. Rachinsky (2005), 'The role of oligarchs in Russian capitalism', *Journal of Economic Perspectives*, **19**(1), 131–50.

Hämäläinen, T.J. (2003), *National Competitiveness and Economic Growth: The Changing Determinants of Economic Performance in the World Economy*, Cheltenham, UK and Northampton, MA, USA: Edward Elgar Publishing.

Hayward, J.E.S. (ed.) (1995), *Industrial Enterprise and European Integration: From National to International Champions in Western Europe*, Oxford: Oxford University Press.

Heep, S. (2008), 'Chinas neuer Staatsfonds: Organisation, Finanzierung und Investitionsstrategie der China Investment Corporation', *Asien*, **108**, 51–66.

Henisz, W. and A. Swaminathan (2008), 'Institutions and international business', *Journal of International Business Studies*, **39**, 537–9.

Henley, J., C. Kirkpatrick and G. Wilde (1999), 'Foreign direct investment in China: recent trends and current policy issues', *World Economy*, **22**(2), 223–43.

Huang, Y. (2002), 'Between two coordination failures: automotive industrial policy in China with a comparison to Korea', *Review of International Political Economy*, **9**(3), 538–73.

Huawei (2004), *Annual Report 2004*, available at http://www.huawei.com (accessed 7 August 2008).

Hwang, K.-k. (1987), 'Face and favor: the Chinese power game', *American Journal of Sociology*, **92**(4), 944–74.

Inkpen, A.C. (2000), 'Learning through joint ventures: a framework of knowledge acquisition', *Journal of Management Studies*, **37**(7), 1019–43.

Jaumotte, F. (2004), 'Foreign direct investment and regional trade agreements: the market size effect revisited', IMF Working Paper WP/04/206, IMF, Washington, DC.

Johanson, J. and J.-E. Vahlne (1977), 'The internationalization process of the firm – a model of knowledge development and increasing foreign market commitments', *Journal of International Business*, **8**, 23–32.

Kedia, B.L., D. Mukherjee and S. Lahiri (2006), 'Indian business groups: evolution and transformation', *Asia Pacific Journal of Management*, **23**(4), 559–77.

Keister, L.A. (1998), 'Engineering growth: business group structure and firm performance in China's transition economy', *American Journal of Sociology*, **104**(2), 404–40.

Khanna, T. and K. Palepu (1999), 'Policy shocks, market intermediaries, and corporate strategy: the evolution of business groups in Chile and India', *Journal of Economics & Management Strategy*, **8**(2), 271–310.

Khanna, T. and Y. Yafeh (2007), 'Business groups in emerging markets: paragons or parasites?', *Journal of Economic Literature*, **XLV**, 331–72.

Khanna, T., R. Gulati and N. Nohria (1998), 'The dynamics of learning alliances', *Strategic Management Journal*, **19**, 193–210.

Kornai, J. (1986), 'The soft budget constrain', *Kyklos*, **39**, 1–30.

Kryshtanovskaya, O. and S. White (2005), 'The rise of the Russian business elite', *Communist and Post-Communist Studies*, **38**, 293–307.

Lall, S. (1982), 'The emergence of Third World transnationals: Indian joint ventures overseas', *World Development*, **10**(2), 127–46.

Lau, J. and M. Dickie (2008), 'China Telecom in $16bn Unicom deal', *Financial Times*, 3 June.

Lecraw, D.J. (1977), 'Direct investment by firms from less developed countries', *Oxford Economic Papers*, **29**(3), 442–57.

Levine, R. (1999), 'Financial development and economic growth: views and agenda, World Bank Policy Research Working Paper No. 1678, World Bank, Washington DC.

Li, S., S.H. Park and S. Li (2004), 'The great leap forward: the transition from relation-based governance to rule-based governance', *Organizational Dynamics*, **33**(1), 63–78.

Lipsey, R.E. (2002), 'Home and host country effects of FDI', National Bureau of Economic Research (NBER) Working Papers 9293, NBER, Cambridge, Massachusetts.

Liu, H. and K. Li (2002), 'Strategic implications of emerging Chinese multinationals: the Haier case study', *European Management Journal*, **20**(6), 699–706.

Liu, X. and C. Wang (2003), 'Does foreign direct investment facilitate technological progress? Evidence from Chinese industries', *Research Policy*, **32**(6), 945–53.

Liu, X., T. Buck and C. Shu (2005), 'Chinese economic development, the next stage: outward FDI?', *International Business Review*, **14**(1), 97–115.

Loree, D.W. and S.E. Guisinger (1995), 'Policy and non-policy determinants of US equity foreign direct investment', *Journal of International Business Studies*, **26**(2), 281–99.

Lu, D. (2000), 'Industrial policy and resource allocation: implications on China's participation in globalization', *China Economic Review*, **11**, 342–60.

Luo, Y. (2000), *Multinational Corporations in China: Benefiting from Structural Transformation*, Copenhagen: Copenhagen Business School Press.

Ma, X. and J.W. Lu (2005), 'The critical role of business groups in China', *Ivey Business Journal*, **69**(5), 1–12.

Makino, S., T. Isobe and C.M. Isobe (2004), 'Does country matter?', *Strategic Management Journal*, **25**, 1027–43.

Meyer, K. (2004), 'Perspectives on multinational enterprises in emerging economies', *Journal of International Business Studies*, **35**(4), 259–76.

Meyer, K. and H.V. Nguyen (2005), 'Foreign investment strategies and subnational institutions in emerging markets: evidence from Vietnam', *Journal of Management Studies*, **42**(1), 63–93.

Michailova, S. and V. Worm (2003), 'Personal networking in Russia and China: blat and guanxi', *European Management Journal*, **21**(4), 509–19.

MOFCOM and NDRC (2007), *Catalogue for the Guidance of Foreign Investment Industries (Amended in 2007)*, Decree of the State Development and Reform Commission, the Ministry of Commerce of the People's Republic of China, No. 57, 31 October, 2007 available at http://www.fdi.gov.cn/pub/FDI_EN/Laws/law_en_info.jsp?docid=87372 (accessed 28 January 2009).

Murtha, T.P. and S.A. Lenway (1994), 'Country capabilities and the strategic state: how national political institutions affect multinational corporations' strategies', *Strategic Management Journal*, **15**, 113–29.

Ng, L.F.Y. and C. Tuan (2001), 'FDI promotion policy in China: governance and effectiveness', *World Economy*, **24**(8), 1051–74.

Ng, L. F.Y. and C. Tuan (2002), 'Building a favourable investment environment: evidence for the facilitation of FDI in China', *World Economy*, **25**(8), 1095–114.

Nolan, P. and J. Zhang (2002), 'The challenge of globalization for large Chinese firms', *World Development*, **30**(12), 2089–107.

North, D.C. (1990), *Institutions, Institutional Change and Economic Performance*, Cambridge: Cambridge University Press.

NWDA (Northwest Regional Development Agency) (2008), 'China town! Wigan to become largest textile centre in Europe', available at http://www.nwda.co.uk/news--events/press-releases/200801/china-town.aspx (accessed 2 January 2009).

Oliver, C. (1997), 'Sustainable competitive advantage: combining institutional and resource-based views', *Strategic Management Journal*, **18**(9), 697–713.

Pack, H. and K. Saggi (1997), 'Inflows of foreign technology and indigenous technological development', *Review of Development Economics*, **1**(1), 81–98.

Park, S.H. and Y. Luo (2001), 'Guanxi and organizational dynamics: organizational networking in Chinese firms', *Strategic Management Journal*, **22**(5), 455–77.

Peng, M.W. (2003), 'Institutional transitions and strategic choices', *Academy of Management Review*, **28**(2), 275–96.

Ramamurti, R. (2001), 'The obsolescing "bargaining model?" MNC-host developing country relations revisited', *Journal of International Business Studies*, **32**(1), 23–39.

Rivoli, P. and E. Salorio (1996), 'Foreign direct investment and investment under uncertainty', *Journal of International Business Studies*, **27**(2), 335–57.

Rugman, A.M. and J. Li (2007), 'Will China's multinationals succeed globally or regionally?', *European Management Journal*, **25**(5), 333–43.

Rui, H. and G.S. Yip (2008), 'Foreign acquisitions by Chinese firms: a strategic intent perspective', *Journal of World Business*, **43**(2), 213–26.

Russell, A. (2008), 'Mauritius offers Asia gateway into Africa', *Financial Times*, 6 March.

Sauvant, K. (2005), 'New sources of FDI: the BRICs. Outward FDI from Brazil, Russia, India and China', *Journal of World Investment and Trade*, **6**, 639–709.

Saxenian, A. (2002), 'Transnational communities and the evolution of global production networks: the cases of Taiwan, China and India', *Industry and Innovation*, **9**(3), 183–202.

Sethi, D., S. Guisinger, D.L. Ford Jr and S.E. Phelan (2002), 'Seeking greener pastures: a theoretical and empirical investigation into the changing trend of foreign direct investment flows in response to institutional and strategic factors', *International Business Review*, **11**(6), 685–705.

Sigurdson, J. (2005), *Technological Superpower China*, Cheltenham, UK and Northampton, MA, USA: Edward Elgar Publishing.

Sornarajah, M. (2004), *The International Law on Foreign Investment*, 2nd revised edn, Cambridge: Cambridge University Press.

Standifird, S.S. (2006), 'Using guanxi to establish corporate reputation in China', *Corporate Reputation Review*, **9**(3), 171–8.

Sun, P. (2005), 'Industrial policy, corporate governance, and the competitiveness of China's national champions: the case of Shanghai Baosteel Group', *Journal of Chinese Economic and Business Studies*, **3**(2), 173–92.

Sun, P. (2007), 'Is the state-led industrial restructuring effective in transition China? Evidence from the steel sector', *Cambridge Journal of Economics*, **31**(4), 601–24.

Taylor, C.T. (2000), 'The impact of host country government policy on US multinational investment decisions', *World Economy*, **23**, 635–47.

Teagarden, M.B. and D.H. Cai (2009), 'Learning from Dragons who are learning from us: developmental lessons from China's global companies', *Organizational Dynamics*, **38**(1), 73–81.

Teng, B.S. (2004), 'The WTO and entry modes in China', *Thunderbird International Business Review*, **46**(4), 381–400.

Thun, E. (2004), 'Industrial policy, Chinese-style: FDI, regulation, and dreams of national champions in the auto sector', *Journal of East Asian Studies*, **4**(3), 453–89.

Tian, L. (2007), 'Does government intervention help the Chinese automobile industry? A comparison with the Chinese computer industry', *Economic Systems*, **31**(4), 364–74.

Tsang, E.W.K. and P.S.L. Yip (2007), 'Economic distance and the survival of foreign direct investments', *Academy of Management Journal*, **50**(5), 1156–68.

UNCTAD (2001), *Home Country Measures*, IIA Issues Paper Series, UNCTAD/ITE/IIT/24, New York and Geneva: United Nations.

UNCTAD (2004), *International Investment Agreements: Key Issues, Volume I*, New York and Geneva: United Nations.

UNCTAD (2005), *South-South Cooperation in International Investment Arrangements*, New York and Geneva: United Nations.

UNCTAD (2006), *World Investment Report 2006 – FDI from Developing and Transition Economies: Implications for Development*, New York and Geneva: United Nations.

Vandevelde, K.J. (1998), 'The political economy of a bilateral investment treaty', *American Journal of International Law*, **92**(4), 621–41.

Wang, H. (2000), 'Informal institutions and foreign investment in China', *Pacific Review*, **13**(4), 525–56.

Wang, H. (2001), 'Implementing vigorously the opening strategy of "going global"', in *Almanac of China's Foreign Economic Relations and Trade 2001*, Beijing: MOFCOM, pp. 94–5.

Wang, J. (2004), 'China's regional trade agreements: the law, geopolitics, and impact on the multilateral trading system', *Singapore Yearbook of International Law*, **8**, 119–47.

Welch, L.S. and R. Luostarinen (1993), 'Inward-outward connections in internationalization', *Journal of International Marketing*, **1**(1), 44–56.

Wells, L.T. (1983), *Third World Multinationals: The Rise of Foreign Investment from Developing Countries*, Cambridge, MA: MIT Press.

World Bank (2008), *China Quarterly Update December 2008*, available at http://siteresources.worldbank.org/INTCHINA/Resources/Quarterly_December_2008.pdf (accessed 14 April 2009).

WTO (2009), Statistics Database, available at http://stat.wto.org/Home/WSDBHome.aspx?Language=E (accessed 6 April 2009).

Xiao, J. and F. Sun (2005), 'The challenges facing outbound Chinese M&A', *International Financial Law Review*, **24**(12), 44–6.

Yeung, H.W.-C. (2006), 'The dynamics of Southeast Asian Chinese business', in H.W.-C. Yeung (ed.), *Handbook of Research on Asian Business*, Cheltenham, UK and Northampton, MA, USA: Edward Elgar Publishing, pp. 356–80.

Yeung, H.W.-C. and K. Olds (eds) (2000), *Globalization of Chinese Business Firms*, London: Macmillan.

Yiu, D., G.D. Bruton and Y. Lu (2005), 'Understanding business group performance in an emerging economy: acquiring resources and capabilities in order to prosper', *Journal of Management Studies*, **42**(1), 183–206.

Zeng, M. and Williamson, P.J. (2003), 'The hidden Dragons', *Harvard Business Review*, **81**(10), 92–9.

Zhang, K.H. (2001), 'What attracts multinational corporations to China?', *Contemporary Economic Policy*, **19**(3), 336–46.

Zhang, W. and R. Taylor (2001), 'EU technology transfer to China: the automotive industry as a case study', *Journal of the Asia Pacific Economy*, **6**(2), 261–74.

Zhang, Y. (2007), *Large Chinese State-owned Enterprises: Corporatisation and Strategic Development*, Basingstoke: Palgrave Macmillan.

Zhao, Z.Y. and L.Y. Shen (2008), 'Are Chinese contractors competitive in international markets?', *Construction Management and Economics*, **26**(3), 225–36.

8. The political economy of infrastructure multinationals: the case of Chinese investment in Africa

Yuxuan Tang and Robert Pearce

INTRODUCTION

In this exploratory chapter we seek to investigate the nature and interaction of two of the most important and enigmatic new forces in international business; the growing role of multinational enterprises (MNEs) in the creation of infrastructure in developing countries and the emergence of MNEs from China. Both of these new types of MNE have been defined within, and are responsive to, important trends in the development of the global economy. In the case of infrastructure the rise of MNEs reflects the widespread privatisation of its creation and provision, but with the position of the sector nevertheless still determined within government-defined development programmes. Though emergence of Chinese MNEs would not be surprising given the growth and opening of the economy, the speed and form of their arrival may, in fact, reflect more specific needs of Chinese development as perceived through government policy. Similarly, the ability of Chinese MNEs to establish international operations may derive institutionally from the wider competitiveness of their home economy; for example, in the form of preferred access to cheap capital.

Here we seek to draw out important aspects of these two phenomena through an investigation of a major context for their interaction; the involvement of Chinese firms in generation of infrastructure capacity in Africa. This context, as indicated above, places the issues raised by participation of Chinese infrastructure MNEs (IMNEs) in Africa beyond the normal concerns of international business, by invoking both the wider needs of economic development in Africa and of Chinese MNEs as players in building the cores of sustainability in China's growth. The manifest interdependencies between the institutional bases for the two sources of competitive dynamism (African and Chinese development) into which these MNEs are projected ultimately provoke issues of political economy.

Both the broad definition of infrastructure and the precise delineation of its component subsectors remain the subject of persistent debate. To a considerable degree such imprecision may be innate to the very nature of infrastructure and its provision, positioned as they would be at the centre of the dynamic processes of development and growth. One facet of this is, as so often, the role of technological change, which is likely to both reformulate the extent and content of the need for infrastructure services and also alter the ways in which these can be supplied. The latter may increase the scope for 'unbundling' of supply and, through this, provide increased potential for marketisation and privatisation of some elements of infrastructure. This has become notably visible in the telecommunications subsector, for example. The understanding of infrastructure, notably in terms of its ownership and market orientation, has also been considerably affected by the wider changes in political and economic structures (nationally and globally) in recent decades. This then allows for the formulation of private infrastructure enterprises and for the international expansion of their operations as foreign direct investment (FDI) and IMNEs.

Within this uncertain territory UNCTAD (2008, p. 87) provides a useful working definition of infrastructure as comprising 'the physical facilities, institutions and organisational structures, or the social and economic foundations, for the operation of a society'. This is useful for our purposes here by encompassing not only the nature of infrastructure but also emphasising its positioning as facilitating the functioning of society in its widest sense. In the processes of development infrastructure improvement is needed both to meet increased consumer demand for particular services and also to build endogenous capacities into the growth process itself. Thus UNCTAD (2008, p. 87) focuses on 'economic' infrastructure which 'directly supports production activities of enterprises at various points of the value chain' and 'underpins the functioning of other economic activities, and is hence directly relevant to the competitiveness of firms and to economic development'. The political economic implications of how infrastructure is developed and its services supplied, therefore, reflect both the efficiency and distribution of important aspects of social welfare provision at a point in time and how the capacity is being put into place to build these into successful and sustainable economic development.

It follows from the previous discussion that improved infrastructure provision is inherently endogenous to achievement of economic growth, whatever the initial level of development of an economy. Nevertheless it will be most decisively crucial for countries which are at early stages of development and targeting the initiation of an industrial sector or the realisation of particular sources of potential comparative advantage (for example, in resource-based sectors). For such countries the challenge is the creation of new infrastructure capacity, in both sufficient magnitude and appropriate forms. The rise of IMNEs can be seen to have the potential to help with both quantitative (financial) and qualitative (appropriate project formulation and implementation) concerns. In the next section we will attempt to formulate a view of the IMNE in terms, mainly, of its ability to address the qualitative issues of infrastructure creation and supply within national development programmes. Part of what these MNEs do, as with all such enterprises, is raise capital, so that they are also relevant to issues of funding of infrastructure. This is also vital as countries at early stages of implementing development programmes face an inevitable financing gap for infrastructure creation.

Though attempts to estimate infrastructure funding gaps vary according to source of calculation,[1] and are in any case inevitably open to wide degrees of uncertainty, UNCTAD's (2008, pp. 92–4) overview demonstrates very clearly that large shortfalls are likely to be endemic for developing countries and regions. Thus a World Bank estimate is quoted to suggest that overall developing countries would need to invest 7 per cent to 9 per cent of gross domestic product (GDP) annually on infrastructure creation and maintenance in order to achieve the rates of economic growth needed to secure the levels of poverty reduction and welfare improvements targeted in the Millennium Development Goals. Actual achieved levels were then estimated as only reaching 3 per cent to 4 per cent of GDP. Indicative figures, particularly relevant to this chapter, are provided (UNCTAD, 2008, table 111.3) for the infrastructure investment needs of sub-Saharan Africa from 2006–15. Overall annual average needs were projected[2] as totalling $40.1 billion; $22.8 billion for new investment and $17.2 billon for operation and maintenance.[3] But plausible funding only totalled $16.5billon, leaving a financing gap of $22.5 billion or 59 per cent of that needed.[4]

This points to China's ability and willingness to provide capital as being at the centre of the participation of Chinese IMNEs in growth of infrastructure provision in Africa. This is, however, only a leading impulsion within a wider nexus of needs, motivations and agents. Ultimately we can see the role of Chinese IMNEs as being major vehicles operationalising precise synergies and interdependencies between the developmental needs and capacities of Africa and China. A central issue emerging in the sustainability of China's growth and international competitiveness is that the focus of this on the manufacturing sector has generated demand for many natural resources and primary product inputs that exceed the scope of domestic supply. A number of positive aspects of this Chinese growth are, however, also relevant here. As already indicated the generation of a surplus of reinvestable capital, alongside a build-up of foreign exchange reserves, is central. Securing the growth already achieved has also led to familiarity with the need for, and thus competitiveness in creating, infrastructure. It has therefore helped to generate an efficient construction sector that is familiar with a positioning in infrastructure creation. In a similar fashion competitive and ambitious firms have emerged in China in other industries that can overlap with infrastructure provision, notably telecommunications.

In Africa we have already observed the crucial existence of infrastructure limitations as a constraint on growth, along with the related infrastructure funding gap. As hinted above two aspects of this constraint, the shortage of capital and the lack of domestic competence in infrastructure creation, could be alleviated through access to Chinese capital and expertise. A precise form of the infrastructure limitations then becomes significantly relevant here; the way in which infrastructure bottlenecks constrains Africa's ability to build development and competitiveness around its extensive and varied resource-supply strengths. Alleviation of these bottlenecks can then provide a point of mutual benefits for Africa and China, with Chinese finance and expertise allowing Africa to realise its resource-supply potentials in ways that very precisely feed back into China's own developmental needs.

The complementarities between the realisation of Africa's resource potentials and the creation of effective infrastructure there thus emerge as vital to the developmental progress of both Africa and China. These interdependencies, therefore, play a role in both Chinese government policy towards Africa and its FDI there. This then draws in the last major player in this network of interdependencies and synergies; the emergence and commitment to Africa of Chinese resource-seeking MNEs. Though these resource MNEs may be either state-owned or private there is no doubt that their commercial viability is positioned within and responsive to the twin needs of African and Chinese development. In many cases the strong innate interdependence between Chinese IMNEs and resource MNEs may be intuitive, or arms-length, in the sense that IMNEs' role in an infrastructure creation programme may help improve a host-location's capacity to support development of its resource potentials in which resource-seeking MNEs then find a viable position. In other cases, however, the two types of Chinese MNEs may be drawn into a specific project, so that the synergistic benefits they can provide are perceived and planned a priori (see Foster et al., 2008, table 10, p. 38, for example).

The strategic synergies inherent in infrastructure creation and the development of primary resource potentials, within the overarching context of Chinese policy and ability to leverage capital availability, have been incorporated in the deal package known as the 'Angola Mode' (Foster et al., 2008, pp. 42–4; Kaplinsky and Morris, 2009) or 'resources for infrastructure'. The central player in facilitating and coordinating the Angola Mode deal structure is the China Export-Import Bank. Here an African government signs a framework agreement for a programme of infrastructure creation and resource development involving two Chinese companies. Firstly, a Chinese infrastructure firm (either state-owned or private) is contracted by the host government to undertake particular infrastructure projects, with loan financing for this provided by the Ex-Im Bank. Secondly, the African government awards to a Chinese resource-sector MNE the rights to develop natural resource opportunities in the country. The circle is then completed when the resource company repays, in kind, the infrastructure loan to the Ex-Im Bank. In this way the operations of the resource MNE becomes a guaranteed source of scarce inputs into China's industrial development. The African country, with perhaps very limited financial credit worthiness, is enabled to secure the development of its resource-based growth potentials along with the creation of infrastructure, which may have spillovers into the economy beyond merely facilitating the associated resource sectors.

CONCEPTUALISING THE INFRASTRUCTURE MULTINATIONAL ENTERPRISE (IMNE)

The increasing visibility of the internationalisation of infrastructure provision, as a subject of systematic analysis and debate, can be attributed to two sources. Firstly, at the macro level, in terms of significant increases in the extent of reported flows of FDI in infrastructure sectors. This can be observed both as increases in the proportion of total FDI flows that the sector accounts for, and the growing share of infrastructure creation and provision that is provided by foreign enterprises in many countries. Secondly, at the level of specific high-profile cases and contexts, such as Chinese participation in infrastructure creation in Africa addressed here. Resistance to privatisation of infrastructure supply, whether at an ideological level or by particular directly affected consumer groups, is often articulated most strongly towards potential foreign ownership. Also notable trends within the wider phenomenon of infrastructure FDI have often attracted speculative contention with, again, Chinese FDI in Africa providing a clear example. It is argued here that in order to address the twin issues of how and why infrastructure FDI has emerged, and what its implications are in terms of achieving a sponsoring government's aims in the creation of infrastructure supply capacity, it is necessary to investigate the nature of the international firms that do it; that is, IMNEs. Such an investigation is facilitated by the adoption and, as necessary, adaptation of analytical frameworks that have already been operationalised effectively in the manufacturing and services sectors.

The creation or expansion of infrastructure supply capacity, especially in very poor countries at the early stages of an articulated development process, can be seen to play two roles, each of which is likely to challenge the normal parameters of private enterprise decision making. Firstly, it is likely to supply direct services to consumers, thus comprising an important facet of what successful development is expected to provide to a population. The social benefits of such improvements to individual welfare, and their potential to provide immediate positive feedbacks into the development process itself, suggests that the pricing of such infrastructure services might not be best left to the market and private enterprise suppliers. Secondly, important elements of infrastructure expansion are intended to provide inputs and spillovers supportive of other value-adding parts of the economy. Thus infrastructure and its enhancement is an inherent part of the process of building for sustainable and self-reinforcing development. But this aspect of infrastructure performance is manifest in externalities that will be realised over long periods of time. How host government planners and potential private infrastructure providers predict and value these outcomes, and determine the firm's reward structures and conditions of operation, are again beyond the scope of normal investment decision processes.

At the centre of this analysis we can place an infrastructure project (IP). Even where it derives from privatisation of an existing source of infrastructure service supply we can consider, as central to an IP, the pursuit of the enhancement of provision in terms of quantity and/or quality. Whatever the ultimate arrangement to secure its implementation an IP will be legitimated through the authorisation of a host-country government or agency, for whom it would be expected to target broadly defined developmental or welfare objectives.

A significant benefit of a coherent commitment to infrastructure creation, and potentially of the participation of IMNEs in it, is likely to be an improved capacity to attract FDI into those wider sectors of the economy that represent feasible sources of development and international competitiveness. Where infrastructure programmes are structured to support realisation of distinctive localised competitive resources (latent sources of comparative advantage) it may often be the case that the most complete fulfilment of these productive potentials may be through participation of established MNEs in the relevant sectors. But for such MNEs to be convinced that a country does represent a significant and viable new source of competitive activity (whether through market-seeking (MS) supply to the local economy or as efficiency-seeking (ES) production for international markets) appropriate forms of supporting infrastructure need to be perceived as central to the host economy's projected development programmes.

Confidence in this regard may be considerably enhanced by the participation of IMNEs in the planning, building and initial operation of those facets of infrastructure on which other foreign investors expect to depend. An important element of this would be expected to derive from the view that where experienced international investors are prepared to commit significant resources to long-term infrastructure programmes, with major sunk costs, it indicates a high level of trust in both the host government's acceptance of private business and its ability to generate sustained economic growth. Such an apparent endorsement by IMNEs should encourage the normally rather smaller and more flexible MNEs of other sectors to also commit to the economy's emerging competitive potentials. Similarly, the co-option of IMNEs by the sponsoring host government can again be seen, by other potential MNE investors, as indicative of the belief that such enterprises' participation will secure the most effective creation of the new infrastructure, in terms of its capacity to support the realisation of the wider-ranging developmental potentials.

The emergence of privatised infrastructure sectors in developing countries can be seen to derive from two possible sources. Firstly, as most frequently predicated as a focus of political-economy debate, through the passing into private ownership and control of previously state-owned infrastructure enterprises. Secondly, through the privately funded and privately organised expansion of infrastructure capacity through new projects that are articulated to address specific aspects of government-perceived developmental targets. For analytical purposes here, in terms of deriving contexts amenable to particular contributions of IMNEs, we can suggest that both origins for privatised infrastructure operations can ultimately be seen as providing the basis of a discrete, development-oriented infrastructure project. Though privatisation of existing state-owned infrastructure firms was often initially projected to reflect ideological motives or a short-term need for capital, a desire to expand and reposition supply of the relevant service was usually also present.[5] Thus our emphasis here is on the capability of IMNEs to implement IPs, whether this constitutes significant regeneration and repositioning of antecedent state-owned enterprises, or the creation of completely new enterprise and capacity.[6]

Therefore at the centre of the decision process of an IMNE we place, almost by definition, an IP. This immediately indicates a key difference with the decisions of MNEs in the manufacturing and service sectors.

Thus in the latter sectors an MNE would normally formulate its own investment project, reflecting its perception of the potential for a country's location advantages (LAs) to support one of its range of strategic objectives (resource seeking; market seeking; efficiency seeking; knowledge seeking) and of the capacity of its existing sources of competitiveness (ownership advantages – OAs) to access and operationalise these factors effectively. In the infrastructure sector the broad parameters of an IP will normally be defined by a host-government ministry or agency, in pursuit of a range of social and developmental objectives that are not inherently amenable to the relatively short-term performance and profitability optimisation of private enterprise. Where there is a realistic acceptance by planners that private, in fact probably foreign private, technologies, skills and practices will be needed to secure successful implementation of the IP it is also likely to be accepted that its details, at least, will need to be bargained with putative IMNE participants, who will have access to these competences and the ability to package them effectively. The extent to which such a bargaining process is able to secure acceptable terms for the effective implementation of the IP in terms of its originally perceived aims, or whether some reformulation of these aims needs to be conceded to an IMNE, is an important facet of assessing the internationalisation of infrastructure creation.

Before substantive bargaining over the terms and detailed structure of an IP an IMNE is likely to assess it in terms of more conventional LAs. Thus the likely initial level, and the potential growth, of demand for the services of the IP would remain a plausible determinant of interest. Within this the extent to which the benefits that an IP provides to the host economy can be marketised in a form that can be appropriated by the IMNE is likely to be crucial and, often, contentious. On the supply side the ability of the host economy to provide adequate access to inputs that an IMNE will need to construct and operate the IP efficiently is also likely to be a significant decision determinant. Potentially relevant here would be the extent to which the IMNE would be permitted to utilise imported inputs in formulating the IP.

A potentially very significant factor in how an IMNE assesses a particular IP is the form in which it is intended to be structured contractually. This is most likely to affect the way in which the IMNE evaluates its scope for appropriating returns from the project, but can also impinge on its expectations for securing its most effective implementation in terms of both creation and operationalisation.

It is useful to see foreign enterprise involvement with infrastructure generation as being implemented through two tiers of IMNE, providing different types of input into IPs' formulation and operationalisation.

Firstly, following Foreign Investment Advisory Service (FIAS) terminology (Donaldson et al., 1997), we can distinguish 'sponsors' ($IMNE_{sp}$), who undertake the negotiations with host-country governments concerning the basic terms under which the IP will be created and then participate, to varying degrees, in formalising strategic details of its aims and structure. From this position at the core of an IP the $IMNE_{sp}$ will derive the responsibility for bringing together the resources and expertise needed to create and (at least initially) run it. This points towards a second tier role in the IP for subcontracted MNEs ($IMNE_{su}$), who will bring specialised capabilities to, in particular, the stages of building the physical supply capacity of the project.

Of course, where an IP is very wide-ranging and complex in its aims, technologies and processes, a consortium may need more than one $IMNE_{sp}$, as well as a varied multiplicity of $IMNE_{su}$. Different $IMNE_{sp}$ may bring different dimensions of existing political association (both in terms of home country and host country) and established connections with different subsets of $IMNE_{su}$.

From the beginning of the analysis it has been almost axiomatic that the privatisation and internationalisation of infrastructure creation in poorer countries has been significantly driven by the need to access new sources of capital. That this is achieved through foreign direct investment, rather than from portfolio sources, suggests that the OAs of IMNEs are built around the need and ability to raise capital competitively. However, the ability of a particular $IMNE_{sp}$ to raise capital to support its participation in a specific IP will reflect distinct firm-level skills and capacities. Thus $IMNE_{sp}$ need to possess particular firm-specific and sector-specific competences that they can leverage to raise project-specific capital. This can involve the ability to clearly articulate and persuasively project (i) the viable rewards (risk/return) of the IP to investors and (ii) its own distinctive firm-level capacity to secure them; in terms of the organisational competences likely to be needed to develop, operationalise and run the IP.

The type of OAs that are central to a successful $IMNE_{sp}$ would then focus on (i) skill in bargaining with the host-country government or agency commissioning the IP and (ii) ability to evaluate and access sources of more conventional types of OAs that are needed to build and operationalise an IP effectively. Alongside potential intra-group sources this places a high priority on locating appropriate $IMNE_{su}$ and building their inputs into a coherent realisation of the IP.

Here OAs directly related to operationalisation of an IP, including those that may be most effectively secured through $IMNE_{su}$ include (i) technologies, (ii) effective familiar engineering and construction practices and (iii) an ability to implement effective markets for infrastructure services where none had previously operated.

The defining attractiveness of an IP, taken over a long but often finite time period (for example, in the case of Build Operate Transfer (BOT) projects) is its projected profitability to the potential IMNE (and its nexus of shareholders and stakeholders). A first, more direct, dimension of how an $IMNE_{sp}$ evaluates an IP will consider aspects of quite conventional LAs and reflect variants of familiar MNE strategic motivations, including (i) the likely demand for its services, reflecting a MS motivation and (ii) the availability of the inputs (including the current state of infrastructure) that will allow the IP to be created and operated effectively, reflecting an ES concern.

However, the extent to which an $IMNE_{sp}$ can develop its commitment to, or evaluate its returns from, an IP in terms of unconstrained MS or ES calculations of normal LAs (that is, as familiar from manufacturing or services sectors) may be compromised by the IP's context. Thus often an IP for which an $IMNE_{sp}$ may tender/bargain may be one component of its host-country's more widely defined development programme, with aspects of its perceived aims represented in externalities/synergies with other parts of the programme. Reflecting this, the social benefits to host-country development, as understood by government planners, may not be fully appropriable in the private rewards offered to IMNEs. The much discussed issue of prices/tariffs for infrastructure services is a prominent manifestation of this (which is likely to take an extra dimension of contention where the services derive from an IMNE).

A potentially important aspect of IMNE host-government tension may be the extent to which an IMNE is allowed to define the specific details of an IP, or to impose changes to the original dimensions of an IP as proposed by a host agency. This would, to some degree, allow an $IMNE_{sp}$ to define aspects of the LAs which its own operations would respond to and activate. In this, however, an $IMNE_{sp}$ may provide an ability to define the specifics of an IP to established levels of international capability in a way that might, indeed, elude local planners. This knowledge of received practice of $IMNE_{sp}$ (or indeed associated $IMNE_{su}$) may be a genuine benefit of their participation (a distinctive OA that adds value to the IP). But host governments may nevertheless have legitimate viable concerns that allowing too much IMNE influence at this stage of project articulation may permit opportunistic behaviour that can compromise the social-developmental contribution of the IP in terms of its wider contexts.

A second dimension of LAs that has a pervasive position in the early literature on IMNEs is the extent to which they will perceive a country's

broader institutional environment as conducive to private and foreign participants as being able to securely realise the performance they expect and
require from a specific IP. As expressed in a FIAS report (Sader, 2000) this
'requires detailed preparation by putting in place an effective institutional
legal regulatory framework, supported by strong political commitment to
sectoral reform and liberalisation'.

The context (defined around analysis of OAs and LAs) in which we have
seen an $IMNE_{sp}$ as operating is, therefore, a very complex and multipar-
tied one. This suggests that an understanding of how such an IP is effectively developed by an $IMNE_{sp}$ would need to incorporate a multitude of
contractual agreements and bargaining situations. This, in turn, indicates
a vital role for transactions cost and internalisation analysis in fully understanding and evaluating IMNEs.

Two elements of this have already been indicated and may be drawn out
here: (i) the $IMNE_{sp}$ will bargain in depth with the host-country government or agency to define the nature of the project, and its expected contribution and rewards. Where this proves difficult (high transaction costs) it
may lead to either the IMNE abandoning the project or going ahead in a
satisficing form that it sees as less than optimal. (ii) The terms of participation of $IMNE_{su}$ needs to be bargained and contracted. Again trying to
lower the transaction costs of this may compromise the achievement of an
ideally configured IP.

In addition to the upfront MS and ES elements of developing its commitment to projects there is an, at least intuitive, knowledge-seeking (KS)
component to IMNEs' (both sponsors and subcontractors) behaviour.
Thus each new IP undertaken by an IMNE is likely to be an entry into
a differentiated and complex situation, representing (i) very distinctive
opportunities and contexts, essentially articulated externally by the host
government and, (ii) a different configuration of consortium partners
($IMNE_{su}$) – some familiar, some new.

So each new project/consortium/context represents a strong learning opportunity, so that there is an innate KS dimension within their
expansion. This, in turn, suggests that more successful IMNEs will
be augmenting their internal sources of competitiveness (OAs) most
quickly. That, then, raises issues of future global industry structure, with
a potential for increased concentration and the emergence of clearly
dominant players.

Ultimately the generation of the modes of analysis and articulation of
issues suggested here should allow us to address a key normative concern.
This would be to discern the extent and ways in which the realisation of
an IP's developmental potentials are enhanced, or compromised, by being
executed by an IMNE.

THE ROLE OF FDI IN AFRICAN INFRASTRUCTURE CREATION

In this section we use data compiled by the United Nations Conference on Trade and Development (UNCTAD, 2008) to draw out aspects of FDI in the creation of infrastructure in Africa, comparing this with similar commitments in Asia and Latin America. Table 8.1 shows the share of infrastructure in the growth of overall global FDI stocks from 1990 to 2006. Though the inter-year comparisons need to be treated with some degree of caution, due to variations in country coverage, important indicative trends clearly emerge. Certainly the status of infrastructure as a major emergent sector for FDI is confirmed, with inward (IFDI) stocks growing at well-above average rates during periods which saw massive expansion of FDI activity globally. Thus IFDI stocks, as a share of all FDI, rose from 1.3 per cent in 1990 to 9.0 per cent in 2000 (that is approximately seven-fold) before falling back marginally to 8.3 per cent in 2006.

Though IFDI into (in fact mainly between) developed economies represented the strongest element in its overall growth, the sector also asserted a notably stronger position in total FDI in developing economies. In Africa the growth in relative status of IFDI matched the global pattern, being around seven times higher (9.3 per cent) in 2000 than in 1990 (1.3 per cent) and achieving some further growth (to 10.4 per cent) to 2006. These growth rates meant that the share of IFDI in Africa became significantly greater than in Asia, though not matching the persisting very notable shares in Latin America.

The growth in FDI into infrastructure creation in developing countries in recent decades (Table 8.1) means that it has also asserted a

Table 8.1   Share of infrastructure in total inward FDI stocks, 1990–2006, by host region

	% share			
	1990	1995	2000	2006
World	1.3	3.4	9.0	8.4
Developed countries	1.5	2.5	9.0	8.3
Developing countries	3.8	6.0	8.8	8.9
Africa	1.3	6.0	9.3	10.4
Latin America and Caribbean	7.4	11.8	23.7	20.1
Asia and Oceania	1.4	3.9	4.4	6.0

Source: UNCTAD *World Investment Report 2008*, Annex table A.111.1.

Table 8.2	*Share of foreign and domestic sources in the investment commitments of infrastructure industries of developing economies, 1996–2006, by industry and host region*

Regional Infrastructure sector	Source of commitment (%)			
	A	B	C	Total
All developing countries[a]				
Energy	30.0	21.4	48.5	100.0
Telecommunications	35.2	21.2	43.6	100.0
Transport	19.3	27.8	52.9	100.0
Water and sewage	25.2	27.7	47.1	100.0
All infrastructure	28.5	23.3	48.2	100.0
Africa				
Energy	32.0	11.9	56.0	100.0
Telecommunications	40.1	11.6	48.1	100.0
Transport	28.4	16.5	55.1	100.0
Water and sewage	41.5	2.8	55.3	100.0
All infrastructure	35.5	12.5	51.9	100.0
Asia				
Energy	21.1	29.3	49.6	100.0
Telecommunications	19.6	31.0	49.5	100.0
Transport	17.4	39.3	43.3	100.0
Water and sewage	21.1	34.1	44.8	100.0
All infrastructure	19.5	32.5	47.7	100.0
Latin America and Caribbean				
Energy	37.6	16.5	45.7	100.0
Telecommunications	42.8	20.0	37.1	100.0
Transport	18.8	21.8	59.4	100.0
Water and sewage	28.8	22.1	49.2	100.0
All infrastructure	33.2	19.3	47.4	100.0

Notes:
Sources of commitments A Foreign[b]; B domestic private; C domestic public.
a.	Data covers all developing countries, except high-income developing economies (for example, Hong Kong, South Korea, Singapore and Taiwan).
b.	Covers all forms of financial commitments by 'private' entities in infrastructure industries of host economies. Some of the investors may be publicly owned foreign enterprises, either entirely or in part. Commitments include both equity and non-equity contributions to investments.

Source:	UNCTAD *World Investment Report 2008*, figure 111.1 derived from World Bank's Private Participation in Infrastructure Database.

significant position as a source of funding for the sector. Table 8.2 presents UNCTAD's interpretation of World Bank data on various sources of commitments to the financing of infrastructure projects in developing countries from 1996 to 2006. In this data the source designated as 'foreign' takes the form of an FDI-type[7] participation in an infrastructure project, even when (as often the case for Chinese MNE investments) there is some degree of public participation in, and influence on, the investing firm. Taken across all developing countries the foreign commitments represent 28.5 per cent of the total, somewhat ahead of domestic private (23.3 per cent) but well below the persisting dominant position of domestic public funding (48.2 per cent).

At the sectoral level telecommunications represents the most distinctive case, with both the highest share (35.2 per cent) taken by foreign commitments and the lowest (43.6 per cent) by domestic public. Thus in telecommunications privatisation per se is strongest, but also most likely to be dominated (62.4 per cent) by foreign investments. Energy then reveals the most similar case, with foreign commitments accounting for 30.0 per cent of the total and for 58.4 per cent of the private funding. It is then transport that provides least room for foreign commitments with only 19.3 per cent of the total and just 41.0 per cent of the overall private contribution.

Africa records the highest shares in total commitments for both foreign (35.5 per cent) and domestic public (51.9 per cent), so that domestic private is squeezed to its lowest share (12.5 per cent). This then means that as a proportion of total private infrastructure commitments foreign accounts for 74.0 per cent in Africa, compared with 63.2 per cent in Latin America and only 37.5 per cent in Asia. In Africa, therefore, the most distinctive tendency is that of substitution of foreign commitments for domestic private funding. This pattern is most visible in the water and sewage subsector but also, at least by comparison with Asia, can be seen in the three other subsectors.

The UNCTAD data presented in Table 8.3 indicates very notable changes in the magnitudes and locations of IFDI commitments between 1996 and 2006. Thus the total IFDI commitments to developing countries were only just over half as large during 2001 and 2006 ($83.9 billion) as they had been between 1996 and 2000 ($162.4 billon). However, this is dominated by one major change in the form of the collapse in commitments to Latin America from $109.4 billon (67.4 per cent of the total) in the first period to only $27.4 billion (32.2 per cent) in the latter.[8] Nevertheless total commitments to Asia also fell marginally, though this still allowed Asia to emerge as the largest host region (37.4 per cent of total) between 2001 and 2006.[9]

These declines for Latin America and Asia mean that the quite modest

Table 8.3   Foreign investment commitments[a] in infrastructure projects in developing economies, by industry and host region, 1996–2006

| | (a) Value $ billon | | | | | | | |
| | Africa | | Asia | | Latin America | | Total Developing[b] | |
	1996–2000	2001–06	1996–2000	2001–06	1996–2000	2001–06	1996–2000	2001–06
Energy	6.8	5.7	20.5	10.7	47.7	13.5	75.1	29.9
Telecommunications	11.5	14.0	5.0	9.7	45.8	2.1	62.2	25.7
Transport	1.2	5.5	6.1	8.7	12.2	9.7	19.6	23.7
Water	0.1	0.2	1.7	2.4	3.7	1.7	5.5	4.3
All infrastructure	19.7	25.5	33.3	31.4	109.4	27.0	162.4	83.9
	(b) Percentage share							
	1996–2000	2001–06	1996–2000	2001–06	1996–2000	2001–06	1996–2000	2001–06
Energy	9.1	19.1	27.4	35.8	63.5	45.3	100.0	100.0
Telecommunications	18.5	54.3	8.0	37.6	73.5	8.0	100.0	100.0
Transport	6.5	23.1	31.1	36.3	62.4	40.6	100.0	100.0
Water	1.6	5.5	31.6	55.0	66.8	39.5	100.0	100.0
All infrastructure	12.1	30.4	20.5	37.4	67.4	32.2	100.0	100.0

Notes:
a.   Covers all forms of financial commitments by 'private' entities in infrastructure industries of host economies. Some of these investors may be publicly owned foreign enterprises, either entirely or in part. Commitments include both equity and non-equity contribution to investments.
b.   Data covers all developing countries, except high-income developing economies (for example, Hong Kong South Korea, Singapore and Taiwan). Asia includes Oceania. Latin America includes the Caribbean.

Source: UNCTAD *World Investment Report 2008*, table 111.7 derived from World Bank's Private Participation in Infrastructure Database.

rise in IFDI commitments to Africa (from $19.7 billion in 1996–2000 to $25.5 billion for 2001–06) in fact represents an increase in the share of total commitments from 12.1 per cent in the first period to 30.4 per cent in the second. Telecommunications has been the main recipient of IFDI commitments in Africa, accounting for 58.3 per cent of the total in 1996–2000 and 54.9 per cent in 2001–06. Taken alongside a collapse of telecommunications commitments in Latin America and the still low commitments in Asia, this means that Africa received 54.3 per cent of all IFDI in developing countries in the subsector in the latter period. The rise in transport

Table 8.4   Origin of foreign investment commitments^a in developing country^b infrastructure sectors, by origin, 1996–2006

Host region and sector	Origin of FDI commitments (per cent)^c	
	Developed economies	Developing economies
Africa		
Energy	91.3	8.5
Telecommunications	42.0	58.0
Transport	82.1	17.9
Water	100.0	–
Total	60.8	38.1
Asia and Oceania		
Energy	78.7	42.8
Telecommunications	24.1	75.7
Transport	43.5	56.1
Water	76.0	24.0
Total	57.1	42.8
Latin America and Caribbean		
Energy	92.3	7.7
Telecommunications	73.8	25.3
Transport	85.8	14.4
Water	97.6	2.4
Total	83.9	15.7

Notes:
a.   Covers all forms of financial commitments by 'private' entities in infrastructure industries of host economies.
b.   Data covers all developing countries, except high-income developing economies.
c.   Where totals add to less than 100 per cent the difference reflects transition economy investments.

Source: UNCTAD *World Investment Report 2008*, table 111.17. UNCTAD estimates, based on data from the World Bank's Private Participation in Infrastructure Database.

IFDI in Africa in the second period (albeit still at low aggregate levels) also increased its share of developing country total from 6.5 per cent to 23.1 per cent. Similarly, in energy Africa also increased its share of developing country total from 9.1 per cent to 19.1 per cent, by merely avoiding the very significant declines experienced in Latin America and Asia.

As Table 8.4 shows, developed country enterprises still account for the majority shares of IFDI commitments in the developing countries. Thus only 38.1 per cent of commitments in Africa originated in other developing economies, compared with 42.8 per cent in Asia and a minimal 15.7 per cent in Latin America. It is in telecommunications that developing country enterprises have asserted themselves as sources for IFDI in other developing regions, accounting for 58.0 per cent in Africa, 75.7 per cent in Asia and for a relatively high (by comparison with other subsectors) 25.3 per cent in Latin America. Compared to Asia, Africa has been relatively limited in attracting IFDI from other developing countries in both energy and transport.

CHINESE CONSTRUCTION FIRMS IN AFRICA

By its very nature the construction industry becomes an inevitable component of the creation of new infrastructure capacity. Therefore construction industry firms will be major players in the generation and implementation of IPs. This is clearly a significant factor in the growth of international operations of leading construction sector enterprises. As our conceptualisation suggests construction firms may become $IMNE_{sp}$, helping in the formulation of important IPs and then recruiting supporting inputs to their operationalisation, as well as supplying their own capacities to implementation. Or they may play the $IMNE_{su}$ role, providing particular specialised competences to complement those of other participants in building up elements of infrastructure capacity.

Two of the trends that have been important drivers of the recent growth of the internationalised construction sector are very relevant to our concerns here. Firstly, the substantial increase in demand for construction services in Africa that derives from the growing commitment to new and upgraded infrastructure. Secondly, the international expansion of Chinese construction industry firms.[10] As Table 8.5 shows the total market in Africa supplied by the 225 leading contractors documented by *Engineering News Record* doubled from $7,640 million in 2000 to $15,139 million in 2005 (or by an annual rate of 14.8 per cent). Within this Chinese contractors' market increased almost six-fold (from $540 million to $3,233 million), so that its share of the total trebled (from 7.1 per cent to 21.4 per cent). This meant that in 2004 (marginally) and 2005 (more clearly) Chinese contractors took more important positions in the African market than US firms.[11]

The understanding of important aspects of the Chinese construction firms that implemented this facet of China's participation in African infrastructure creation has benefited from a survey/interview study by Chen et al. (2007). The 35 firms with African operations covered were believed to constitute over 90 per cent of all large-scale Chinese construction firms, with 23 of them featuring in *Engineering News Record*'s top global operations in the sector in 2006. Though respondents suggested that they rarely

Table 8.5   *Shares, by home country, of leading international contractors**
        in the African market, 2000–05

Origin of contractor	Market size ($million)					
	2000	2001	2002	2003	2004	2005
China	540.0	654.1	1,103.9	1,492.1	2,106.8	3,233.5
Japan	422.5	456.6	1,059.5	1,304.3	778.0	466.9
Korea	152.0	372.0	308.4	5,56.6	643.3	598.6
Europe	3,953.4	4,111.0	4,951.4	5,883.1	7,129.5	7,467.7
USA	1,364.2	2,362.4	2,650.2	2,009.4	1,976.6	2,334.3
Total	7,639.9	8,819.3	11,138.2	12,655.5	14,283.8	15,139.1
	Market Share (%)					
	2000	2001	2002	2003	2004	2005
China	7.1	7.4	9.9	11.8	14.8	21.4
Japan	5.5	5.2	9.5	10.3	5.5	3.1
Korea	2.0	4.2	2.8	4.4	4.5	4.0
Europe	51.8	46.6	44.5	46.5	49.9	49.3
USA	17.9	26.8	23.8	15.9	13.8	15.4
Total	100.0	100.0	100.0	100.0	100.0	100.0

Note: * Figures based on *Engineering News Record* top 225 international contractors.

Source: Derived from Chen et al (2007), table 1, p. 452.

saw market entries as part of wider strategic (for example, continental) perspectives Chen et al.'s evidence does imply extensive Africa-wide operations for many of them. Thus on average the surveyed Chinese firms operated in 7.26 African countries (5.06 in sub-Saharan countries and 1.20 in North Africa). In a similar manner some individual host countries attracted quite an extensive range of the Chinese construction enterprises.[12]

A familiar issue in discussion of Chinese expansion into Africa has been the extent to which individual participants, notably in construction and/ or infrastructure creation, reflect wider Chinese strategic interests and, therefore, benefit from home-country financial or diplomatic support. Reflecting this Chen et al. (2007) investigated the sources from which Chinese construction firms procured their participation in individual projects. Here, in line with a broader strategic positioning, 40 per cent of the firms' projects in Africa derived from 'bidding among Chinese contractors' for projects financed by Chinese funds. Most likely here the projects' broad aims, format and funding will be determined through intra-government bargaining and opened to tender to Chinese contractors. Very notably though a larger proportion of African projects (49 per cent) were secured by Chinese contractors through international bidding.[13] These are then projects funded and approved by multilateral or regional organisations, for which the Chinese contractors have to compete with other international construction enterprises. The extent to which the Chinese contractors' ability to compete may still derive, to some degree, from home-government support remains an open question, however. The remaining 11 per cent of projects were secured through 'sole source negotiations', which seems to imply a more direct independent involvement in articulating a project (rather than bidding for one *ex post*).

The Chen et al. survey also aimed to investigate the familiar allegation that Chinese construction firms employ relatively small amounts of local labour in Africa. Though finding a very wide variation between respondents, so that criticism cannot be generalised, they nevertheless reported that almost half the firms' total labour forces did come from China. Also less than 10 per cent of skilled work force positions were filled by African workers. In a similar manner they reported relatively limited sourcing of raw materials and equipment in Africa, with quality and efficiency factors determining their acquisition from, in the main, China. This suggests that there are quite limited spillover benefits from how Chinese firms operationalised construction/infrastructure projects, though the main sustainable developmental benefits would be intended to come from the subsequent performance of the completed facilities.

ICT PROVISION IN AFRICA: THE ROLE OF CHINESE MNEs

It is inherent to the close relationship between infrastructure creation and economic development that as development proceeds the relative importance of different types of infrastructure provision will change. Thus the need for ICT provision is likely to emerge more strongly once industrialisation processes become more complex and interdependent. Similarly consumer demand for the services of the sector will become increasingly strong and sophisticated as average income levels grow. But it is also likely to often be the case that these ICT demands emerge at a stage before the country's indigenous technological and enterprise capacities can provide for them adequately. Logically this can then open up an important opportunity for international firms in the ICT sector to supply the equipment and build up the backbone of initial provision in such countries. It may then also be plausible that the foreign firms most likely to play this role effectively may be ones that have emerged in other countries that have themselves recently been through similar formative stages in their industrial and technological evolution. The extensive participation of two Chinese ICT firms (Huawei Technologies Co. Ltd and Zhong Xing Telecommunications Co. Ltd (ZTE)) in the formulation of this type of infrastructure provision in African countries may be a precise manifestation of this scenario. This again indicates the hybrid context of such countries' infrastructure provision since, in ICT, the technological progress and innovation that drives the dynamics of the sector are most effectively secured within commercially motivated enterprise, whilst the services it supplies retain very strong externalities and social aspects.[14]

In their detailed review of Chinese financing of infrastructure creation in sub-Saharan Africa Foster et al. (2008) provide extensive documentation drawn from the Chinese Projects Database compiled by the World Bank Public Private Infrastructure Advisory Facility (WB-PPIAF). This database initially assembled all press reports of Chinese participations in Sub-Saharan African infrastructure projects and then sought to verify details from more formal (Chinese and international) sources. From the verified sources the WB-PPIAF database located 124 new Chinese financed projects initiated in sub-Saharan Africa from 2001–07[15] (57, that is, 46.2 per cent, in the two years 2006/07). The aggregate value of Chinese financing commitments to these projects was $15.97 billion (of which 72.3 per cent was in 2006/07).[16]

The two most prominent sectors for those projects were power (especially hydropower) and transport (especially railroads), both of which had 36 (29 per cent) projects and accounted for 33 per cent of Chinese financing. Though ICT reported almost as many projects (34) it only accounted for 17 per cent of Chinese funds. Thus of these three dominant infrastructure sectors ICT operates through distinctly smaller projects (in terms of Chinese funding, at least) than power and transport. The fourth designated sector, water, recorded 15 projects (12 per cent) but only 3 per cent of Chinese financing. Finally, by contrast, three multi-sector projects accounted for 14 per cent of the Chinese finance.[17]

Of the 34 ICT projects in sub-Saharan Africa that involved Chinese financing the WB-PPIAF database suggests (Foster et al., 2008, table A.3.3.) that 27 involve the participation of two Chinese contractors: ZTE and/or Huawei. Of the remaining projects the Chinese contractor for two was not known, China Mobile and China Great Wall Industry Corp accounted for one each, whilst the French-Chinese Joint venture (JV) Alcatel-Shanghai Bell (ASB) participated in five (including a JV that also involved both ZTE and Huawei).[18]

Table 8.6   ZTE participation in Chinese financing commitments[a] in confirmed ICT projects in sub-Saharan Africa, 2001–07

Country	Year	Project details	Project cost $million	Chinese commitment $million
Angola	2005	An agreement between ZTE and Mundo Startel to install a new fixed line network in eight states in Angola	69	38
Benin	2004	Provision of complete GSM national network in Benin – including GPRS capability on its existing GSM network[b]	–	–
Central African Republic	2005	Supply and installation for mobile and fixed networks covering the whole country	79	67
Dem. Rep. of Congo	2001	China-Congo (CCT) network project	20	10
Cote d'Ivoire	2006	Build the network covering Abidjan and its adjacent areas – Phase 1	30	30
Eritrea	2005	200,000 lines fixed telecom network rehabilitation project	21	–
Ethiopia	2003	Expansion of Ethiopia's existing mobile network capacity in Addis Ababa and regions[b]	29	–
Ethiopia	2006	Expand and upgrade Ethiopia's telecom network	–	822
Ethiopia	2007	First phase of fibre transmission backbone, expansion of mobile phone service for the Ethiopian millennium and expansion of wireless telephone service.	200	2,000
Ethiopia	2007	GSM project phase 2	478	478
Ghana	2005	Build a CDMA 2000 IX network for Kasapa Telecom[b]	–	–
Ghana	2007	Communication system for security agencies project	–	(3)
Lesotho	2007	Rehabilitate the Telecom Agricultural network	–	30
Mali	2005	Rehabilitate CDMA 2000 IX WLL network in Bamako	2	1

Table 8.6   (continued)

Country	Year	Project details	Project cost $million	Chinese commitment $million
Niger	2001	Equip Niger Telecommunications Company (SONITEL) with GSM mobile system covering the city of Niamey[b]	8	[c]
Niger	2001	Tender for 51% ownership of SONITEL and its mobile arm, Sahel Com[d]	–	24
Nigeria	2002	National Rural Telephony Project (NRPT) Phase 1[e]	200	200
Sudan	2005	Sudan Telecom purchasing equipment from ZTE	–	200
Zambia	2006	Deploy fibre-optic lines over ZESCO power transmission network[b]	11	–

Notes:
a.   Chinese financing from Ex-Im Bank unless otherwise noted.
b.   Chinese financing source not specified.
c.   Unconfirmed.
d.   ZTE own financing.
e.   Joint venture with Huawei and ASB.

Source: Foster et al. (2008), table A3.3. Originally derived from World Bank PPIAF Chinese Projects Database, 2007.

The 19 projects involving participation of the state-owned contractor ZTE (Table 8.6) covered 14 different sub-Saharan African countries, with Ethiopia the most notable multi-project host with four. This reflected a particularly strong role for ICT in China's financial commitment to Ethiopia, with three of the projects positioned within Ethiopia's $1.5 billion Millennium project. This aimed to 'create a fibre optic transmission backbone across the country and roll out the expansion of the GSM network, with estimated 8,500,000 new connections' (Foster et al., 2008, p. 21). Of these 19 ZTE projects the Ex-Im Bank was the confirmed Chinese financier in 12 cases, with ZTE itself financing two cases and the other five cases not identified. It is also noted (Foster et al., 2008, p.19) that, in support of its worldwide operations, ZTE also had access to a standing line of credit of $500 million from the Ex-Im Bank issued in 2004.

The privately owned Huawei participated in eight projects, including

Table 8.7   Huawei participation in Chinese financing commitments[a] in confirmed ICT projects in sub-Saharan Africa, 2001–07

Country	Year	Project details	Project cost $million	Chinese commitment $million
Burundi	2004	Burundi GSM mobile telecommunications project	9	8
Gambia	2005	CDMA network for Gamtel[b]	–	–
Ghana	2006	National fibre backbone project	70	31
Nigeria	2002	National rural telephony project[c]	200	200
Senegal	2007	Build the e-government network[d]	51	51
Sierra Leone	2005	Provision of CDMA fixed wireless	17	17
Sierra Leone	2006	Upgrade the rural telecom network	–	18
Zimbabwe	2004	Two contracts for telecom equipment supply with Zimbabwe's state-owned fixed line operator Tel One and mobile Operator Net One	332	[e]

Notes:
a. Chinese financing from Ex-Im Bank unless otherwise noted.
b. Chinese financing source not specified.
c. Joint venture with ZTE and ASB.
d. Joint venture with CMEC.
e. Unconfirmed.

Source: Foster et al. (2008), table A3.3. Originally derived from World Bank PPIAF Chinese Projects Database, 2007.

the JV with ZTE and ASB in Nigeria and another (with China National Machinery and Equipment Import and Export Co.) to build the e-government network in Senegal. The other projects were in separate countries, except for two in Sierra Leone In all seven cases where the source of Chinese funding was known it was the Ex-Im Bank. However, as with ZTE, Huawei had auxiliary access to finance for its overseas operations in the form of $600 million export sellers credit from the Ex-Im Bank (granted in 2004) and $10 billion in credit financing from China Development Bank (also 2004).

It is important to observe, of course, that few of the projects listed in Tables 8.6 and 8.7 represent acts of FDI by ZTE or Huawei as this is normally defined. The finance for the projects is usually, in effect, government to government with very rare and limited participation by the firms. The projects themselves are set to be owned and controlled by African (often government) entities. Nevertheless, in terms of opening up the research agendas suggested in this chapter, we can still see these operations in Africa as an integral part of the international expansion of Chinese MNEs. At the broadest level this simply reflects the now established view, in analysis of International Business (IB), that a wide range of entry, ownership and operational modes are available to MNEs in their international expansion. The choice of mode for individual overseas operations is then contingent on industry, location and firm factors.

Here familiar aspects of infrastructure constrain the degree to which its creation and service provision can be amenable to normal competitive market forces. These idiosyncratic elements include the massive initial fixed costs of establishment to initiate supply, with then a likely long period over which revenue returns will spread and the potential complexities of determining these revenues flows that can reflect the externalities of many infrastructure services. A vital aspect of these externalities, central to discussion here, is that particular IPs are often integral to wider development programmes, which crucially conditions the terms on which IMNEs can participate. Through diplomatic support agreements, Huawei offers lower bid than rivals at 20 per cent–30 per cent on core technology, which reduces the monopoly of products and service of western providers (Qie, 2010). This can be further complicated when, as again in this discussion, the IMNEs emerge from a positioning in their home country's recent development and often remain, in their international expansion, to some degree agents of that home-country development. In elaborating the growth of Chinese IMNEs, and their involvement in African IPs, the sources and nature of their firm-specific OAs becomes a major issue in research agendas in IB and political economy.

We can suggest that the firm-specific competences that Chinese IMNEs may leverage to assert their position in African IPs can take two forms. Firstly, traditional asset OAs in the form of their mature products or service specific sources of competitiveness embodying the firm's realised types of distinctive technology and expertise.[19] Secondly, something closer to the recently introduced institutional OA (Dunning and Lundan, 2008; Lundan, 2010), in the form of unique skills and expertise in dealing with governments, during participation in infrastructure creation, learnt during their own evolution within Chinese development. Though we have noted that Chinese firms such as ZTE and Huawei (or construction firms) do not finance the projects they operate within, their capabilities may be far from irrelevant to project funding, however. Thus it may be that the potential participation of a particular Chinese IMNE in a project (that is, the commitment of specific OAs whose strength has been already proven in operations in China) can underpin the willingness of the Ex-Im Bank to finance that project.

DISCUSSION AND AGENDA

As we have described them here the participation of Chinese IMNEs in the creation and provision of infrastructure in Africa can be seen to be mediating between two differently phased processes of economic development. From the Chinese side we can discern several factors innate to the process of development that have proved to have a crucial influence on the involvement in infrastructure creation in Africa. At the macro level the sustained high rates of economic growth in China have generated enormous savings and foreign exchange surpluses that can be leveraged towards particular forms of international expansion. At a more micro level the processes of securing, and widening the sustainable scope of, economic development in China have led to the generation of forms of knowledge and expertise specific to particular enterprises that can then provide them with the capacity to play distinctive roles in such Chinese international economic expansion. In terms of sectors that can feed positively into early stages of development elsewhere we have seen that such enterprise-level competences can be significant elements of China's African involvement, from construction of very basic transport infrastructure through to creation of ICT networks which laid the foundation of future expansion in the ICT market. But even if the emergence of internationally competitive ICT firms, such as Huawei and ZTE, is clearly indicative of an upgrading of the frontiers of Chinese economic development there remains an overwhelming need for externally accessed sources of energy and raw materials. This, too, has decisively conditioned the essential parameters of China's involvement with Africa's development agendas.

On the African side there are, of course, a large number of national economies with different sources of developmental potentials and different mixes of the bottlenecks that may constrain the realisation of these potentials. Generalising from this diversity into particular scenarios of Chinese participation in African development we can distinguish two particularly relevant sources of potential. On the supply side we can see the capacities to meet needs for various primary resources as being at the core of the early-stage developmental opportunities of many African economies. More towards the demand side we can perceive an opportunity, inherent in the deepening of development itself, emerging in the need for services, such as ICT, that have a significant public-good nature. The positioning of infrastructure provision in development is innate to both these potentials in Africa. Thus ICT is, in itself, a crucial facet of the deepening of infrastructure scope that becomes essential as development proceeds and needs to encompass greater complexities and industrial and service interactions.

For the realisation of resource potentials as a basis of internationally oriented development complementary infrastructure, notably related to transport facilitation, needs to be constructed (roads; ports, airports, and so on).

Central to the existence and persistence of these infrastructural bottle-necks are two constraints on the capacity to alleviate them from indigenous sources; shortage of capital and the lack of relevant types of knowledge and expertise. The need for infrastructure improvement to drive the devel-opment process means it cannot normally wait for endogenous generation of reinvestable capital and appropriate competences. As indicated earlier Chinese development has progressed to the point where it has the capacity to provide both factors to unlock the infrastructure constraints in Africa. At the macro level the developmental complementarities between China and Africa is well understood. The successes of Chinese development have already generated surplus capital as a leverageable resource, whilst these same high growth rates increasingly emphasise the need to secure from external sources supplies of energy and primary resources. These latter, in turn, represent the most immediately leverageable comparative advan-tages of many African countries.

But if the macro-level political economy of the finance/resource interaction explains Chinese commitment to participation in African IP less is known, at a more micro level, about the nature and sources of Chinese IMNEs' positioning in the implementation of many of them. In an agenda to understand this the vital question here is, in effect, whether the precise forms of Chinese IMNEs' participation in African IPs can help alleviate the second constraint noted above, by providing access to the most relevant and competent sources of necessary knowledge and expertise. In terms of our perspective on the differential phasing of Chinese and African development we have invoked, as a generalised line of argument, that Chinese enterprises (in, for example, construction and ICT) will have learnt, from their involvement within China's earlier development, types of expertise and competence that can underpin logi-cally their extension into African infrastructure creation.

This points to the central concerns in projecting this area of investi-gation forward. These are to understand the origins and nature of the particular competitive advantages now possessed by Chinese IMNEs and to approach an evaluation of the implications of the application of these specific types of firm-level competences to African IPs that will have very context-specific objectives.

NOTES

1. For a detailed review of various estimates of aspects of infrastructure shortage and their implications see Foster et al. (2008, pp. 23–6).
2. The estimates assume an annual growth rate of 7 per cent and an annual investment in infrastructure of 9 per cent of GDP, so as to achieve the region's Millennium Development Goals poverty reduction targets.
3. By sector the totals were Electricity \$8.8 billion, Telecommunications \$5.2 billion, Roads \$17.2 billion, Rail \$0.8 billion, Water and Sewage \$8.0 billion.
4. These sources comprised \$8.0 billion from internally generated funds, \$5.0 billion from external funding and \$3.5 billion from financial institutions, loans and overseas development assistance (ODA).
5. Thus whilst privatisation often raised capital for the government's other budgetary needs, it often also occurred at a point where more capital for expenditure on infrastructure expansion was perceived as a major developmental priority. Additionally, of course, when infrastructure privatisation is carried out by IMNEs the capital committed will be imported and thus help alleviate balance of payments and foreign exchange constraints on development.
6. Ramamurti (1996, pp.11–12) points out that in the case of privatising state-owned enterprises in some more advanced sectors (for example, telecommunications and airlines) securing the aims of macro-economic benefits (alleviation of budgetary and balance of payments constraints) and projection of an attractive environment may be best secured by sale of already successful and efficient operators. In other cases in such sectors it is also suggested (Ramamurti, 1996, p.13) that restructuring and efficiency improvements are imposed before sale to secure better terms.
7. That is the foreign investment derives from a legally-instituted independent enterprise, rather than aid funding or some form of government-to-government financial transfer.
8. This reflects massive declines in commitments in the two infrastructure subsectors (energy and telecommunications) that had dominated (85.5 per cent of total) investments in 1996–2000.
9. The source of this decline focuses on the halving of commitments in the energy subsector which had dominated commitments (61.2 per cent) in the first period. Thus, though at lower aggregate levels, commitments to Asia in the other three subsectors all increased marginally.
10. Chen et al. (2007, p. 452) provide two indicators of this. Firstly, that in 2006 *Engineering News Record* found that two Chinese construction firms had entered the top ten global constructors list, with five more in the top 50. Secondly, that the 11th five-year plan period (2006–10) was projected to see an annualised 15 per cent growth in turnover from overseas contracting business, which would have implied a total value of \$50 billion in 2010.
11. European contractors held their relative position in the African market over time, with French contractors dominating this (25.4 per cent of the total market in 2000 and 24.0 per cent in 2005; the latter making it the only country with a larger share than the Chinese in that year). British contractors increased share notably (from 1.7 per cent to 5.0 per cent) and the Italian more marginally (5.1 per cent to 7.0 per cent) whilst the German faced some share decline (9.8 per cent to 6.1 per cent).
12. Thus 13 of the firms (almost 40 per cent) operated in Algeria and 12 in Sudan, with ten in Angola and Nigeria, nine in Botswana and eight in Congo.
13. For detailed analysis of Chinese construction contractors competitiveness in bidding for internationally funded projects see Foster et al. (2008, pp. 26–9). This source also draws attention to notable differences between multilateral agency-funded contracts awarded to Chinese firms and those implemented within Chinese-funded operations. Thus multilateral projects were predominant in transport (including roads) and water sectors and located in Ethiopia, Mozambique, Tanzania and Democratic Republic of Congo, whilst Chinese-funded projects were more likely to be in hydropower, rail and

information and communications technology (ICT) and located in Angloa, Sudan and Nigeria.
14. This is well expressed by UNCTAD (2008; box 111-2, p. 90).
15. It was indicated (Foster et al., 2008, p.14) that the number of press-reported projects tended, on average, to be around 50 per cent higher than these verified ones. This, they suggest, 'reflects the existence of a large tail of such projects that could not be readily verified through official sources'.
16. The differences between the number and value shares indicate that new projects in 2006 (the Chinese 'year of Africa') and 2007 were much bigger (in terms of Chinese financial commitments) than those of earlier years. A significant contribution to this is the 82 billion Ex-Im Bank loan to Angola in 2007 that is not allocated to any specific sector, or, therefore, Chinese contractor.
17. This funding is dominated by the unallocated $2 billion Ex-Im Bank standby loan to Angola for infrastructure support.
18. This JV, implemented in 2002, involved the first phase of Nigeria's National Rural Telephony Project.
19. Though much discussion of MNEs from emerging economies, such as ZTE and Huawei (Sun, 2009) considers that entry into developed industrialised economies may invoke elements of KS, here it seems plausible that entry into African countries, at earlier stages of their development, can invoke a more traditional application of established OAs.

REFERENCES

Chen, Ch., P-C. Chiu, R.J. Orr and A. Goldstein (2007), 'An empirical analysis of Chinese construction firm's entry into Africa', *The CRIOCM International Symposium on Advancement of Construction Management and Real Estate*, Sydney, Australia, pp. 451–63.
Donaldson, D.J., F. Sader and D.M. Wagle (1997), 'Foreign direct investment in infrastructure: the challenge of Southern and Eastern Africa', Foreign Investment Advisory Service Occasional Paper, No. 9, World Bank, Washington, DC.
Dunning, J.H. and S.M. Lundan (2008), *Multinational Enterprises and the Global Economy*, 2nd edn, Cheltenham, UK and Northampton, MA, USA: Edward Elgar Publishing.
Foster, V., W. Butterfield, Ch. Chen and N. Pushak (2008), 'Building bridges: China's growing role as infrastructure financier in Africa', Public Private Infrastructure Advisory Facility, *Trends and Policy Options*, No. 5. World Bank, Washington, DC.
Kaplinsky, R. and M. Mormis (2009), 'Chinese FDI in Sub Saharan Africa: engaging with large dragons', *European Journal of Development Research*, **21**(4), 551–69.
Lundan, S.M. (2010), 'What are ownership advantages?', *Multinational Business Review*, **18**(2), 51–70.
Qie, Y. (2010), 'Go abroad: the internationalising strategy of Chinese enterprises', China Economy Press.
Ramamurti, R. (1996), 'The new frontier of privatisation', in R. Ramamurti (ed.), *Privatising Monopolies: Lessons from the Telecommunications and Transport Sectors in Latin America*, Baltimore, MD: Johns Hopkins University Press.
Sader, F. (2000), 'Attracting foreign direct investment into infrastructure – why is

it so difficult?', Foreign Investment Advisory Service, Occasional Paper No. 12. World Bank, Washington, DC.

Sun, S.L. (2009), 'Internationalization strategy of MNEs from emerging economies: the case of Huawei', *Multinational Business Review,* **17**(2), 129–56.

UNCTAD (2008), *The World Investment Report 2008*, New York and Geneva: United Nations.

9. The overseas expansion of Chinese multinational corporations

Bersant Hobdari, Evis Sinani, Marina Papanastassiou and Robert Pearce

INTRODUCTION

As it is clearly stated in one of latest World Investment Reports (WIR) published by the United Nations Conference on Trade and Development (UNCTAD), large multinational corporations (MNCs) from emerging economies are appearing as global investment leaders. While only 19 featured among the Fortune 500 in 1990, 47 such companies did in 2005. The top five MNCs from emerging economies are also among the top 100 global MNCs, that is Hutchison Whampoa (Hong Kong, China), Petronas (Malaysia), Singtel (Singapore), Samsung Electronics (Republic of Korea) and CITIC Group (China) (UNCTAD, 2006, p. 24, pp. 31–2).

Over the last two decades China is one of the economies that is leading the emerging countries in generating foreign direct investment (FDI) abroad. Based on recently published information in the UNCTAD (2010) China is ranked among the top ten host and home countries for FDI. In particular, mainland China is ranked second (after the USA) with $95 billion as final destination for FDI in 2009 and sixth (following the USA, France, Japan, Germany and Hong Kong, China) with $48 billion as investor country.

Looking also at the top 100 non-financial MNCs from developing economies as published by UNCTAD in 2008, we observe that Hutchison Whampoa Limited (from Hong Kong, China) is ranked in the first place whilst in the list we find 13 more companies such as the CITIC group, the China Ocean Shipping Group Company, the China National Petroleum Corporation, SinoChem Cor., Star Cruises and so on indicating the industrially diversified presence of Chinese MNCs. All 14 MNCs (which state as home country either mainland China or Hong Kong, China) report 609 overseas subsidiaries which employ approximately 460,000 people. Thus it is becoming evident that the emergence of Chinese MNCs is attracting the attention for further study. In this chapter we aim to provide some empirical background on the key characteristics of Chinese outward FDI through the network of leading Chinese MNCs' overseas subsidiaries.

CHARACTERISTICS OF CHINESE OVERSEAS SUBSIDIARIES

In this section we aim to present key characteristics of Chinese MNCs' overseas operations at a subsidiary level. The data we present in this chapter are obtained from the spring 2008 edition of *Corporate Affiliates Directory*, Lexis Nexis. Data information shows that 147 Chinese parent companies are reported in the Directory. The average number of subsidiaries of included parent firms in the 2008 sample is about 3 per parent, with the number of subsidiaries per parent firm ranging from 1 to 57. The top five firms, namely, China National Chemicals Import and Export Corporation, China Minmetals Corporation, CITIC Group, Gold Peak Industries (Holdings) Limited and Bank of China account for 49 per cent of all subsidiaries, while 36 per cent of firms have only one subsidiary (see Hobdari et al., 2008).

Regarding the geographical distribution of Chinese FDI the evidence, as presented in the literature, is somewhat mixed. Wang (2002) claims that Chinese overseas subsidiaries reflect an extensive geographical expansion which goes beyond the neighbouring Southeast Asian region and includes a range of developed economies as well. On the other hand, Morck et al. (2008) argue that Chinese subsidiaries are mostly located in neighbouring economies. They also underline the special preference for locating in Hong Kong in order to capitalize on the favoured tax treaties.

Our data, as depicted in Table 9.1, bridge the two views. As can be seen in Table 9.1 Chinese MNCs expand through their subsidiaries in a wide range of countries well beyond the Southeast Asia region. In particular, the USA, the UK and Germany are among the developed countries that seem to attract a substantial number of overseas subsidiaries out of the total of 297 overseas units included in our sample. At the same time, what it not reported in this table (as it is focused exclusively on locations outside China) is the significant presence of subsidiaries in Hong Kong (see Hobdari et al., 2008 for an extensive analysis of Chinese subsidiaries location including Hong Kong). Actually 265 subsidiaries are reported to be located in Hong Kong providing support for Morck et al.'s (2008) arguments on the preferential positioning of Hong Kong as a host region to mainland China FDI (Rugman and Li, 2007 reach a similar conclusion as per the regional rather than global nature of Chinese MNCs' overseas

Table 9.1   Geographical distribution of number of Chinese subsidiaries by host country

Host country	Number of subsidiaries
Australia	15
Austria	1
Belgium	1
Brazil	3
Canada	11
Colombia	1
Cyprus	2
Denmark	1
Finland	1
France	4
Germany	19
India	2
Indonesia	3
Italy	4
Japan	10
Korea (South)	4
Malaysia	4
Netherlands	6
New Zealand	2
Norway	1
Philippines	1
Russia	1
Singapore	27
South Africa	2
Spain	2
Sweden	12
Switzerland	11
Taiwan	12
Thailand	2
USA	115
UAE	1
UK	16
Total	297

Source: Adapted from Hobdari et al. (2008), table 4, p. 145; authors' calculations.

expansion). This diversified geographical spread of Chinese subsidiaries can be explained either through Buckley et al. (2007) who show how specific host-country location advantages – that reflect similarities to the Chinese market – boost Chinese FDI into these host markets or through

Table 9.2   Size and regional distribution of investment by Chinese firms

Sales	Host Region					
	Africa	Asia-Pacific	Europe	Middle East	North America	South America
Up to $US100 million	2	40	44	1	39	1
$US 100–500 million	0	15	17	0	34	2
$US 500 million–1 billion	0	4	0	0	5	0
$US 1–1.5 billion	0	0	1	0	0	0
More than 1.5 billion dollars	0	2	1	0	6	0
Total	2	61	63	1	84	3

Source: Adapted from Hobdari et al. (2008), table 5, p. 146; authors' calculations.

the findings of Duanmu and Guney (2009) who argue that Chinese FDI is attracted to countries with 'better institutional environments'.

What is obvious though, in Table 9.2, is that the majority of Chinese overseas subsidiaries are of relative small size regardless of the host region (see Deng, 2004 for a confirming observation). It is only the North America region that attracts relatively larger subsidiaries reflecting potentially the dynamic competitive environment Chinese subsidiaries face in this market.

Looking at the top 100 MNCs from emerging economies in the recent WIRs we do see a widespread industrial diversification among them. In particular as is stated in WIR 2007 we could group these MNCs into three groups:

1. Primary sector MNCs which mainly includes oil, gas and mining and related manufacturing such as metals.
2. Non-tradable services and specific manufacturing sectors such as cement and food and drink which are more investment oriented.
3. Industries 'exposed to global competition' which include electronics, IT, automotives which are dominated by Southeast Asian MNCs (UNCTAD, 2007, p. 26).

As can be noticed in Table 9.3, the Chinese subsidiaries in our sample follow the pattern described above with subsidiaries specializing in

Table 9.3   Industrial distribution of outward investment by Chinese MNCs' overseas subsidiaries

Industry	Number of Chinese overseas subsidiaries
Resources and construction	54
Food production, textile and apparel	11
Wood, paper products, chemicals and pharmaceuticals	12
Other manufacturing	22
Electronics, transport equipment and instruments	19
Total manufacturing	64
Trade	42
Finance, insurance and real estate	52
Other services (includes business, legal, health and hotel services)	85
Total	297

Source: Adapted from Hobdari et al. (2008), table 1, p. 142; authors' calculations.

resource-based industries as well as electronics and services and thus creating a quite diversified industrial profile.

Another important component in the understanding of Chinese MNCs' emergence and expansion is the identification of motivation to invest abroad. Previous research has indentified the complexity of strategic motivations of Chinese FDI which reflects both their geographical as well as their sectoral diversification. Early work by Li (1993) and Young et al. (1996) underline the impact of economic reforms in China (confirmed more recently by Luo et al., 2010) and market seeking and strategic seeking, respectively, to promote the expansion of Chinese MNCs. In recent work, knowledge seeking is emphatically related to investment in developed countries (Ding, 2000; Deng, 2007, 2009; He and Lyles, 2008; Rui and Yip, 2008, Cheung and Quian, 2009) whilst Hong and Sun (2006) place emphasis as well on resource-seeking motivations.

In previous work (see Hobdari et al., 2008; and Oladottir et al., 2009, Hobdari et al., 2010) the authors have developed a methodology building on the theoretical traditions of Caves (1996) and Dunning (2000) as well as Yeaple (2003) where the expansion strategy is related to the motivation to invest abroad through FDI. This is then measured following the empirical modelling of Palepu (1985) in order to identify the motivation/strategy of outward FDI at the subsidiary level. As such, subsidiaries are considered a vital vehicle in the organic growth of the MNC as they assume specific responsibilities reflecting the needs of the group, their

China and the multinationals

Table 9.4   *Strategy and regional distribution of investment by Chinese overseas production units*

Strategy	Host Regions						
	Africa	Asia-Pacific	Europe	Middle East	North America	South America	Total regions
Horizontal Integration	2	31	43	0	49	4	129
Vertical Integration	0	17	13	0	24	0	54
Lateral Integration	0	16	14	1	20	0	51
Risk Diversification	0	18	14	0	31	0	63
Total	2	82	84	1	124	4	297

Source: Hobdari et al. (2010), table 2, p.71.

own capabilities and, last but not least, the potential of the host market or region (Papanastassiou and Pearce, 2009). The methodology developed thus reflects the MNC's complex organizational structure and is based on firm-level information, that is, headquarter and subsidiary. As the ultimate aim is to discern the different strategic motivations which overseas subsidiaries are performing, firm-level information provided by The Lexis Nexis *Corporate Affiliations Plus Directory* allowed the authors to discern the primary industrial specialization of each overseas unit and thus to compare it with that of the ultimate parent. Based on this, the strategy is deemed to be 'horizontal integration' if the overseas unit operates in the same core or related industry as its parent. The strategy is deemed to be 'vertical integration' if the overseas investment is taking place in natural resource industries, whilst it is 'lateral integration' if the overseas investment is taking place in different stages of the value chain, forward or backward (compared to that of the parent). Finally, a fourth strategy is identified, that is, that of risk diversification if the overseas unit and its parent operate in unrelated industries (Hobdari et al., 2010, pp. 68–9).

As can be seen in Tables 9.4 and 9.5, the motivation/strategy to invest abroad is varied by both the geographical location as well as the sectoral diversification of the overseas subsidiary, respectively. Whilst horizontal integration (which reflects market-seeking motivations) appears as a dominant motivation across regions (Table 9.4) we do notice that lateral

Table 9.5   Distribution of Chinese overseas operation units by strategy and industrial classification

Strategy industry	Horizontal integration	Vertical integration	Lateral integration	Risk diversification	Total
Resources and construction	24	11	2	17	54
Food production, textile and apparel	6	0	1	4	11
Wood, paper products, chemicals and pharmaceuticals	6	1	2	3	12
Other manufacturing	4	6	5	7	22
Electronics, transport equipment and instruments	4	4	6	5	19
Total manufacturing	20	11	14	19	64
Trade	18	8	10	6	42
Finance and real estate	30	12	8	2	52
Other services	37	12	17	19	85
Total	129	54	51	63	297

Source: Hobdari etal. (2010), table 1, p. 70

integration (reflecting efficiency-seeking motives) as well as risk diversification (reflecting knowledge–seeking motives) to be dynamically present in particular in the North American markets.

Not surprisingly, we observe in Table 9.5 that 'globally competing industries' such as electronics, transport equipment and instruments tend to be predominately efficiency and knowledge seeking as they pursue, through their overseas subsidiaries, lateral integration and risk diversification respectively. Services are opting for horizontal integration as the primary goal there is market seeking.

CONCLUSION

It is evident that Chinese MNCs are rapidly growing in the global economy as international investors. It is equally evident that the Southeast Asia region is only part of their geographical expansion which includes developed countries such as the USA and European Union countries as well as other emerging markets. In the case of Chinese MNCs geographical diversification is linked to sectoral diversification which includes highly competing global industries such as electronics as well as other industries such as primary resources and services. This variation reflects different strategic motivations when investing abroad and results in multiple subsidiary profiles. In this chapter we identified four different strategic motivations using a sample of 297 overseas subsidiaries of leading Chinese MNCs, that is, horizontal, vertical and lateral integration and risk diversification and we showed how these strategic choices vary among host regions and sectors. These findings are confirmed empirically in Hobdari et al. (2010, p. 79) against a set of location and ownership specific variables where results showed 'that Chinese MNEs realize their strategic choices through an integrated network of overseas units and that each strategic choice is distinctively determined by a set of location and firm specific variables'.

This outcome leads us to conclude that 'Chinese MNCs do not differ from their global competitors coming mainly from developed economies as all MNCs face a common denominator when it comes to competitiveness, i.e. the need to be innovative and efficient. The only way to secure access to new sources of creativity and improve performance is through the effective application of the network of overseas production units. Thus, the roles of overseas units can no longer be either static or predetermined. They must evolve in such a way that will reflect the internal dynamics of the MNE and the changes in the external environment, i.e. that of host country or region that are called to serve' (Hobdari et al., 2010, p. 79).

REFERENCES

Buckley, P., J. Clegg, A.R Cross, X. Liu, H. Voss and P. Zheng (2007), 'The determinants of Chinese outward foreign direct investment', *Journal of International Business Studies*, **38**, 499–518.

Caves, R.E. (1996), *Multinational Enterprise and Economic Analysis,* 2nd edn, Cambridge: Cambridge University Press.

Cheung, Y.-W. and X. Qian (2009), 'Empirics of China's outward direct investment', *Pacific Economic Review*, **14**(3), 312–41.

Deng, P. (2004), 'Outward investment by Chinese MNCs: motivations and implications', *Business Horizons*, **47**(3), 8–16.

Deng, P. (2007), 'Investing for strategic resources and its rationale: the case of outward FDI from Chinese companies', *Business Horizons*, **50**(1), 71–81.

Deng, P. (2009), 'Why do Chinese firms tend to acquire strategic assets in international expansion?', *Journal of World Business*, **44**(1), 74–84.

Ding, X.L. (2000), 'Informal privatization through internationalization: the rise of nomenclature capitalism in China's offshore businesses', *British Journal of Political Science*, **30**(1), 121–46.

Duanmu, J.L. and Y. Guney (2009), 'A panel data analysis of location determinants of Chinese and Indian outward foreign direct investment', *Journal of Asia Business Studies*, **3**(2), 1–15.

Dunning, J.H. (2000), 'The eclectic paradigm as an envelope for economic and business theories of MNE activity', *International Business Review*, **9**, 163–90.

He, W. and M. Lyles (2008), 'China's outward foreign direct investment', *Business Horizons*, **51**(6), 485–91.

Hobdari, B., M. Papanastassiou and E. Sinani (2008), 'Micro-evidence on investment patterns and motivations of Chinese multinationals', in V. Worm (ed.), *China-Business Opportunities in a Globalising Economy*, Frederiksberg: Copenhagen Business School Press.

Hobdari, B., E. Sinani, M. Papanastassiou and R. Pearce (2010), 'Micro-evidence on investment patterns and motivations of Chinese multinationals', *Review of Market Integration*, **2**, 61–86.

Hong, E. and L. Sun (2006), 'Dynamics of internationalisation and outward investment: Chinese corporations' strategies', *China Quarterly*, **187**, 610–34.

Li, P. (1993), 'Chinese investment and business in Canada: ethnic entrepreneurship reconsidered', *Pacific Affairs*, **66**(2), 213–43.

Luo, Y., Q. Xue and B. Han (2010), 'How emerging market governments promote outward foreign direct investment: experience from China', *Journal of World Business*, **45**(1), 68–79.

Morck, R., B. Yeung and M. Zhao (2008), 'Perspectives of China's outward foreign direct investment', *Journal of International Business Studies*, **39**, 337–50.

Oladottir, A.D., B. Hobdari, E. Sinani, M. Papanastassiou and R.D. Pearce (2009), 'Global expansion strategies for Icelandic, Irish, and Israeli multinationals', mimeo.

Palepu, K. (1985), 'Diversification strategy, profit performance and the entropy measure', *Strategic Management Journal*, **6**, 239–55.

Papanastassiou, M. and R. Pearce (2009), *The Strategic Development of Multinationals; Subsidiaries and Innovation*, London: Palgrave Macmillan.

Rugman, A. and J. Li (2007), 'Will China's multinationals succeed globally or regionally?', *European Management Journal*, **25**(5), 333–43.

Rui, H. and G. Yip (2008), 'Foreign acquisitions by Chinese firms: a strategic intent perspective', *Journal of World Business*, **43**(2), 213–26.

UNCTAD (2006), *World Investment Report 2006: FDI from Developing and Emerging Economies: Implications for Development*, New York and Geneva: United Nations.

UNCTAD (2007), *World Investment Report 2007: Transnational Corporations, Extractive Industries and Development*, New York and Geneva: United Nations.

UNCTAD (2010), *World Investment Report 2010: Investing in a Low-carbon Economy*, New York and Geneva: United Nations.

Wang, M.Y. (2002), 'The motivations behind China's government-initiated industrial investment overseas', *Pacific Affairs*, **75**(2), 187–206.

Yeaple, S.R. (2003), 'The complex integration strategies of multinationals and cross country dependencies in the structure of FDI', *Journal of International Economics*, **60**(2), 293–314.

Young, S., C.-H. Huang and M. McDermott (1996), 'Internationalisation and competitive catching-up: case study evidence on Chinese multinational enterprises', *Management International Review*, **36**(4), 295–314.

Index

knowledge transfer 144
see also external knowledge; internal
   knowledge
Korea *see* South Korea

laboratories 10–13, 16, 27, 37, 42–57,
   87
laser technology 90
lateral integration 22, 192–3
Latin America 169–74
Lexis Nexis 188, 192
Li, P. 191
license arrangements 145
Liebherr 145
local supply 25, 30–31
locally integrated laboratory (LIL) 47,
   49–50, 57, 72–4
location advantages (LAs) 43, 165,
   167–8
Logistic Regression 95
low-carbon technologies 107

Macau 37
machinery industry 29–30
Makadok, R. 118
Malaysia 144, 187
marine technology 117
market liberalization 104–5, 116, 121,
   127
market research 28
market scope 27
market seeking (MS) 10–11, 16, 26–34,
   38–9, 163–5, 168
   Ericsson 65–6
   R&D 52–4, 79
marketing 27, 37, 51, 67, 83, 87
mature product 10, 47, 65, 181
mature technology 11
Mauritius 143
medical instruments 90
MERCUSOR 142
metal industry 97
MG Rover 139
Michailova, S. 149
migrants 144
Millennium Development Goals 160
Millennium Project 179
minerals industry 149
mining industry 190
Ministry of Commerce of the People's

Republic of China (MOFCOM)
   44, 128
Ministry of Finance 137
Ministry of Foreign Trade and
   Economic Cooperation
   (MOFTEC) 116
MMC exchange 73
Mobile Communications Ltd Centre
   72
mobile multimedia 72
mobile phones 62, 65–9, 72, 77, 79, 133
modern R&D 60
Morck, R. 188
motor vehicle industry *see* automotive
   industry
MP3 74
multilateral agreements 142–3, 176

NAFTA 142
Nanjing Automobile Corporation
   (NAC) 139
National Bureau of Statistics in China
   44
national champion policies 136
National Development and Reform
   Commission (NDRC) 128
National Development Plan 105
National Science and Technology
   Ministry 108
National System of Innovation (NSI)
   3, 13–14, 16, 23, 42–57, 73
   see also innovation
Netherlands 143
network 117–19
   global market 24
   government-business 18, 128, 135,
     147
   innovation 68–9
   knowledge 87
   social 20, 125–6, 147–8
Nigeria 143
non-metallic mineral product industry
   97
North, D. 120
North America 22

OCO Consulting 60
OFDI *see* foreign direct investment,
   outward
oil and gas industry 149, 190